They Went To College

THE COLLEGE GRADUATE IN AMERICA TODAY

They Went To

THE COLLEGE GRADUATE

ERNEST HAVEMANN

PATRICIA SALTER WEST

College

IN AMERICA TODAY

Based on a survey of U.S. college graduates

made by Time *Magazine*

and analyzed by

the Columbia University Bureau

of Applied Social Research

HARCOURT, BRACE AND COMPANY

NEW YORK

Foreword

While collaborating with Mrs. West on this book I have often thought about Sir Isaac Newton. He sat under the apple tree and the law of gravity fell into his lap. I sat in my office one day, catching up on the newspapers, and this book fell into my lap. One of the editors of *Time* magazine, to which I had once given the best years of my life, called me up, told me that the magazine had hold of what it believed to be the world's first thorough collection of facts about the U.S. college graduate, and asked me if I would be interested in helping to make them into a book. The reason he happened to call me instead of someone else was fairly simple and accidental, like the path of a falling apple. He knew that the material contained a lot of statistics, and he remembered that my chief fame at the magazine consisted in being able to divide up a lunch check correctly when six people were going Dutch. (This is a minor accomplishment, but not among writers.)

I looked at the material; it turned out to be a vast and full-scale survey made by the magazine and analyzed by Mrs. West—Dr. West—as a member of the Columbia University Bureau of Applied Social Research. By my lights it constituted a surprising and endlessly fascinating store of information about the college man and the college woman. It had taken scores of people and goodness knows how much money to gather the facts, and an even greater effort to turn the great raw bundle of facts into the kind of data that make sense. I felt much as an historian must feel upon opening a trunkful of lost letters from Napoleon.

My own part in the book has been not only accidental but ex post facto. The real job was done by the *Time* magazine people in gathering the data; by Dr. Robert K. Merton of the Bureau of Applied Social Research in recognizing their possibilities and turning them into a major research project, and by Dr. West. *Time* planted the apple tree;

v

Dr. Merton watered it, and Dr. West did the pruning, cultivating, spraying, and chasing away of birds. The factual content of the book is the product of Dr. West, a sociologist with no special interest in writing. I—a writer with an interest in but no talent for statistical analysis—just happened along when the apple was ripe.

It should be pointed out, in all fairness, that the role of *Time* magazine was not completely altruistic. (In fact I happen to be a small stockholder, and I *hope* they're not going completely altruistic.) The magazine conceived the survey in the first place as an analysis of its reading public, which happens to be about 77% college trained. It was only as an afterthought that the data, which seemed too good to keep, were turned over to the Columbia University Bureau of Applied Social Research. For this reason there are certain unavoidable gaps in the book; I am sure that James Linen, the publisher of *Time*, would agree with the authors and with you that the study leaves quite a few questions unanswered, and that it would have been nice if these questions had been anticipated and pursued. It would also have been better if the facts in the book, which were obtained by questionnaire in 1947, could have been presented a little sooner. However, all the really important questions do seem to be answered. As for the time lag, most of it was unavoidable anyway in a study of this scope, and at any rate it is our hope that the information will still be pertinent and useful twenty years from now.

The authors are very grateful to *Time* magazine for providing the survey material, and to Dr. Merton and the rest of the staff of the Bureau of Applied Social Research for guidance, direction, and assistance in making the best possible use of it. We should especially like to express our appreciation to Frank Stewart who assembled the sample, built the questionnaire, saw the survey through initial tabulation and analysis, and tested the various waves for significant statistical differences; to Dr. C. Robert Pace, Syracuse University, who developed many of the activity and attitude questions used; to David Wallace, Director of Market Research for *Time* magazine in 1947 and 1948, under whose over-all guidance the study was conducted; and particularly to the presidents of the 1,037 colleges without whose cooperation this entire book would have been impossible.

Ernest Havemann

Contents

Charts

PART ONE

What This Book Is About

A Lot of Buildings Have Ivy

The folklore about the American college is endless. During the 1920's there was a well-accepted theory, propagated by a magazine called *College Humor*, a musical comedy called *Good News*, and a song titled *The Varsity Drag*, that male college students spent all their time shopping for raccoon coats and college widows, and that coeds spent all their time doing the Charleston and reading Havelock Ellis. During the 1930's the campus was popularly considered to be a hotbed of Communism, where the students did nothing all day but sign petitions, stage pacifist demonstrations, and throw stones at the R.O.T.C. teachers. Immediately after World War II the campus was known in folklore as a place inhabited solely by young married veterans, attending for free under the G.I. Bill of Rights, terribly busy drying diapers between the pages of their textbooks, but not too busy to make straight A's in such abstruse subjects as atomic energy and the role of the citizen in the United Nations.

As a nation we spend a great deal on our colleges: something over $2 billion a year in public and private funds. We have 1,301 colleges, universities, teachers' colleges, professional schools, and technical schools qualified to grant degrees in higher education—which is just about as many as can be found in all the other nations of the world combined. Some 2,500,000 of our young folks—about one boy and girl out of six between 18 and 21—have been attending them. Never in the history of education has there been anything like this. Never in any other time or country has the college degree been so commonplace, or considered a prerequisite for so many jobs and careers. All the recent talk about more federal aid to education has tended to put the emphasis in the other direction: on the number of young men and women who are *not* going to college. But whatever further growth is necessary or desirable, the really amazing thing about the American college is the growth it has had already.

Yet most of us, despite statistics which seem to be a prima facie vote of confidence, view our colleges with extremely mixed emotions. Many adults believe that girls go to college simply to find husbands. On the other hand they will argue all summer with a daughter desirous of marrying the neighbor boy, who is established as a first lieutenant in the Air Force, rather than "completing her education." Many fathers are absolutely convinced that boys learn nothing in college but how to paddle the younger fellows in the fraternity, play football and basketball, and write home for more money. Yet if a male offspring shows inclinations to go direct from high school to a job, these same fathers exhibit a distress which is a pitiful thing to watch. Parents who have never been to college ordinarily send their children with half a hope that it will be the key to a new and better world, but with half a fear that it will merely turn them into social butterflies. Parents who have been through it themselves sometimes send their children in the earnest conviction that it is their greatest hope for a happy, useful, and prosperous life. But often they merely feel that, since they themselves lived through it without permanent damage, the children can probably do the same.

In a way college has become at least partly a social habit; it is "the thing to do" and practically every parent who can afford it tries to give it to his children. The motives can range from pure dedication to the same thing that makes people buy a larger television screen than the neighbors'. In another way college has become very mysterious and magical, a kind of talisman which nobody really understands but which everyone respects—either wholeheartedly or with a self-conscious cynicism about his own superstitions. There must be thousands of parents who, if pressed, would admit that they firmly believe college to be a complete waste of time—yet who are somehow afraid not to send their children. There are thousands of youngsters every year who approach the campus in the same spirit, as if saying, "I don't believe there's anything here, but I don't want to miss it." There are also parents who practically starve themselves for years in order to give their children a college education, and students who work almost unbelievable hours at jobs which help them earn their own way.

The folklore is endless. The facts have been pretty scarce. What *does* college do to its students? What kind of breadwinners does it turn out, and what kind of citizens with what kind of political and social attitudes? What happens to the marriages of college graduates? What kind of families do they have? Has their education made them happier or has it just made them restless? What happens to the A students and to the C and D students, to the Big Men on Campus and to the wallflowers, to the boys who own their own convertibles and the boys who have to wait on tables to earn their board? What happens to the girl who goes from college to a career, and to the girl who gets married on graduation day? In short, is college really worth all the time and trouble?

These are not easy questions, and probably no one will ever know the full, complete, and final answers. But one way of getting at the facts is to select as large a group of college graduates as possible, picking them carefully to represent a cross section of all the graduates now alive, and then to ask them as many questions as time permits about their college careers and their lives since they left the campus. With the help of 1,037 of the American colleges, this has now been done. A group of 9,064 of their graduates, young and old, men and women, good students and bad, has taken part in this survey. They were queried in detail, in a manner explained in the appendix, then some of them were invited to submit their own comments on the college problem, and did so in letters ranging from one to many pages. The data were analyzed at the Columbia University Bureau of Applied Social Research, and this book is a report on the findings. In it we cannot hope for all answers but we can discover some of them, and get the best available clues to many others.

There is one thing, unfortunately, that we cannot do. Looking at our college graduates we can never be completely sure whether they got where they did—in terms of breadwinning, citizenship, family life, or personal happiness—because of their education or in spite of it. Our 9,000 subjects have gone to college and that is that. They are forever stamped as college graduates, and there is just no telling what would have happened to them if they had stayed away. For real accuracy in any kind of scientific experiment you need a control group, and in this study there is no such thing. In case anyone is interested, we can offer a method of remedying this defect sometime in the future. Somebody with the time, patience, money, and influence could pick out 20,000 high school graduates some year, match them into two groups equal in intelligence, grades, family background, religion, and economic standing in the community, and persuade one group to go to college while sending the other off to work. If a careful record were then kept of their progress, at the end of their lifetimes the world would have the perfect comparison of the college graduate with the non-college citizen. Pending such a study, we shall have to be satisfied with what we have here.

There is one other qualification that must be borne in mind while reading the book, and this is the fact that going to college involves all kinds of pre-selection. The graduates tend to have come from families of above-average economic status, and to have all the various social and cultural benefits that go with greater wealth even in a democracy. Moreover it takes better than average intelligence to acquire a college degree— at the very least, the graduate group is certainly free of the extremely dull-witted people, the border-line morons and worse, who as a matter of fact make up about 11% of the population at large. While by no means all intelligent people have gone to college, all people who have been graduated from college are reasonably intelligent. Thus in every respect the graduates must have started life with a considerable advantage over the average man.

The first fact to consider—a fact which became apparent to the researchers who worked on this study even before they had sent out their first questionnaire—is that the word college covers a lot of ground. It was probably a little unfair of one of our contemporary wits to define college as "any building with ivy on it." Nevertheless our 1,000-odd institutions of higher learning do run the gamut. To some of our 9,000 subjects, college meant an Ivy League men's school like Princeton, with its $45 million endowment. To others, college was a struggling little Midwestern coeducational school which was barely able to afford a few microscopes for the zoology laboratory, and where the professors' names were completely unknown even ten miles away. College can mean—and has meant to our subjects—such diverse places as a Big Ten university with an enrollment of 28,000 or a teachers' school with 100 students; a rich "finishing" school in the East or a modest little women's college in the South; a denominational college run by the Methodists or Lutherans or Catholics; a school existing in such strictly college towns as Champaign, Illinois, and Columbia, Missouri; a school surrounded by a big city like

Chicago University or Columbia University in New York. Just to pick three colleges with similar names, there are 3,000 miles and a whole world of differences between George Washington University in the District of Columbia, Washington University in St. Louis, and the University of Washington on the West Coast.

In these widely varied colleges our graduates were able to get their degrees in a widely varied range of subjects. They could specialize in Latin or in automotive engineering; they could study Shakespeare or oil drilling. They could learn about Aristotle or, to pick some of the oddest courses from the school catalogues, about Bait Casting, Sewerage and Sewage Treatment, Cosmetic Manufacturing, Tearoom Service, Massage, Fundamentals of Camping, and Radio Gag Writing.

Chart 1 shows the subjects in which our graduates "majored"—i.e., to which they devoted the most attention while obtaining their degrees. The outstanding thing about it is the proof it offers of the diversity of what is commonly called the college education. A graduate who majored in the humanities, in other words the type of student who usually has an A.B. as proof of the "broad, general education" which was once considered the major purpose of the college, has had a very different experience from the graduate pharmacist. In the matter of textbooks and professors, the home economics students have had very little in common with the doctors, the science graduates with the students of the fine arts, or the engineering students with the dentists. Even within the categories listed in Chart 1 there can be wide differences. A humanities major may have specialized in the dead languages or in French and Spanish; in Shakespeare or in modern poetry; in ancient history or the social trends in modern Europe. The civil engineers have followed a curriculum along quite different lines from the chemical engineers.

Thus a college education can mean any one of a hundred things, or perhaps even thousands of things. Not only do the colleges vary greatly among themselves in size of student body, wealth, faculty, physical equipment, and environment, but also the college courses are much more diverse than ordinarily considered. It would be possible for twin brothers to go to the same big university, join the same fraternity, go to all the same social functions, and date the same girls, and yet—by virtue of taking different courses—never meet the same professors, read the same books, or be exposed to the same set of facts. It will not be enough to discuss the college graduate as distinguished from the non-graduate. Since college

CHART 1

"College educated" means many different things

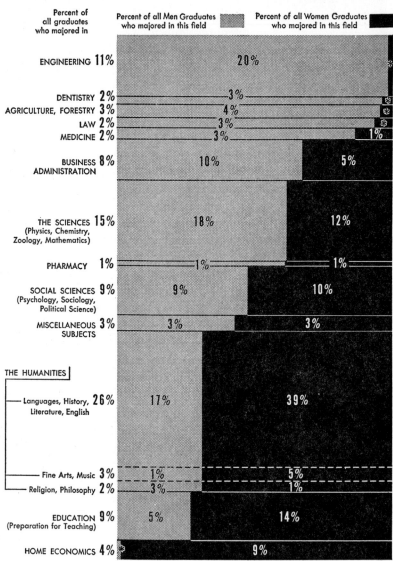

Percent of
all graduates
who majored in

Percent of all Men Graduates
who majored in this field

Percent of all Women Graduates
who majored in this field

ENGINEERING 11% — 20% — *

DENTISTRY 2% — 3% —

AGRICULTURE, FORESTRY 3% — 4% —

LAW 2% — 3% —

MEDICINE 2% — 3% — 1%

BUSINESS 8% — 10% — 5%
ADMINISTRATION

THE SCIENCES 15% — 18% — 12%
(Physics, Chemistry,
Zoology, Mathematics)

PHARMACY 1% — 1% — 1%

SOCIAL SCIENCES 9% — 9% — 10%
(Psychology, Sociology,
Political Science)

MISCELLANEOUS 3% — 3% — 3%
SUBJECTS

THE HUMANITIES

— Languages, History, 26% — 17% — 39%
Literature, English

— Fine Arts, Music 3% — 1% — 5%

— Religion, Philosophy 2% — 3% — 1%

EDUCATION 9% — 5% — 14%
(Preparation for Teaching)

HOME ECONOMICS 4% — * — 9%

* Less than ½ of 1%

means so many different things, we shall have to make some further comparisons between the graduates of different types of schools and different types of courses.

Before we leave Chart 1, we can make a few other observations about it. Our sampling shows that the broad general training of the humanities still predominates; but this wide margin of leadership is accounted for mostly by the women graduates. Among men, there are practically as many graduates in engineering and also in the physical sciences as there are in the humanities. The social sciences like psychology and sociology, a fairly recent addition to the college curriculum, rank surprisingly high among both men and women. Business administration, one of the more or less practical and vocational subjects which no college would have deigned to teach a hundred years ago, and against which many educators are still fighting, ranks fourth for male graduates. Home economics, a sort of counterpart for the practical female, ranks fifth among women graduates. For better or worse, we have obviously come a long way from the day when a college course consisted mostly of Latin and Literature.

CHAPTER 2

Mortarboards Come in All Sizes

It takes all kinds of people to fill the campuses; in a way it is an over-simplification to talk about the college graduate as if he were a recognizable type. At any college at any given moment there is likely to be one group of young men and women who seem to have nothing on their minds but their books. They study hard, earn mostly A's, get Phi Beta Kappa keys—and are seldom seen outside the classroom or the library. They appear to have very little interest in the common frivolous pursuits of youth; their lack of concern with social life, dating, athletics, and bridge seems somewhat unnatural to their less studious classmates, and partly from contempt and partly from envy they have become known in folklore as the Greasy Grinds. The folklore further maintains that they will all wind up as bad poets, sadly in need of haircuts and money. There is another group which, although also making Phi Beta Kappa, is much better accepted on the campus. These are the young folks who seem to be brilliant in every respect—scholastically, socially, athletically, and at bridge, poker, or conversation. They go out for a lot of campus activities, often become president, stay out all night at dances, and yet make fine grades on the next day's examination. They are known in folklore as the All-Around Students, and are commonly expected to be the bright shining stars of the class in later life; they are the people chosen in the college annuals as most likely to succeed.

There are also the Big Men on Campus, and the Big Women on Campus. These are the students who seem to feel that social contacts are the chief thing to be gained in college—the go-getters and the natural-born politicians. They choose the snap courses to save time, and at that they barely get passing grades. But the energy they save on studying goes into making friends and influencing people. They get invited to all the dances

10

and elected to all the offices. Everybody knows them and considers them mighty important. As the campus phrase has it, they "get around."

Then there is another group, often quite large, which scarcely gets around at all. Its members never make an impression of any kind on the campus. Their names are barely known, except perhaps among a few close friends. They are not popular; they do not engage in the social life or the extra-curricular activities, and yet they do not distinguish themselves scholastically. In the college annuals they are the students whom the editors pass over rapidly, with a few vague and noncommittal lines, and the folklore does not even bother to give them a name. We shall have to coin our own term for them, and call them The Students Who Just Sat There. Their number is legion and their motives are many. They include the girl who is so in love and so close to marriage as to consider everything else as secondary. They also include the people who are too young for the campus, or too old, and the students who are so busy trying to earn their own way at a hard job that they can barely stay awake during classes and have to rush to work immediately afterward. When the folklore considers them at all, it expects them to wind up as grocery clerks. (In this as in most matters, as later chapters will show, the folklore has some surprises coming.)

The campus—at least the composite campus—has students from all types of backgrounds. Among our graduates are the Greasy Grind, the All-Around Student, the Big Man on Campus, The Student Who Just Sat There; the Protestant, the Catholic, and the Jew; a smattering of Negroes and members of other races; the wealthy students who drew their allowances during the school term and rested during the summer, and boys and girls who worked their way at varying jobs and to varying extents. Our college graduate, it turns out, represents almost a bewildering array of people. Yet right now, before we consider what college has done to its various types of students, we can make a few generalizations.

Generalization No. 1: The Matter of Age

As the proponents of more and bigger colleges like to point out, college graduates still constitute a very small minority in the U.S. At the moment, according to census figures, there are about six million of them; this is an impressive number by any previous standards of mass education but it still amounts to only 6% of all the population old enough to have got through college.

One reason the figures are so low is that the expansion of the American campus is a relatively new thing. In the last century a college degree was a real rarity, making its possessor an object of much curiosity and respect. Even by 1900, only four boys and girls out of every 100 of college age were actually going to school, and of course not all of them continued to the point of graduation. The proportion increased slowly up to World War I, and then moved up fast. By 1940, about 16% of all youngsters in the suitable age brackets were going to college. The number dropped during World War II, when most young men were busy fighting, but was back to around 16% by 1947. The trend since then, barring such circumstances as the draft, seems to be toward even higher percentages.

This increasing popularity of the college education is amply reflected in our group of 9,000 graduates. Among our subjects only 1.5%, or 15 of every 1,000, received their degrees before 1900. (This very low figure, of course, is caused not only by the rarity of the nineteenth-century college degree but also by the attritions of age; the pre-1900 graduates had to be near or past 70 at the time of the study.) From that point the percentage rises rapidly, as follows:

Year of Graduation	Percent of Graduates
Before 1900	1.5%
1900-1909	4.3
1910-1919	8.6
1920-1929	20.0
1930-1939	34.4
1940-1947 (eight years)	31.2
	100.0

What this means, in considering college graduates as a group, is that there are many more young people than old. Among our subjects slightly less than one of five was past his fiftieth birthday, and only slightly more than one of five was in his forties. The majority—three out of five—were in their twenties or thirties. The median age of all graduates—to use a statistical term which will be very convenient throughout the book—was 36.9. This means that half were older, and half were younger. And even this median does not tell the whole story. In the age bracket of 25 to 29, there was just about the same proportion of graduates as people in the population as a whole. In the bracket of 30 to 44, the proportion of graduates was far higher than in the population at large. In all the 45-

and-over brackets, there were fewer graduates than non-graduates. Our graduate group contains a disproportionately large number of people in the young and younger middle-age groups, and a disproportionately small number of older folk. In general we can say that the college graduate, as a type, is distinguished by his youth.

Generalization No. 2: The Matter of Sex

College started out, in the days before the feminist movement, as an institution for men only. The women, of course, have now infiltrated en masse, as they have infiltrated almost everything else. But most of their gains took place in the last century, leaving them far short of equality. In our sample 58.3% are men, and only 41.7% are women. This would indicate that if you pick out a college graduate at random, by sticking a hatpin through a list, the chances are just about three out of five that you will come up with a man.

It has sometimes been assumed that the women are catching up, or at least that they are getting onto an equal footing in the current crops of graduates. But this impression is due mostly to the peculiar circumstances of the last decade. During World War II, naturally, the colleges were turning out quite a few more female graduates than male. After the war the G.I. Bill of Rights sent the men flocking back, and the women were badly outnumbered for a while. Then just when things were starting to return to normal, to a point where a trend-spotter might have been able to see through the fog, the new post-Korean draft bills clouded the glasses all over again.

Certainly there is nothing in our sample to indicate any trend toward a 50-50 basis between the sexes in college. Indeed in this century the proportion of women by age groups is remarkably constant, once allowance has been made for what happened during World War II. Among the under-30 graduates in our group, women are in the majority due to the wartime experience. But of the graduates in their thirties, women make up 37%. They also make up 38% of the graduates in their forties and 37% of those 50 and over.

The college graduate is distinguished not only for his youth but also for his masculinity.

Generalization No. 3: The Matter of Birthplace

Although our college graduates come from all kinds of family back-grounds, from all parts of the nation, from big cities, small towns, and farms, they do not come in equal proportions. As a matter of fact birth-place has played a large part, at least up to the time of the study, in de-termining a child's chances of going to college. As Chart 2 shows, if he was born in the East, his chances were excellent; if he was born in the South, his chances were poor. The smaller cities under 100,000 population —and especially the villages with fewer than 2,500 inhabitants—have con-tributed far more than their share of graduates. The farms have contrib-uted far less.

The mathematical odds implied by Chart 2 could be made into a parlor trick. If you are introduced to a stranger about whom you know nothing except that he has a college degree, you will be right nearly seven times out of ten if you guess that he came from one of the twenty-one states in the East or Midwest. Although fewer than a fourth of all Americans grow up in small towns or cities of less than 25,000, the chances are nearly 50-50 that your new acquaintance did. You can be almost perfectly sure, with only one miss in ten, that he did not grow up on a farm.

Generalization No. 4: The Matter of Dad's Education

The parlor game can be carried a little farther. As we have mentioned before, only about 6% of all Americans old enough to have a college de-gree actually do have one. Moreover, it is generally assumed to be an axiom (about which we shall have some things to say later both pro and con) that college graduates are not the big breeders in our society. Thus the chances that your new acquaintance came from parents who also had college degrees would seem to be pretty remote. The truth is quite the opposite; the chances are very good indeed.

Of the men graduates in our sample, a full 32%, or nearly a third, came from families in which at least one parent had gone to college. (In 6% the mother had gone although the father had not; in 15% the father although not the mother, and in 11% both parents.) For the women graduates the figures are even more impressive. Of the women 10% had a mother who went to college, 18% a father, and 16% a mother and father who were both college-trained—for a total of 44% from college families.

A substantial number of college graduates are the offspring of women who went to college, or of men who went, or of both mothers and fathers who themselves have degrees. Of all the people who want their children to attend college, the college graduates seem to want it the most—and to be best able to afford it. And the higher education of girls, still considered a luxury on many levels of our society, is the especial prerogative of the college-trained people.

In the case of the first woman you meet the next time you walk down the street, the chances are certainly no better than one in ten that either of her parents went to college. But the next time you meet a woman college graduate, the chances are almost 50-50.

Generalization No. 5: The Matter of Where the Money Came From

There is one more fairly safe guess about the college graduate which more or less violates the folklore. College is usually thought of as an alternative to any kind of economic usefulness in the years between 18 and 21. Indeed young parents nowadays, when they try to plan for sending the children to college, are most often inclined to think of it as an all-or-nothing proposition—to wit, how can we keep supporting the children until they have their degrees, how can we pay their tuition and buy their clothes and send them an allowance for room, board, and spending money?

Actually the facts about our now living graduates are quite different. The next time you meet one you can safely assume that his parents did *not* support him completely during his college years. Of all our graduates, only 29% never turned a hand at gainful labor until they got their degrees.

The other 71% worked their way, in whole or in part. Some of them, of course, worked only during vacation. But of all the graduates in our sample more than half had jobs after classroom hours right during the school term. It is the rule, rather than the exception, to pay at least part of the expenses through one's own labor.

There are some significant sex differences here. Young women of college age have fewer opportunities for jobs, either in the summer or during the school year. Young men apparently feel more strongly about the value of a college education, and are more willing to sweat for it. Moreover there are some factors of parental psychology and finances involved. A middle-income family is probably more willing to give full-time support to a young woman of college age than to a young man—the young

CHART 2

Where Graduates come from.
Primarily from East of the Mississippi,
North of the Ohio

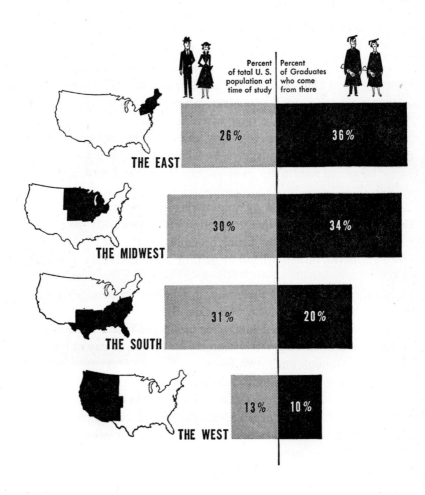

and small towns

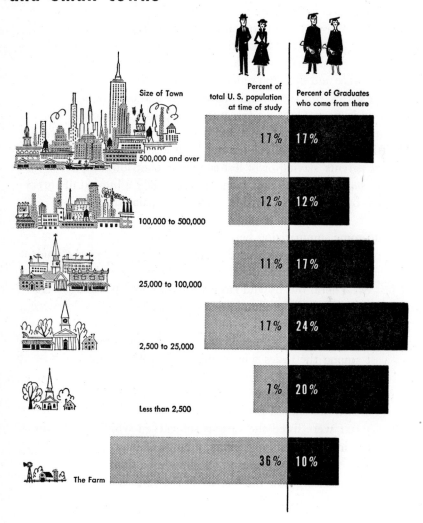

Size of Town	Percent of total U. S. population at time of study	Percent of Graduates who come from there
500,000 and over	17%	17%
100,000 to 500,000	12%	12%
25,000 to 100,000	11%	17%
2,500 to 25,000	17%	24%
Less than 2,500	7%	20%
The Farm	36%	10%

man seeming much more capable of earning all or part of his way. On the other hand it seems a reasonable assumption that many lower-income families will strain their budgets to help a son through college, while declining to pay any part of a girl's expenses; it is likely that many girls from poorer families, given no help at home and realizing the difficulty of earning all their own expenses, simply give up the idea. At any rate we had better stop talking about our graduates as a group at this point, and consider them by sexes as in Chart 3.

As the chart shows, the folklore about how young people go to college is true only in part. By and large, the girls do get sent there at their parents' expense; nearly half our women graduates got their degrees as a gift from mother and dad, and only about one in six earned half her own expenses or better. But the boys, in remarkable numbers, send themselves, in whole or in part. Only a sixth were completely supported by their parents during their college days, and better than one in three earned at least half his own way. College has not been nearly so great an expense, in terms of parents' slaving or of lost economic contributions, as the folklore would suggest. It does cost money; it is usually a burden of sorts on the parents—but it is not so terrible a burden as painted.

We can do some summarizing here. The term college graduate covers a lot of ground. We have with us the Phi Beta Kappas and the students who barely made it; we have the Big Men on Campus and The Students Who Just Sat There. But by and large we have a group distinguished by its youth, its maleness, its predominance of Easterners and Midwesterners and its lack of Southerners and farm boys. It is also notable for its tendency to come from college-trained parents, yet at the same time its ability—at least among the males who dominate it—to have got there by its own effort and earnings.

On the subject of youth, which is one of the big things about the college graduate, we should now bring our Chart 1, from page 8, up to date. In Chart 1 were listed the various subjects in which our graduates majored, as an indication of how diverse a range of interests is covered by the term college education. We can now draw up a similar list, which becomes Chart 4, showing how the interest in the various broad educational fields has changed through the years. It turns out that as a group the younger graduates, who so greatly outnumber the older ones, have been getting a significantly different type of education.

CHART 3

Who paid the bill?

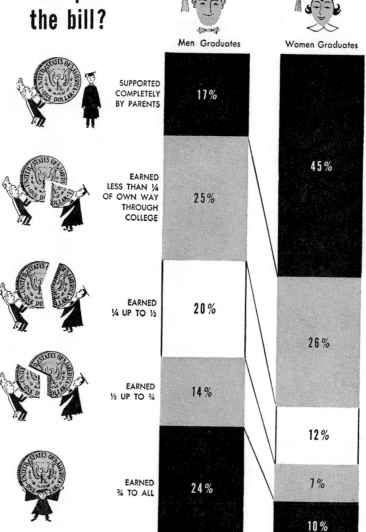

Men Graduates | Women Graduates

SUPPORTED COMPLETELY BY PARENTS — 17% / 45%

EARNED LESS THAN ¼ OF OWN WAY THROUGH COLLEGE — 25%

EARNED ¼ UP TO ½ — 20% / 26%

EARNED ½ UP TO ¾ — 14% / 12%

EARNED ¾ TO ALL — 24% / 7% / 10%

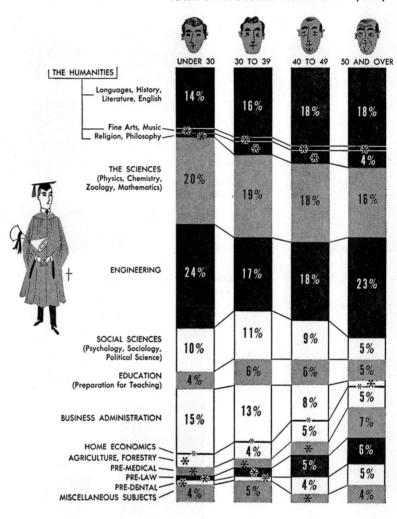

CHART 4 # The long term trend— away

Percent of Men Graduates who list it as their specialty

	UNDER 30	30 TO 39	40 TO 49	50 AND OVER
THE HUMANITIES				
Languages, History, Literature, English	14%	16%	18%	18%
Fine Arts, Music Religion, Philosophy	❋	❋	❋	❋
				4%
THE SCIENCES (Physics, Chemistry, Zoology, Mathematics)	20%	19%	18%	16%
ENGINEERING	24%	17%	18%	23%
SOCIAL SCIENCES (Psychology, Sociology, Political Science)	10%	11%	9%	5%
EDUCATION (Preparation for Teaching)	4%	6%	6%	5%
			8%	5%
BUSINESS ADMINISTRATION	15%	13%	❋	7%
			5%	
HOME ECONOMICS	❋	4%	❋	6%
AGRICULTURE, FORESTRY			5%	
PRE-MEDICAL	❋	❋		5%
PRE-LAW	❋	❋	4%	
PRE-DENTAL				
MISCELLANEOUS SUBJECTS	4%	5%	❋	4%

from the humanities and professions

Percent of Women Graduates who list it as their specialty

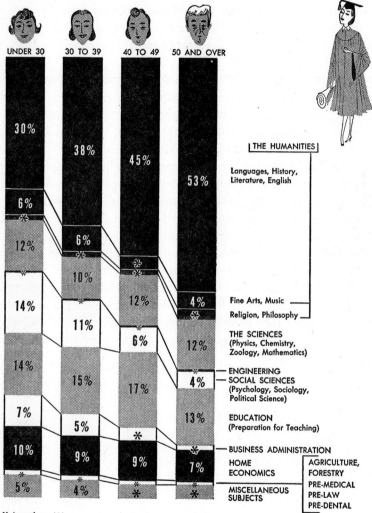

UNDER 30	30 TO 39	40 TO 49	50 AND OVER	
30%	38%	45%	53%	THE HUMANITIES — Languages, History, Literature, English
6%				
❀				
12%	6%	12%	4%	Fine Arts, Music
	❀	❀	❀	Religion, Philosophy
14%	10%	6%	12%	THE SCIENCES (Physics, Chemistry, Zoology, Mathematics)
	11%			ENGINEERING
14%		17%	4%	SOCIAL SCIENCES (Psychology, Sociology, Political Science)
	15%			
7%		✱	13%	EDUCATION (Preparation for Teaching)
10%	5%		❀	BUSINESS ADMINISTRATION
	9%	9%	7%	HOME ECONOMICS
✱	✱	✱	✱	AGRICULTURE, FORESTRY, PRE-MEDICAL, PRE-LAW, PRE-DENTAL
5%	4%	✱	✱	MISCELLANEOUS SUBJECTS

✱ Less than 4%
✱ Less than ½ of 1%

If you meet a college graduate who is over 50, the chances are 18 out of 100 that he was a pre-medical, pre-legal, or pre-dental student. But if he is under 30, the chances are just four in 100. This is only to be expected, of course, for our college population has been growing much more rapidly than the need for professional men. (In the case of doctors, perhaps the difficulty and expense of increasing training facilities, rather than the question of job markets, have been determining factors.) However the decline percentagewise does represent a substantial change on the campus and in our graduate group.

The position of the humanities has been declining steadily among both men and women; if the "broad, general education" is really the chief goal of the college, then the educators are right in worrying on this score. Among the newest crop of graduates, only 16 men out of 100, and 37 women out of 100, have majored in this old traditional field.

On the other hand there has been a substantial rise in the proportion of graduates trained in the social sciences, and a really spectacular rise in the proportion who have studied business administration. Among the graduates over 50, only one in 100, male and female, majored in this field. Among those under 30, the figures have jumped to 15 men out of 100 and 7 women out of 100. Ignoring the women graduates for the moment, we can make an even more dramatic comparison. In our oldest group of graduates, there are 18 men who took pre-medical, pre-legal, and pre-dental courses for every specialist in business administration. In the youngest group, there are about four business majors for every man who majored in those three professions. It just goes to show, once again, how times and graduates have changed.

PART TWO

Portrait of the Old Grad

(Masculine Division)

3

The Matter of Money

They come from all kinds of places and all kinds of homes; they go to many different types of campuses, meet many breeds of professors, and study everything from Aristotle to zoology, including, as we have noted, bait casting and tearoom service. Yet in life after the campus, the college graduates have one trait very much in common. Viewed strictly from a materialistic point of view, they are conspicuously successful. They hold the best jobs, the positions of greatest prestige. They make a great deal more money than their non-college contemporaries. By all conventional standards of worldly attainment they have made good almost to the man.

This fact is not exactly news. It has been reported before in various independent studies, and also in periodic analyses of data from the U.S. Census Bureau. But the margin of economic success attained by our graduates is so striking that our portrait of the Old Grad has to begin with this elemental observation: Whatever else he may be, he is exceptionally well off.

One of our subjects wrote enthusiastically of his college training, "I place the value in money (if that is possible) at $100,000." This graduate may have been treading on dangerous statistical ground; there can be no way of telling how successful at earning a living he and his fellows, obviously at least somewhat privileged from the start, would have been without their training. But he was merely dramatizing an opinion which most graduates have reached and which is given ample support, if not actual proof, by our study.

Within our group at the time of the survey, less than ½ of 1% of the men were among the unemployed; you would have had to hunt far and wide for a college graduate without a job. Nor would you have found very many working at manual labor or even in the lower-grade white collar jobs. Most of them by far were at such high levels as the professions, or semi-professional, managerial, or entrepreneurial posts. Chart 5 shows the remarkable contrast between the type of work done by the male college graduate and by the non-college worker at the time of the study. If the line through the center of the chart can be considered the water line, the figures for non-college men are like an iceberg, with only 16% in the top-ranking positions and all the rest submerged in routine or minor jobs. The college graduates, on the other hand, float up like a high-riding ship, with 84% on top and only 16% submerged.

There can be no mistaking the import of the table: the college graduates hold the key jobs in our society. The non-college man who rises to the top is a relative rarity. On the other hand it is unusual to find an Old Grad who is not at the top.

Holding the more important jobs, the graduates naturally earn more money than the average man. At the time of our study the men graduates earned a median income of $4,689. (Again that statistical term: half earned more, half earned less.) For all American men at work that year, the median income was less than half that, or $2,200. And for all the contrast that there seems to be in these two figures, the actual disparity between the college man and the non-graduate was even greater. In the first place the figure for the population as a whole comes from census data and includes the college men, who help lift the sum. Moreover, the census figure for all Americans includes all income whether earned or not, and thus is raised by such items as interest on savings, rents, or dividends from investments, none of which are included in the earned income of the college graduates. (The median total family income, earned and unearned, of the college man was $5,386.)

Even our "submerged" graduates—those who did not attain the positions of highest prestige—have done far better as a group than the average worker. The clerical workers and sales persons reported a median income of $3,610 a year, which was still 64% above the median for all U.S. workers. The graduates who had wound up in manual jobs of one sort or another—the skilled, semi-skilled, and unskilled workers in our group— had a median income of $4,200 a year, nearly twice the national median.

There is every reason to believe from the figures we have, although exact and unequivocal statistical comparisons cannot be made in every case, that the college graduates earn considerably more money than their non-college colleagues *job for job*—in other words that college men who

CHART 5

Men who graduated from college and men who didn't— the jobs they hold

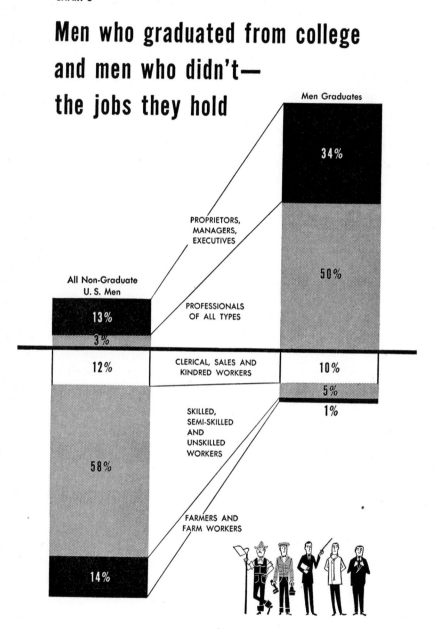

Men Graduates

34%

50%

PROPRIETORS,
MANAGERS,
EXECUTIVES

All Non-Graduate
U. S. Men

13%

3%

PROFESSIONALS
OF ALL TYPES

12%

CLERICAL, SALES AND
KINDRED WORKERS

10%

5%

1%

SKILLED,
SEMI-SKILLED
AND
UNSKILLED
WORKERS

58%

FARMERS AND
FARM WORKERS

14%

become sales clerks have higher earnings on the average than non-college sales clerks, and the same for college men who become office clerks or private secretaries or mechanics. For an example in which we have sufficient evidence for a pretty good statistical comparison, we can return to the skilled, semi-skilled, and unskilled workmen among our graduates. Their median income at the time of the study, as was mentioned, was $4,200 a year. Census reports show that in the same year all the craftsmen, foremen, and kindred workers in the population—a roughly similar group—had a median income of $2,746.

This is an especially interesting fact—or perhaps we should hedge here and say an especially interesting probability—in view of the concern which many people have had about over-educating our population. The Chancellor of the New York State Board of Regents, William J. Wallin, summed up this concern rather neatly in a speech made during the very period when our data were being analyzed. "We are likely," he said, talking of all the moves to further expand higher education, "to educate . . . many more men and women than can earn a living in the field in which they have chosen to be educated—and too often anywhere else—and we shall find that, embittered with their frustration, these surplus graduates will turn upon society and the government, more effectively and better armed in their destructive wrath by the education we have given them!"

These are strong words, but they do reflect something that our folklore has been wondering about. We wondered about it in a somewhat similar way—although with more cynicism and less ponderosity—during the years of the Great Depression of the thirties when jobs for young people were almost non-existent and a college education seemed to be merely a rather expensive postponement of unemployment. At that time the folklore maintained that all law students were bound to wind up as filling station attendants, and as a matter of fact quite a number of them did. Our study seems to indicate that all this is not quite so bad, in sheer materialistic terms, as Chancellor Wallin or anybody else might think. At least the people we educated for filling station jobs seem to be making more money than any other filling station attendants around.

There is another fact about the earning power of our graduates that is worthy of special mention, and as the best way of discussing it we have drawn up Chart 6, which shows the median earnings of college graduates and U.S. workers as a whole at various age levels. There are two very striking things about Chart 6. In the first place, it appears that our college

CHART 6

The cash value of the degree.
It increases with age

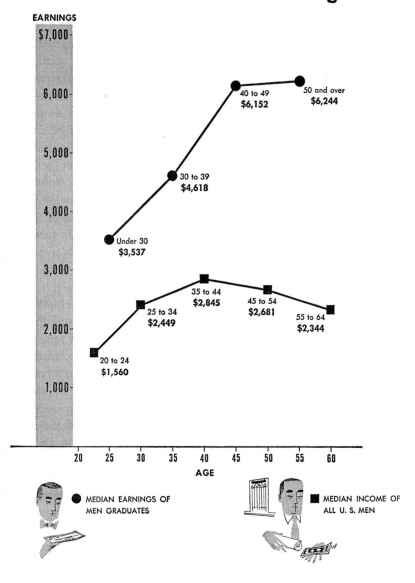

EARNINGS

50 and over
$6,244

40 to 49
$6,152

30 to 39
$4,618

Under 30
$3,537

35 to 44
$2,845

45 to 54
$2,681

25 to 34
$2,449

55 to 64
$2,344

20 to 24
$1,560

AGE

● MEDIAN EARNINGS OF
MEN GRADUATES

■ MEDIAN INCOME OF
ALL U. S. MEN

graduates earn more money almost from the first year on the job than the average man makes at the peak of his earning power. In the population at large, the peak period comes in a man's late thirties and early forties, when the median is $2,845 a year. But our very youngest and least established graduates, those under 30 years of age, have a median income of $3,537. In the second place our graduates get wealthier as they get older, while the average man begins declining after 45. Among our graduates the very oldest group, the 50-and-overs, have the best incomes. In the general population, the 50-and-overs are losing ground fast to younger men.

Everything that we have said heretofore about the earning power of the college graduate, as opposed to the earning power of the non-college man, therefore deserves a further emphasis. Our graduates, as we noted in Chapter 2, are an exceptionally young group; well over half of them are below 40. Thus as a group they are as yet nowhere near their peak earning power. Our under-30 graduates already have a median income which is 60% above the national median. The graduates in their thirties are 110% above the national median, i.e., a little better than twice as well off. And if past experience is any criterion these graduates will increase their advantage as they grow older. Our graduates in their forties are 180% better off than the average man, and our graduates over 50 years old are 184% better off—in other words, doing nearly three times as well as average.

To put it still another way—the material success of the graduates being outstanding no matter how you look at it—our graduates excel the non-college worker not only job for job but also age for age. Even in their earliest productive years they earn far more than the average man at the peak of his earning power. After 45 the disparity becomes even more pronounced. At that age the average man's earning power is dropping fairly fast. The college graduate's earning power is still going sharply up.

Of course many writers on the subject of college education have expressed the opinion in recent years that the cash value of the diploma is declining. These writers feel that the great expansion of the colleges in this century has resulted in lower standards of admission and lower standards of performance all around, so that the graduates of today are by and large not nearly so carefully selected or thoroughly trained as those of the past; they also feel that the college degree has lost its scarcity value. The people belonging to this school of thought might want to place their own interpretation on Chart 6. They would probably say that the consistent rise of earnings with increasing age among our graduates means just this: that the older graduates are a quite different and superior breed as compared with the younger ones. They would probably also be inclined to make the forecast that our younger graduates, those in their thirties and particularly those under 30, will *never* attain the income levels of the older graduates.

On the validity of this argument, our survey cannot possibly provide the answer. (In fact there is probably no way at all, except waiting for time to tell, to get a definitive answer.) Our graduates were questioned about their incomes as of a given moment; we cannot be sure that the older graduates have been making progressively more money as they went along, and we have no way of knowing how much our younger graduates will be making in the future. But at least the pattern of the past, as revealed by Chart 6, is a very consistent thing. And the fact that our very youngest graduates are already making more money than the average man at the peak of his earning power seems sufficient proof that the diploma has not altogether lost its economic value.

At this point we had better digress for a moment. It happens to be a fact in the U.S.—and all our generalizations might turn out to be wrong if we ignored it—that salaries for comparable jobs increase in steady progression with the size of the city in which the job exists. Big-city residents make more money, man for man, than the residents of medium-sized cities, and the people in medium-sized cities make more than people in small towns. (They have to, if they are to continue eating.) Now it almost stands to reason that college graduates tend to congregate in big cities—and as we shall see in Chapter 20, this is one assumption about college graduates that is actually borne out by the facts. Our Old Grads do tend to be big-city people. Can this be the only difference between the earning power of the graduate and of the average man?

Without belaboring the statistics, we can say flatly that the answer is no. This possibility has been explored, and the findings are negative. The college graduate makes more money wherever he lives. In fact we can add one more notch to the gun and say that the college man makes more money not only job for job, not only age for age, but also town for town. No matter how the statistics are grouped and regrouped, they always lead to just one conclusion: the financial success of the college man is a truly impressive thing.

With this fact established, we can now turn to some of the differences in earning power among our various types of male graduates. All the types earn more; it will be interesting to inquire which of them earn most. As a starter, we can point out the kind of fields in which they have landed. Just about 53% of our graduates have established themselves in one phase or another of business life, from business administration or engineering down to routine white collar jobs. About 16% of them are doctors, lawyers, and dentists. Some 9% of them have government jobs, ranging from the top positions downward. About 4% are clergymen and 1% earn their livings in the arts, while another 1% classify themselves as scientists—i.e., professional chemists, physicists, geologists, etc. The remaining 16% are teachers; and as indicated by all the recent bitter complaints about the sad financial plight of the teacher, they constitute a rather special case.

As to how well our various types of graduates are doing, Chart 7 contains the answer. The clergy, as might be expected, are at the bottom of the list—although it should be remembered that their positions usually include perquisites which do not show here in their cash income. The big group of teachers also ranks very low. The really big earners among our graduates, at least in terms of the numbers getting into the highest income brackets, are the doctors, well over half of whom earned $7,500 or more at the time of the study. On the other hand, however, more doctors are in the lowest, or under-$3,000, bracket than is the case for most of our other types of graduates. (This may be due to the difficulty a young doctor has getting started.) For avoiding the lowest bracket, the law and dentistry appear to be the safest routes, and while not nearly so many lawyers and dentists reach the highest bracket as do the doctors, all three of these professions produce more high-paid men than any other field.

In the business field, which draws so many graduates, we can make a further breakdown of the statistics, as has been done in Chart 8. The chart indicates that proportionally more of our graduates who went into banking have reached the $7,500-and-over bracket than the men in any other business. Manufacturing and wholesale-retail trade are close behind, and then the other types of business fall off gradually. The public utili-

CHART 7

Financial rewards differ by occupation

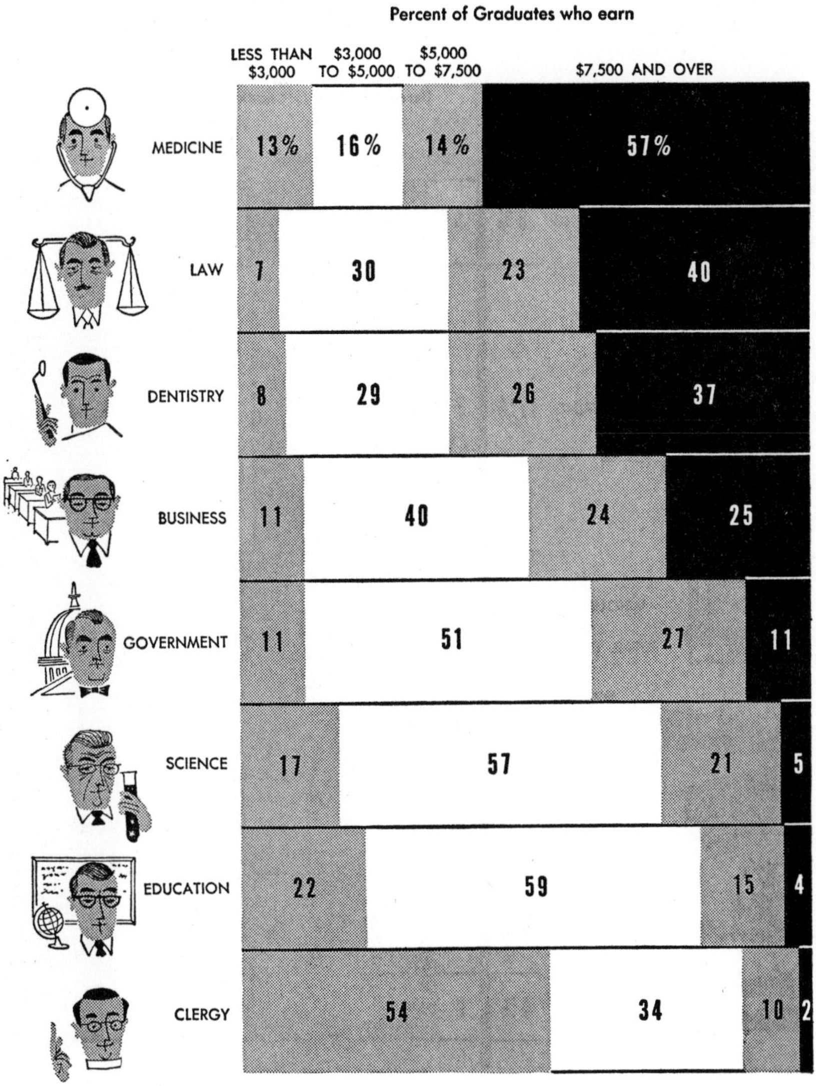

Percent of Graduates who earn

	LESS THAN $3,000	$3,000 TO $5,000	$5,000 TO $7,500	$7,500 AND OVER
MEDICINE	13%	16%	14%	57%
LAW	7	30	23	40
DENTISTRY	8	29	26	37
BUSINESS	11	40	24	25
GOVERNMENT	11	51	27	11
SCIENCE	17	57	21	5
EDUCATION	22	59	15	4
CLERGY	54	34	10	2

CHART 8

How business pays graduates

Type of Business	Percent of all graduates	Percent of Men Graduates in the field who earn			
		LESS THAN $3,000	$3,000 TO $5,000	$5,000 TO $7,500	$7,500 AND OVER
BANKING	5%	10%	39%	21%	30%
MANUFACTURING	17%	7	41	24	28
WHOLESALE AND RETAIL TRADE	9%	14	37	21	28
MINING, PETROLEUM PRODUCTION	2%	9	43	22	26
SERVICE BUSINESSES	8%	14	39	24	23
CONSTRUCTION, ENGINEERING, ARCHITECTURE	6%	10	42	27	21
PUBLIC UTILITIES	4%	9	41	31	19

ties field, which is at the bottom, has only 19% of $7,500-and-up earners as compared to 30% for banking.

So much for a comparison of the earnings of our graduates by occupational field. It will be interesting while we are on this bread-and-butter subject, however, to look at the figures from a somewhat different viewpoint. Let us divide our graduates into some well-known occupational types, as follows:

The Professional Man: in which we include doctors, lawyers, dentists, and scientists.

The Business Executive: namely, all owners or partners of businesses, as well as executives down to the status of department heads.

The Business Professional: that is, the engineers, accountants, etc.

The Rank-and-File Business Worker: including sales, clerical, and all manual workers.

For the purposes of this particular comparison, we can best confine our study to the over-40 graduates, since it is not until after 40, as we have seen, that the college graduate begins to approach his maximum earning power.

With a group limited to the over-40's, and divided in the fashion mentioned above, we get the picture of earnings shown in Chart 9. One thing that the chart demonstrates, all over again, is the preferred financial position of the professional man, notably the doctor, lawyer, and dentist. These graduates fully share with the business executives the top economic success in our group; not quite so many of them get into the $5,000-$7,500 bracket, but even more of them reach the $7,500-and-over category. The business professionals—the engineers, accountants, etc.—do not do nearly so well as the other professional types or as the business heads. The people who wind up in subordinate business jobs, of course, are the least successful of all our four types.

The most striking thing about the chart, however, is the additional evidence it offers of the graduate's earning power, no matter where he winds up in our society. If we recall that the median income of all male workers at the time of the study was $2,200, and that the average worker's earning power begins to decline around 40, it is quite remarkable that our over-40 graduates should show the pattern of Chart 9. Even among

CHART 9

Who earns the most?

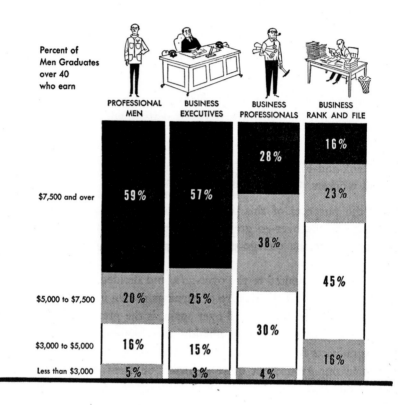

Percent of Men Graduates over 40 who earn	PROFESSIONAL MEN	BUSINESS EXECUTIVES	BUSINESS PROFESSIONALS	BUSINESS RANK AND FILE
				16%
			28%	23%
$7,500 and over	59%	57%		
			38%	45%
$5,000 to $7,500	20%	25%		
			30%	
$3,000 to $5,000	16%	15%		16%
Less than $3,000	5%	3%	4%	

our rank and file workers, only 16% were earning less than $3,000, and well over a third of them, or 39%, were making $5,000 or more. When you get up to the various types of professional men and business executives who comprise more than half our group of graduates, you find that the man earning less than $3,000 a year is a rarity and that even the man under $5,000 a year is uncommon.

The graduates who go into teaching or the clergy do not share in the general prosperity of the college man; the median income for all graduates in what might be called the learned professions is $3,584 a year, which, while a good deal higher than the median for non-college men, is below the level of even the manual, sales, and clerical workers among the graduates. Thus the graduate who considers his diploma as preparation for the learned professions is settling for a relatively low income all his life. But for the graduates who avoid this field, the diploma has a pretty substantial cash value. It may be that college did it or it may only be that the degree proves the graduate had it in him from birth—but the evidence is overwhelming that the Old Grad is the income tax man's best customer.

4

The Matter of Marriage

The 1940's were a fine decade for Cupid. The young men going off to war rushed right from the recruiting station to the marriage license bureau, or proposed to the first girl they met in the PX at their army camp, or failing that dashed home and married their old home-town sweethearts on the last furlough before going overseas. A great many women who had shown no previous interest in or attraction for men were caught up in the whirl. Romance was in the air, and even a good many fairly confirmed bachelors and spinsters, getting along in years, succumbed to the fever. There were more June brides, not to mention May and December brides, than ever before in our national history.

Along with the matrimonial boom went the well-publicized baby boom, which was possibly the outstanding social phenomenon of the decade. In the peak year, which happened to be 1947, our national birthrate was up by 37% over the best year of the 1930's, to the point where many phases of our existence were substantially affected. It became obvious that baby foods, infants' wear, and children's shoes were destined to be major industries, for a time at least; and that schoolroom space and grammar school teachers were going to be in short supply.

Our college people were not immune to the spirit of the times; indeed, as we shall see, they were possibly more enthusiastic than anyone else. And of course when the war ended, and the G.I. Bill of Rights made college more attractive and accessible than ever before, the veterans who descended upon the campus took a full quota of wives and babies with them. In the years just after 1945, the campus underwent a significant change. All of a sudden the universities had to worry about such things as housing for married veterans, and ample clothesline space for the diapers—whereas in the pre-war years it had been rare to find any married students at all, except possibly in the ranks of the football players.

The folklore about the campus changed in accordance. Once considered by many people to be a kind of dating bureau, it became in popular thinking a baby factory.

The unusual events of recent years, however, should not dim the memory of a tradition of much longer standing. Before the war years it was commonly believed that college graduates did much less marrying than the average citizen, and that even when they did marry they seldom produced any children. A girl in her late teens or early twenties, undecided between casting her lot with a college student and a boy who went right from high school to a steady job, would have been advised by most people to forget the student and concentrate on the worker, as a much safer choice. The folklore seemed to hold that college men were too highbrow to be interested in a family, or perhaps just too busy striving for success, or that they were ladies' men but not the marrying type. At any rate they were considered far below par as matrimonial material, and they were also held guilty, even when married, of practicing race suicide.

The folklore had a considerable basis in fact. When *Time* magazine made a survey in 1940 of some of the points covered in the present questionnaires, it found that only 71% of the Old Grads of that period had ever been married, whereas the percentage of all adult American men was 76%. This was not exactly a shocking discrepancy, but it did seem to indicate a trend. Moreover it was found that the college graduates had far fewer children than the non-graduate family.

By the time the present study was made, the percentage of all adult American men who had gone to the altar had jumped to 81%, just a little better than four out of five. The increase, of course, reflects the extraordinary mating activities of the wartime years. But the remarkable thing is that of our men graduates in the study, the number who had married was even higher—namely 85%. Now it may be that this margin of the graduates over the average man is too small to be significant, especially when it is considered that the figure for all U.S. males includes everyone 20 or older, while the graduates are mostly 22 and over. But the figures do seem to show that the college man today is at least every bit as likely to get married as the non-graduate, if not actually a little more likely. At any rate there are certainly no indications of any pronounced trend to bachelorhood.

As a matter of fact we have fewer bachelors in our group at all age

CHART 10

It's a rare Old Grad who lives alone

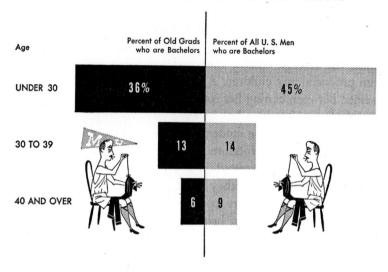

Age	Percent of Old Grads who are Bachelors	Percent of All U. S. Men who are Bachelors
UNDER 30	36%	45%
30 TO 39	13	14
40 AND OVER	6	9

brackets than will be found in the population as a whole, as demonstrated by Chart 10. Nearly two-thirds of our graduates are already married by the age of 30. From that point on the remaining bachelors succumb rapidly, until there are only 5% among graduates who have reached their fifties. All along the line the average man appears more determined about evading marriage—or at least more successful at evasion—than our theoretically footloose graduate.

Our college men not only have married more generally than the average, but also have stayed married more generally. This is one of the most interesting of all the facts our study shows, and although the figures are quite simple they deserve being placed in a chart of their own. This has been done in Chart 11, which is recommended to any young woman who happens at this moment to be hesitating between student and worker, or to any friend or parent called upon to give advice in such a situation. The comparison which Chart 11 makes between the current marital status of our graduates and of all American men is quite striking. Of the graduates who ever got married 96 out of 100 were married and living with their wives at the time of the survey, while for married men at large the figure was about 89 out of 100. Fewer of the graduates were currently living alone as the result of separation or divorce, and far fewer were living alone as widowers.

Although Chart 11 is a very brief one it raises all sorts of speculations. But our questionnaire did not dig quite deep enough in this area, and we can only wish that we could do the whole thing over—or that somebody else will see fit to follow up this fascinating lead.

Are the marriages of our college men really more stable than the average? Or can it be that the college men are merely more decisive about recognizing a marital failure—and because of their greater income more able to get a divorce and try again? For example, our Chart 11 indicates that of all men who have been married, three times as many average men as college graduates (proportionally speaking) are separated from their wives. Does this mean that college men leave their wives so very much more seldom—or merely that once having decided on a parting of the ways they hasten to get the whole thing over through divorce? Our table also indicates that twice as many average men as college men currently classify themselves as divorced. Does this mean that there are fewer divorces among the college men—or does it merely reflect the fact, well established by census data, that after they get divorced they remarry more quickly than the average?

Of all the figures in Chart 11, the most provocative is the one about widowers. Looking at the wide discrepancy between widowers in the general population and among our graduates—which is a matter of three to one—it is only natural to wonder whether the wives of college graduates simply outlive the average wife, and if so why. Is it just a matter of the well-known fact that rich people live longer than poor people? Or can it be merely that our graduates, being younger than the adult population at large, have wives who have not yet suffered the inevitable mortalities of advancing years? Or perhaps that the college man who becomes a widower is quick to remarry?

Unfortunately we cannot answer these questions. The best we can do is offer a few clues. On the matter of how common divorce has been among our graduates, our survey shows this: of the Old Grads who married, 5.8% have been divorced—5.3% once, and 0.5% (or one in every 200) twice or more. As can be seen by comparing these figures with Chart 11, most of the divorced graduates had remarried at the time of the survey, and were living with their new wives. As to how the inci-

CHART 11

The Old Grad stays married

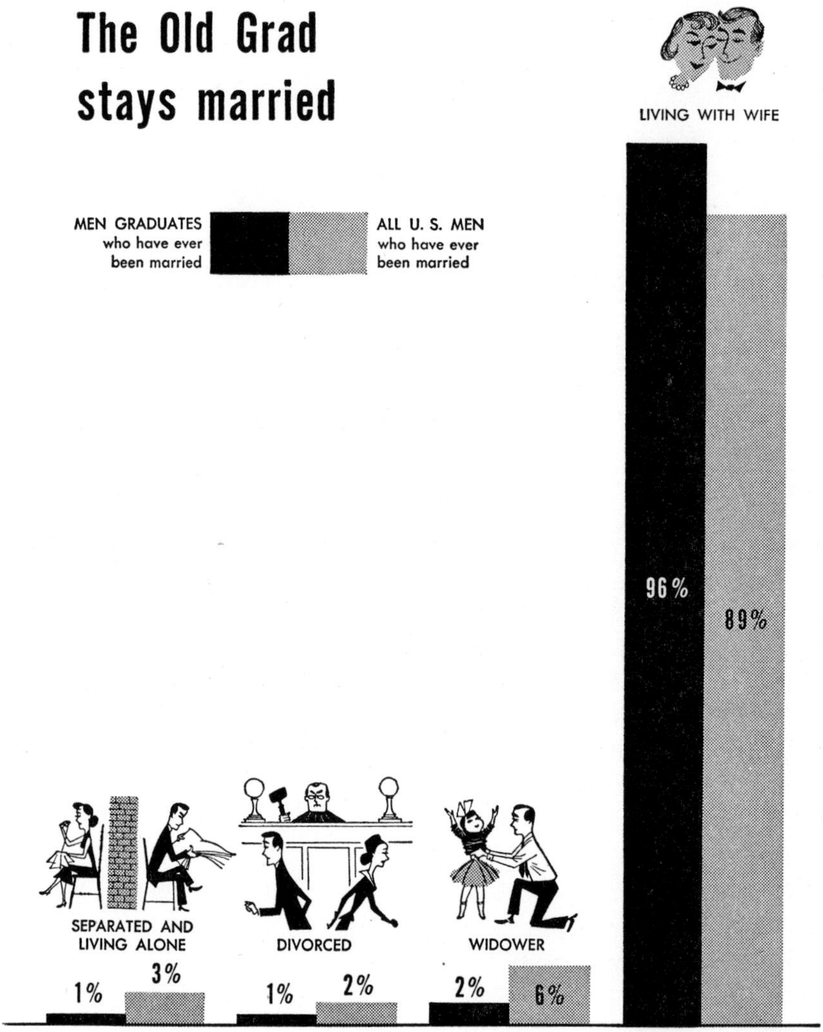

LIVING WITH WIFE

MEN GRADUATES
who have ever
been married ALL U. S. MEN
who have ever
been married

96%

89%

SEPARATED AND
LIVING ALONE

DIVORCED

WIDOWER

1%   3%

1%   2%

2%   6%

dence of divorce among our graduates compares with the population at large, we can only surmise, because nobody keeps national statistics listing the number of men who have ever in their lives been divorced. However the figure of 5.8% for our graduates—about one out of 17— does not seem unduly large when we consider that four million divorces were granted in the U.S. in the decade of the 1940's.

The proportion of working marriages among our graduates is better than average even age for age. The proportion due to divorce and quick remarriage does not seem to be unduly large—if anything, the best guess would be that it is probably small. Chart 11 may not be the final and exact guide to a young woman torn between two swains—but certainly if there is any moral at all to be drawn from these figures, the edge as a matrimonial prospect must go to the college man. It would appear—we cannot possibly guarantee this but the evidence we have is along this line—that the woman who marries a college graduate is less likely to wind up separated, divorced, or in an early grave!

Among our Old Grads who do number themselves as bachelors, of either the eligible or the confirmed type, the figures form an interesting pattern. This can be seen at a glance in Chart 12, which shows that at every age level, it is the graduates in the higher income brackets who do the most marrying—and the least successful graduates who are most likely to be bachelors. Even the youngest of the graduates, those under 30 who have had the least time to succumb to the matrimonial urge, are found to have married just as frequently if they are in the $5,000-and-over income bracket as have the graduates in their forties who earn less than $3,000. Indeed Chart 12 is a statistician's delight in its consistency; no matter how you look at it, the figures show that the Old Grad's matrimonial possibilities run in direct proportion to his amount of worldly success.

There is another observation which can be made in this connection: among our Old Grads in the lower income brackets, the type of city in which they live seems to have a great effect on whether they marry or remain bachelors. Our figures show that of all those earning less than $3,000 a year, 42% of those living in big cities (100,000 population and over) have remained bachelors. But in smaller cities (2,500 to 100,000) the proportion of bachelors is down to 26%, and in the villages under 2,500 it is only 18%. Thus the under-$3,000 graduate, while much less likely to be married than the more successful graduates no matter where

CHART 12 # Income— age— and bachelorhood

Percent of Men Graduates who have never married

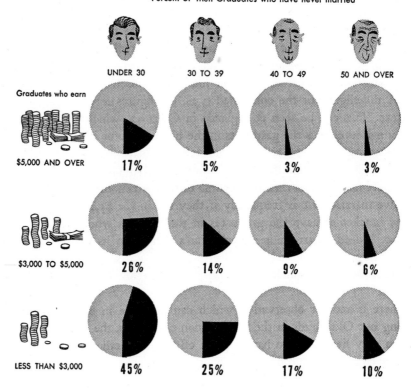

	UNDER 30	30 TO 39	40 TO 49	50 AND OVER
Graduates who earn $5,000 AND OVER	17%	5%	3%	3%
$3,000 TO $5,000	26%	14%	9%	6%
LESS THAN $3,000	45%	25%	17%	10%

he lives, has a fairly good chance of being married if he lives in a very small town, and a very poor chance if he lives in a big city. His own matrimonial possibilities, in other words, run in inverse ratio to the size of his town. On the other hand the $7,500-and-over graduate appears to get married no matter where he lives: the proportion of bachelors in this earnings bracket is 2% in the villages, 2% in the cities from 2,500 to 100,000, and 4% in the cities of 100,000 and over.

Undoubtedly the explanation lies in the lower living costs in the small town and the higher living costs of the big cities. It is probably safe to assume that the Old Grad is unwilling to marry unless he can maintain a certain standard of living for his family—and of course any given standard of living requires less and less salary as you go down the scale of city population. We can also hazard the guess that the standard of living the college man demands before venturing on marriage is less a matter of absolutes than of comparisons. In a big city, where large incomes and the physical evidences of wealth are so common and so conspicuous, the college man earning less than $3,000 a year at the time of the study might well have become obsessed by the thought of failure—failure in comparison with his classmates even though not with the population at large. On the other hand an under-$3,000 graduate in a village or rural area, where life is simpler and wealth is not only less frequent but also much more likely to be hidden under a bushel, would have considerably less provocation for odious comparisons.

This whole matter raises a speculation—unfortunately one on which we have no further clues. It may be that Chancellor Wallin, in the speech from which we quoted on page 28, was correct in thinking that the college graduate who fails to make a good living in his chosen field does become a very embittered and frustrated man. If bachelorhood can ever be considered a criterion for bitterness and frustration, our statistics on the graduates earning less than $3,000 a year would tend in that direction. At the time of our study, most of even our under-$3,000 men were doing better financially than the average American breadwinner. Very few of them were unemployed or otherwise impoverished by average standards. So it is certainly startling to discover from our data that 42% of all college graduates earning less than $3,000 in the big cities were bachelors, and that 26% fell into the same category even in the smaller towns from 2,500 to 100,000. This is not an especially big part of the college problem—our figures show that only 14% of all male college graduates in-

cluding the youngest were in the under-$3,000 bracket at the time of the
study—but it may be an extremely significant one.

We come now to the matter of children. It is a well-known fact,
publicized and deplored for years, that in our modern society it is the
uneducated who rear the big families, and the educated who go childless.
This is one opinion on which there is unanimous agreement, regardless
of religious creed or scientific viewpoint. Underlying this unanimous conclusion, of course, is a vast disagreement about causes and cures. The
Catholic Church blames birth control among the well-off. The Margaret
Sangers blame the lack of birth control among the poor.

The theoretical controversy is none of our business here, but the
statistics are. And the statistics are established beyond doubt. At the time
of our study, the Census Bureau issued a report which was fairly complicated in origin but crystal-clear in import. The Census Bureau chose
to regard the amount of monthly rent (or of its equivalent if the family
owned its own home) as the criterion of financial success. The Census
Bureau further decided to study the amount of breeding going on in
the U.S. by counting every child under 5 years old to be found in a
family where the wife was between 15 and 49—which seems to sum up
the breeding ages if you are willing to give the over-40 women the benefit
of the doubt, as of course any politically supported organization must do—
and where the husband was right on hand at the moment.

The findings were a gem of consistency. Taking all American wives
between 15 and 49, living with their husbands at the time, the number of
children in the family under 5 years old varied as follows:

	Monthly Rent			
	Under $10	$10-29	$30-49	$50 and more
Children per 1,000 women	649	551	433	326

In other words, the more rent—which means the better off the family—the
fewer children right down the line.

Among our graduates the situation is exactly the reverse. As Chart 13
shows, the more money the graduate makes the more children he has.
The statistics here are not quite so consistent as those we have been getting
used to, but this is due mainly to our under-30 group. After 30, the point
at which the graduates really get going in the matter of having children,

CHART 13

Finances and fatherhood

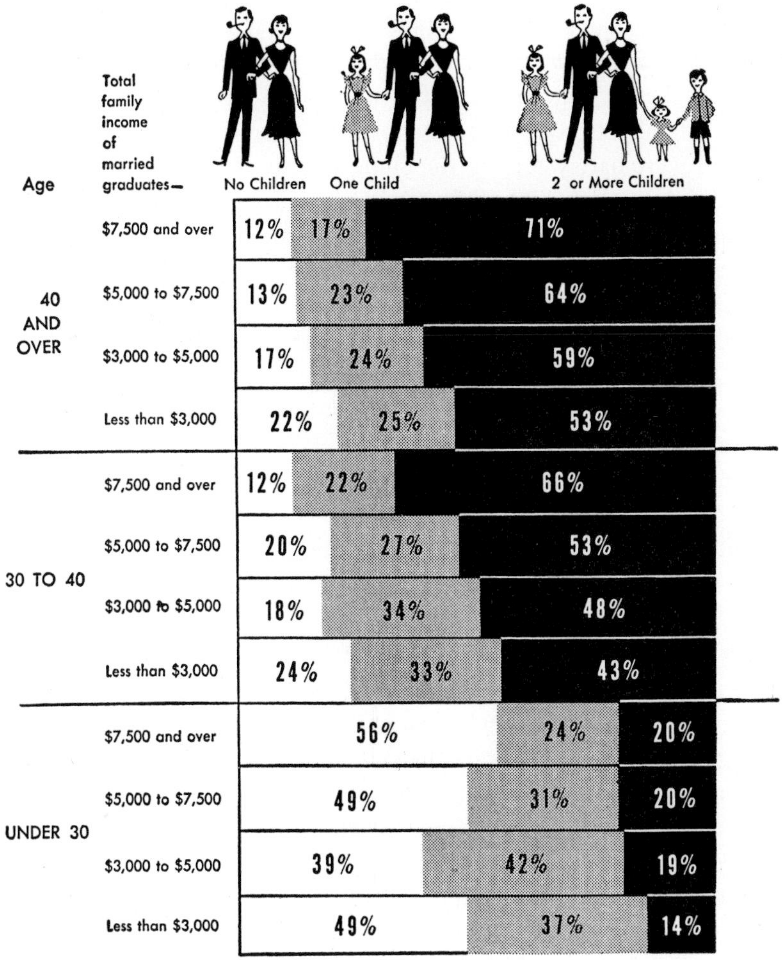

Age	Total family income of married graduates—	No Children	One Child	2 or More Children
40 AND OVER	$7,500 and over	12%	17%	71%
	$5,000 to $7,500	13%	23%	64%
	$3,000 to $5,000	17%	24%	59%
	Less than $3,000	22%	25%	53%
30 TO 40	$7,500 and over	12%	22%	66%
	$5,000 to $7,500	20%	27%	53%
	$3,000 to $5,000	18%	34%	48%
	Less than $3,000	24%	33%	43%
UNDER 30	$7,500 and over	56%	24%	20%
	$5,000 to $7,500	49%	31%	20%
	$3,000 to $5,000	39%	42%	19%
	Less than $3,000	49%	37%	14%

the increases in size of family by income are remarkably steady. We can therefore add another matrimonial generalization about the low-income vs. the high-income graduate. Our successful man is not only more likely than his less prosperous classmate to be married. He is also more likely to be a father—and in addition to that is likely to have a larger family.

Just as we analyzed the figures for bachelorhood and its relation to income by the size of the city in which the graduates were living, we ran off similar figures for fatherhood by the size of city. It is perhaps not at all surprising that our findings should follow a quite similar pattern. It is *the low-income man in the big city* who drags down the averages.

We had better digress here for a moment with some generalized statistics. Of all our Old Grads who had ever been married, including those who were barely leaving the church doors at the time of the study, 79% had at least one child. This is regardless of age or earnings; it is the figure for all the graduates who had been to the license bureau. Of these graduates the high-income group, as we have mentioned, did by far the best at fatherhood, and we can report at this point that they did it without much regard for the size of the cities in which they lived. In the villages up to 2,500 approximately 85% were fathers; in small cities from 2,500 to 100,000 the percentage was 86%; in the big cities of 100,000 and over the figure was 83%.

Among our under-$3,000 Old Grads, however, there is a startling difference between the small-town and small-city man and the big-city resident. In this income bracket, 72% of the married men in villages and in cities under 100,000 were fathers. But in the cities of 100,000 and over, only 53% had a child. Thus the under-$3,000-a-year man in the big city deviates again from the marital pattern of his wealthier colleagues. As we saw on page 43, only 58% of these Old Grads marry. Now we must add the fact that even of those who are married, only 53% are fathers. This means that of all the college graduates who settle down in the big cities, but do not achieve the kind of financial success that was represented by a $3,000-a-year income at the time of the study, only about 31 out of 100 have children.

We started out in this chapter to assay the matrimonial possibilities of the Old Grad in general. Despite our digressions in the last few pages, on the matter of the part which income and size of city seem to play, our goal is still the same. Let us therefore set up a scale of from 0 to 7 on which we can judge our Old Grads as family men. We shall give points in three fields as follows:

Marriage: For having married and being married still—in other words never divorced and not now separated—3 points. (We shall eliminate our small number of widowers from the competition.)

For being married and living with a wife now, although divorced in the past, 2 points.

For having married, but at the present time being divorced or separated, 1 point.

For being a bachelor, no points—a zero.

Children: For each child, 1 point—to a maximum of 3 points for fatherhood.

Home Ownership: For owning one's present home, 1 point. (The part of home ownership in family stability is fairly well established.)

This scale, of course, is strictly our own, and if you sit down for the next five minutes to think of criticisms you will doubtless come up with plenty. However, whether the scale is good or bad, it does represent one kind of test of matrimonial success—and those of us who have worked on this book like it rather well. Obviously the first point in matrimonial success is getting married, and there can be little argument with scoring the bachelor at zero. Perhaps a man who has once been married but is now separated or divorced is equally deserving of a zero, at least on the matter of current performance—but we feel that he deserves one point for trying. To the once-divorced man who is currently making a marriage work, we may be doing an injustice by giving him only two points—because he may have had all the legitimate grievances in the world.

Moving on to our other categories, we may have scored children too high or too low, and the same for home ownership. The whole matter of what constitutes a successful and stable relationship between the sexes is the subject of considerable speculation, not to mention of all the novels ever written. There are even some people who will argue that a bachelor can take up with a lady artist in Greenwich Village, live with her in sin in a rented apartment, never sire a child, and thus score zero on our test—and yet contribute a great deal to the sum total of human happiness, especially his own. We have chosen here, rightly or wrongly, to select a more conventional standard, and one which we think is considerably more realistic by majority view.

On our scale the Old Grads over 40—an age at which the marital mold has had time to set—come out as follows:

Points	Percent of Graduates
7	23%
6	29
5	22
4	14
3	6
2 or less	6

In other words, nearly a fourth of our Old Grads have the perfect score—they are still living with the girls they married, they have at least three children, and they own their own homes. Another 29 out of 100 are near perfect. They too have kept their marriage a going concern, and their only omission is that they have two children instead of three, or that they rent instead of own their houses. Or that they had a perfect score on the present marriage but had once been divorced.

At the opposite extreme, we have only 6% who were bachelors at the time of the study, or divorced or separated, or were engaged in a second marriage without the stability of children or of owning a house.

Our graduates are not notably prolific; it is obvious that the vast majority are practicing birth control, and that they tend to limit the size of their families by their income and by the size of the town they live in. The average number of children for all our married grads is only two, which is below the average for all married men in America. But nevertheless, on every matter except the production of large families, they are doing quite well.

PART THREE

Portrait of the Ex-Coed

CHAPTER 5

The Ubiquitous Spinster

We have almost forgotten it, in this last half of the twentieth century, but the most important question about the coed at one time was simply this: Why should women go to college at all? A great many people believed, in all sincerity, that undue mental strain would cause women to have "brain fever"—a disease which was once very popular even though defying diagnosis by any modern-day medical standards. Many others, unable to imagine any other role for women but that of housewife and mother, felt that higher education was a complete waste of time and effort. And a third group, doubtless composed of the real benighted conservatives of the day, felt that college could only result in de-sexing the woman—that is, rendering her unfit or unwilling for marriage and motherhood, while not giving her any worthwhile alternative in the way of economic usefulness.

It is strange how the prejudices of one generation sometimes become the facts of life of the next. Women have now been to college by the millions, and not one has yet died of "brain fever." Thousands of fathers—without necessarily feeling that they should demand their money back—have watched their daughters show up for commencement exercises, grab their diplomas, and dash off to the marriage license bureau. Yet the third and probably most outlandish of the old prejudices is still very much a matter of concern among us. Just as we began the portrait of the Old Grad with a discussion of his ability to make a living, we must begin the portrait of the Former Coed with a discussion of spinsterhood.

Since we have just finished rating our Old Grads as family men on a scale of 0 points to 7 points, in the last few pages of Chapter 4, we can best start the discussion by applying the same standard to our Former Coeds. The results are quite startling. In fact we had better put down the men's scores once more, alongside the women's, to get the full force of the contrast:

	Percent of Men	*Percent of Women*
Points	*over 40*	*over 40*
7	23%	12%
6	29	19
5	22	15
4	14	13
3	6	7
2 or less	6	34 (!)

On this scale, remember, 7 points represents the ideal family situation—married to the original spouse, owning a house and having three children or more. And 2 points or less represents practically no family success at all; the majority with this score have never married or have made one attempt, never repeated, which ended in divorce or separation. The very best that any of the 2-points-and-under people have done is to marry, divorce, and remarry—without having children or buying a home. Yet into this 2-and-under group, where only 6 of 100 male graduates are found, fall more than a third of all the women graduates. At the opposite end of the scale, only half as many women graduates as men have the perfect score.

For many coeds, it would appear, college amounts to an education for spinsterhood. Of all adult U.S. women at the time of the survey, only 13 out of 100 were unmarried. But of our women college graduates, 31 out of 100 were unmarried. Thus while college men were actually more prone to marry than the average, as we saw in Chapter 4, the college woman was avoiding marriage—or being cheated out of it—in almost alarming numbers.

These figures, of course, only bear out an observation that many people have made and speculated upon from time to time: the old maid among college graduates has been simply too common a phenomenon to escape notice. One common theory has been that expounded by sociologist Paul Popenoe, to the effect that there is "a widespread tendency of women to seek to marry above their own level, and of men to seek to marry below." It may be that college women are simply too choosy to compete successfully in the competition for husbands.

There are other possible theories. It may be that the kind of woman who goes to college, and stays there until she gets her degree, is simply by nature the self-sufficient type who does not regard marriage as woman's ultimate destiny—and will not embark upon it except under the most promising circumstances. It may be that college women become so interested in knowledge, and in careers, as to shun the role of the housewife and mother.

It may even be that this whole phenomenon can be related to the modern U.S. over-emphasis upon personal appearance. It seems to be an obvious fact, not requiring any statistical proof, that the modern male has been taught to have an undue regard for certain types of face and figure popularized by the movie stars, fashion models, and advertising models of our time. The more privileged he is by personality and pocketbook to shop around for a wife—and we have seen how extremely privileged the male Old Grad is in every respect—the less likely he may be to settle for the sort of girl known today as a Plain Jane, or a stylish stout. But what passes today for chic is not necessarily correlated at all with the ability to master a college course. In fact today's parents, sensing that one of their daughters is less attractive by conventional standards than the other, may actually be more inclined to help her through college and into a career than they would in the case of her more marriageable sister. In many instances, the mere fact that a girl obtained a college degree may mean that her parents have already earmarked her for spinsterhood. Or that she herself, sensing her deficiencies in the present-day marital competition, has gone to great lengths to send herself through college in search of independence.

All this is mostly speculation, and we had better move along to the facts which have been revealed by our survey. The first—and most surprising—is this: the chances that a coed will marry depend more than anything else upon her religion. Among Jewish coeds the proportion of unmarried career women is only 23 out of 100. Among Protestants, the proportion is the same as for all coeds—that is, 31 out of 100. Among Catholic women, the proportion jumps to 48 out of 100, or very close to half.

This is probably the most ironic of all the findings in our survey. Of all the groups in our society, the Catholics have the strongest tradition of family; no other church group has taken any such official position against divorce or birth control. Yet the fact remains that of all the Catholic girls who go through college, nearly half are unmarried and have no families of their own.

Some possible explanations may occur to the reader. The difference may be merely a matter of age, or of economic status before college as indicated by working one's way or being sent by one's family. But the fact is that none of these possible explanations holds water. When our statistics are controlled for all possible extraneous factors, the findings are still the same. Age for age, family for family, college for college, and course for course, the Catholic girls are still overwhelmingly the most likely to remain spinsters. They do so in almost exactly equal numbers whether they go to Catholic colleges or non-sectarian schools. Our statistics give no clue as to the reason. But the fact is eminently clear.

There is also a strong correlation between spinsterhood and earning one's own way through college (even though this correlation does not explain the findings about Catholic girls). As can be seen in Chart 14, the girls most likely to marry are those who were supported through college by their parents, or who were supported at least to such an extent that they only had to earn part of their expenses. Between these two groups the differences in marriageability are very small; those who worked their way in part are not so quick to get married, but after 30 they catch up and actually go ahead by a few percentage points. The girls who had to rely mostly on their own resources, however, earning from more than half to all their expenses, are much more likely to remain spinsters. Even among those 30 and over, nearly half are unmarried career women, compared with only 31% of the 30-and-over women who were supported by their families.

We know, of course, that the great majority of girls who work their way through college do so out of sheer economic necessity; they come from families which simply do not have the money to send them. We also know that they must be pretty determined to get a diploma and the cultural, social, and economic advantages that go with it, for it is not easy for a young woman to work her way through school and all but the most ambitious are likely to fall by the wayside. Perhaps these young women, having worked so hard for their knowledge, have a tendency to want to use it—to carve out a career instead of settling down as housewives. We may even surmise that many of them are the first women in their families ever to gain a college degree—and that they scorn to become merely wives and mothers just like any non-college woman.

On the other hand their tendency to spinsterhood may not be a matter

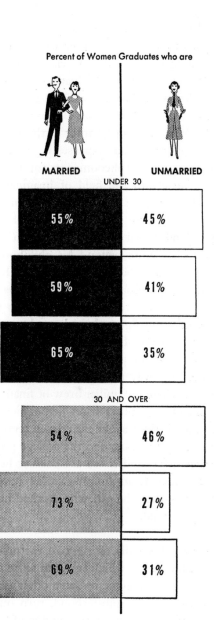

CHART 14

Chances of marriage for the girl who works her way

Percent of Women Graduates who are

MARRIED | UNMARRIED

UNDER 30

EARNED MORE THAN HALF THEIR OWN WAY — 55% | 45%

UP TO HALF — 59% | 41%

WERE COMPLETELY SUPPORTED BY PARENTS — 65% | 35%

30 AND OVER

EARNED MORE THAN HALF THEIR OWN WAY — 54% | 46%

UP TO HALF — 73% | 27%

WERE COMPLETELY SUPPORTED BY PARENTS — 69% | 31%

of choice at all. Certainly during their college careers they are bound to have less time than the other coeds for the kind of social contacts that often lead ultimately, if not sooner, to marriage. They may get out of the habit of—or indeed never acquire any taste or skill for—the boy-and-girl dating pattern. In other words they may have established very early a lifelong leaning toward being quite independent and rather lonely.

Among the men graduates, however, working one's way through school seems to have no effect whatever on marriage prospects. Indeed while the proportion of all married male graduates in our sample is 85%, as we saw in Chapter 4, the figure for the men who earned more than half their own expenses is 86%. But of course marriage is a completely different phenomenon for the man and for the woman. Entering a little into the field of imagination here, we can easily picture a boy from a poor family working his way through school, acquiring a diploma, moving rapidly into the above-average earnings brackets—and very proudly taking unto himself a wife, very possibly a girl from a social class quite beyond his childhood experience. On the other hand the girl from the poor family can hardly use her new post-graduate economic position to support a husband; she marries only if she meets and is attracted to a man who wants to support her.

Perhaps our figures have brought us back, in a rather roundabout way, to the theory of Dr. Popenoe. Perhaps the woman graduate is indeed too "choosy" about possible husbands—and very possibly the girl who has worked her way through school, risen above her class origins, and tasted the heady and unfamiliar brew of financial independence is the "choosiest" of all. On the other hand her choice is probably quite limited. If Dr. Popenoe is right about many men tending to "marry down," to the point of looking right beyond the college girl to her less tutored and more admiring sister—and if we are correct here in surmising that many of the college men from poorer families have a tendency to marry the boss's daughter—then the girl who worked her own way stands on particularly lonely ground.

We have been discussing two factors—religion and working one's way through college—which turn out to be definitely correlated with spinsterhood. Now we come to some other matters which, while often believed to contribute to spinsterhood, turn out to have no correlation at all.

The first of these is the matter of "brilliance" among women, which is popularly supposed to be almost fatal. Countless newspaper columns, magazine articles, and even whole books have been written warning the woman with brains to keep them well hidden, and the suggested techniques have been elaborated into what amounts to a new branch of social science. The theory is that men shy away from the intelligent woman—in fact are scared to death of her—and that if she wishes to acquire a husband she must keep her mouth shut and her eyes glazed over with a baby stare until she is safely to the altar. Not until then does she dare reveal that she knows how to count her change, poke holes in her husband's favorite political prejudices, or read without moving her lips.

Closely akin to "brilliance"—because the two are often confused—is the matter of persistence along the lines of scholarship. In other words, the matter of being a "Greasy Grind." To anyone who has been to college, the very words call up an immediate mental picture: a girl with flat shoes, horn-rimmed glasses, and a shiny nose which she keeps buried in Shakespeare, Schopenhauer, and Shelley; a girl who is not interested in dancing, sports, or small talk; a girl who has the musty air of the library instead of a drop of perfume behind her ears. To date her or court her would be just like having to stay after school, and therefore unthinkable. Obviously, while her former classmates traipse off one by one to be fitted for their wedding gowns, she will be sitting at home reading a good book.

Of all the campus types—the Greasy Grind, the All-Around Students, the Big Woman on Campus, and The Girl Who Just Sits There—the folklore considers the Greasy Grind to be the poorest of all matrimonial prospects. Next worst is the All-Around Girl, who may attract wide envy for her ability to make straight A's while engaging in a spectacular whirl of social and extra-curricular activities—but whose brilliance will prove her undoing unless she can pull off the difficult trick of hiding it from some poor misguided stranger who knows nothing of her academic career. The best bet of all, of course, is the Big Woman on Campus—the girl who hates books, barely qualifies for her diploma, but is a whiz on the dance floor or at running a campus political campaign. Being so eager to date her, the men must also be eager to marry her. Next most likely to marry is The Girl Who Just Sits There; in not attracting much attention, for either scholarship or extra-curricular energy, she at least does not inspire any antagonism.

Thus goes the folklore. The facts do not bear it out at all. Among the graduates whom we can identify from their college careers as Big Women on Campus, 28% are unmarried. For the All-Around Girls the figure is 29%, for the Greasy Grinds 31%, and for The Girls Who Just Sat There 35%. These differences are quite small, and it appears that for practical purposes the chances of marriage do not depend very much on the type of campus career. Certainly the Greasy Grinds and the All-Around Girls do as well or better than the average. If any group shows a significant lag, it is The Girls Who Just Sat There.

Another popular notion that we can knock down right here is the suspicion of women's colleges as breeders of a new race of tweedy, masculine, ardently feminist women who would rather die than submerge themselves in the subordinate role of wife and mother. On the face of it, this suspicion seems to make a lot of sense. The woman's college does appear to be a kind of intellectual nunnery, with its students isolated from all the casual, day-by-day contact between the sexes that is routine in the life of a co-educational school. Even without going quite so far as to fear the students might learn to look upon men as strange and rather fearful interlopers, it is easy to imagine that they might never learn the technique of give-and-take relations with boys of their age.

The facts belie the fears. It is true that in the years just out of college, the graduates of women's schools do lag behind the coeds; among our graduates under 30, fully 47% of the girls' school products are unmarried as compared with only 38% of the students from co-educational schools. But this is just a temporary phenomenon, perhaps accounted for by the number of co-educational school friendships that quickly ripen into marriage after graduation. Among the graduates over 30, there are no significant differences at all in the proportion who are married. Not only do the graduates from women's colleges marry in just as large numbers, but their marriages are equally stable; they are in no sense more prone to wind up in the divorce courts, and they actually seem to produce more children than the women from co-educational schools.

On the general subject of educating yourself to be an old maid, the most important question is probably this: Are the colleges turning out more and more spinsters, or is the number on the wane?

We can get one clue by examining what happened to college women during the 1940's, which as we have seen were the greatest years for marriage in American history. Like the Old Grads, the Ex-Coeds married in far greater numbers than the population as a whole in those hectic war years. The proportion of all adult women who had ever been married rose from 83 out of 100 in 1940 to 87 out of 100 in 1947. Among women college graduates the increase was from 51 out of 100—which was the proportion found in the *Time* magazine survey of 1940—to the 69 out of 100 which we have found in our present sample. This is an extremely impressive rise and indicates that while the woman graduate is still much more likely to wind up an old maid than the non-college woman, nevertheless she is doing far better than in the past.

We cannot let the matter rest there, however, because the wartime marriage boom was admittedly a sociological freak, one that may never be repeated again. With no more evidence than this to go on we should have to concede a strong likelihood that the present improvement in the college woman's marriage rate is just a temporary phenomenon, and that she will return to her solitary habits in the future.

The best way to reach a sensible conclusion is to break down the figures for college and non-college women by age groups, as has been done in Chart 15. At first glance the chart merely seems to be another proof of how many more old maids are found among the graduates than in the population at large; the figures for our graduates are notably higher in every age bracket from youngest to oldest. There is another message here, however, which can be puzzled out without too much difficulty. Among the general population, the percentage of unmarried women goes down steadily by age—from 25% in the group under 30 to 11% among those who are in their thirties, and then leveling off at around 8% among those who are 40 or older. In other words, the average woman's chances of marriage appear to depend largely on how long she has been around and therefore how many men she has had an opportunity to meet. The pattern for the college women is quite different. The number of un-married graduates drops sharply from the twenties to the thirties but then starts to rise again—quite noticeably among graduates in their forties, and then almost spectacularly among those in their fifties. By all standards of logic and of everything we know about women in general, these graduates in their forties and fifties should have had the most chance to marry. But in remarkable numbers, they either did not have the chance or did not take it.

This can only mean that the college women of several decades ago—

CHART 15 **Age and Spinsterhood**

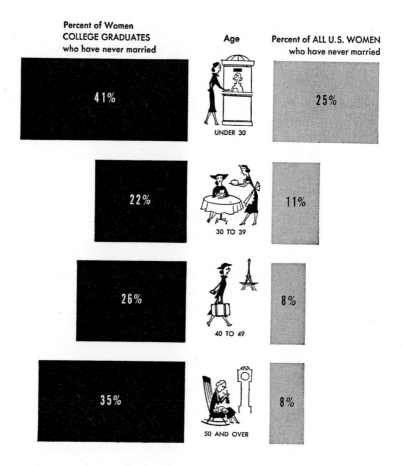

Percent of Women
COLLEGE GRADUATES
who have never married

Age

Percent of ALL U.S. WOMEN
who have never married

41%   UNDER 30   25%

22%   30 TO 39   11%

26%   40 TO 49   8%

35%   50 AND OVER   8%

those who are now in their forties and particularly those who are over 50—were a somewhat different breed from the current crop. When you think about it, this is not surprising. Feminism was a much more ardent crusade in the early part of the century than it is now. Careers for women, representing a relatively new idea, appeared much more exciting and glamorous. It seems only logical that what we now call the older generation of college women should have been much more doubtful about the advantages of marriage—and also have been viewed with considerably more suspicion by male contemporaries who had not yet fully reconciled themselves to the thought of higher education for women.

And it is this "older generation," much more than the newest one, which casts its weight on the side of spinsterhood.

True, spinsterhood is an outstanding characteristic of our women graduates, young as well as old. But our evidence indicates that the trend is away from it. Among graduates the career woman seems to be giving way to the housewife, slowly but surely.

CHAPTER 6

College as a Prelude to Marriage

One of our Former Coeds has written, in connection with our survey,* this provocative letter:

My college training, plus an early and prolonged study of music outside of academic work, has helped greatly in my enjoyment of life. As to my career, that of housewife and mother, college trained me very ill. When I married, I had no training for coping with either a house or children. These things I have had to learn the hard way—and believe me, it has been hard. Because of my liberal education, I would much rather read a book than cook a meal, and I would much prefer to play a Bach fugue than can peaches or scrub the kitchen floor. I have needed all my philosophy courses to reconcile myself to accepting the monotony of household chores. . . . I have tried to systematize my household duties so that I will have some free time daily to express my own personality—be it writing a letter, attending a concert, reading a magazine or book, composing, or playing the piano. Sometimes it seems I am waging a losing battle because there just aren't enough hours in the day to do everything I would like to do. The only consolation is that I never have any time to be bored. . . .

The same points have been made, in one form or another, by many of the Former Coeds who are now wives and mothers. Witness the following comments:

Many college women, like myself, make the mistake of not training for that most important career, marriage.

* After the formal survey had been completed, the graduates were asked by letter if they cared to comment further and in a less impersonal and statistical way on any of the issues raised by the survey. A number of leading questions were suggested, and in addition the graduates were invited to discuss anything that came to mind. From this point on in the book we shall quote frequently from the letters that resulted. The letters have no statistical validity, of course, but they do contain some interesting sidelights on the problems we are considering.

I would ask for one more thing which I believe few liberal colleges give and which I think is very important—courses to teach women to be household managers and mothers . . . I would want courses in homemaking, budgeting, home nursing, child psychology, etc.

College could have helped me more in preparation for marriage and home management. Some of my interests and attitudes were so very academic that I didn't take to the routine of a homemaker for quite awhile.

I am interested to see that marriage courses are being held now in the college.

College could help more, I am convinced, by offering good courses in marriage since that is the way the larger percentage of graduates live—and more study and discussion of child training and family life. I think, as a parent, a college graduate is not as successful as one could be mostly because one expects too much from one's children. I only hope I shall be wise enough to realize that my children are not college material, if that should be the case, and not force them into something beyond their mental powers.

Even the housewives who are more lighthearted about the whole subject, and have apparently never sat down to gloom about the present value of their college courses, sometimes have the same feeling. The following comment, for example, is from a young wife who obviously feels pretty good about her college experience and about life in general, and yet even while jesting seems to be making a serious point:

My college training was far from a disappointment to me, and I can think of very few courses that I'd change if given the opportunity to do so. On second thought—I'd trade History of Civilization for a practical cooking and nutrition course!

To a certain extent, criticisms of this type have to be discounted, for lack of specific training for marriage and motherhood is by no means confined to the college graduate. Our social pattern of recent years, centering more around the movie theater and the automobile than the home, has tended to make domestic skills very unfashionable among young folk, whether or not they have college training. It is simply a fact of life that young women who can dance, swim, or talk well have more dates than young women who have spent a lot of time learning to bake homemade bread, and all young women know it. Therefore the bride who wonders how long to boil a three-minute egg is no mere fiction of the movie script writers. On a possibly even more serious level, a tremendous number of young women embark upon marriage with only the most casual sex education or preparation for childbirth, much less any knowledge of how to rear a child. This is simply a characteristic of our society, having nothing whatever to do with the college.

The only way the college is ever drawn into the picture is in the theoretical arguments that hover over the social phenomenon. Some educators and critics of education maintain that since society fails so signally to educate the young woman for marriage, the college should fill the gap. According to this line of thinking, the home economics courses that have become popular at many colleges in recent years are just a beginning. In addition, the colleges should teach pre-natal and post-natal care, the practical psychology of dealing with husbands and children, gardening, interior decorating, the repair of home appliances, and the technique of balancing a checkbook.

The counter-argument, of course, is that in such an event college would become a very different place from the cultural center that it now represents (or tries its best to represent). Our survey can add very little to this debate; we do not even know whether the letter writers whom we have just quoted would actually be willing, if given the hard choice, to trade what they did get at college for the practical home-making knowledge they wish they had obtained. (It is very easy to wish that one had had certain experiences; it is much more difficult to decide whether one would have given up the alternative experiences.) Perhaps right here we had better settle for a few letters from the other side of the fence—from women who do feel that their college education, for all its lack of practical homemaking advice, has helped them to be wives and mothers:

My life now is not a dull routine as I rather expected housekeeping would be. I have no children as yet to keep me occupied, but I find that I always manage to keep my time occupied by reading or by devoting it to studies in music.

I have found that the time that I do have free during the day is very enjoyable to me. I have read much of the works of authors we studied in our college courses. I have also become more familiar now with the problems of our times.

As for college training in general—it has definitely given me assurance as a woman interested in homemaking and motherhood as a career. I do not feel that commonly discussed inferiority of the housewife. I am able to enjoy friendships with interesting people as well as groups.

To be a good companion, wife, mother, neighbor, and world citizen must naturally call on all of one's resources and unless one can be one and all of these in these times, all the energy of growing and being alive will have gone for nothing. The better prepared we are the better we can fill our place in the world today.

These letters, it will be noted, seem to express feelings rather than facts; it is understandably hard for a college woman, especially one who has taken a general cultural course in the humanities, to say exactly why she feels she is happier and more competent with a whisk broom or an ailing child than she would have been without her education. Indeed many of the letter writers, in trying to explain, find they have to go on at some length, and touch on all sorts of matters which are only indirectly connected with the problem at hand. Thus the following comments, while longer and more tangential than the preceding ones, seem well worth considering here:

Now as a housewife and mother, I think my college training is valuable in keeping my interests above the always present dishpan and diaper level and in helping me investigate or study some new subject. My basic courses in physiology, psychology, and sociology are of tremendous help as my present interest in children stimulates me to pursue child study.

College was one step in training for good citizenship. An excellent high school started the process and the League of Women Voters has stimulated my interests since graduation. College made me aware of the whole community picture and the need for subordinating purely personal interests to it.

To anyone looking for tangible results, I am afraid that my college training must seem to have been a shameful waste of time, since I was married three weeks after I graduated, and the only time the teacher's certificate I was granted was put to use was for a very short period during the war when my husband was overseas. But I have never felt that my time and effort at college were wasted. My marriage was postponed for a whole year solely so that I could finish college, and I have had five years in which to decide whether that supreme sacrifice was a foolish one or not. Intending no disrespect for the institution of marriage or for my dear husband, I would do it all over again.

It isn't easy to analyze the reasons. The degree and diploma are comfortable things to have. I am trained for a profession, should it ever become necessary for me to rely on my own resources. I am sure that I am a little better able to enjoy cultural activities, to get along with people, to help my husband, to understand my child.

My college training has helped me to be of assistance to my two children both in their high school and college work and has given me an understanding of some of their problems. . . .

Had I not gone to college myself I should likely not have realized the importance of a college education and not been so likely to see to it that they had the opportunity for it.

College made me a better mother for my children. The training in child psychology gave me insight into their behavior problems and the solution for many. Granted that there can be good mothers without college training, there isn't one whose instinctive skill or real enjoyment could not have been improved with it. Moreover the valuable habit of checking facts and authorities before jumping to conclusions or forming opinions—one of the most important of disciplines—is passed along naturally when children are very young, making it an integral part of their character development and future good citizenship.

Education's most important function will never be the simple accumulation of facts. The evaluation of thoughts, the substantiation of what seem to be facts, the objectivity of analysis, the recognition of logic, the correlation of detail—the list is endless—but the net result is a mental discipline integrated with character to produce a capacity for service—otherwise education is a selfish dead-end street.

The world's most desperate need today is not food—desperate though that is—but *knowledge*. Not just a mess of facts but the discipline to assess them and the training to take steps for betterment. Intolerance will be no problem, war will be no threat—once a majority of the peoples of the world have the opportunity to obtain a mental discipline as thorough as the physical training offered in most of the nation's armed services.

As it develops, the letters are an admirable introduction to the whole subject of the college-trained wife. Expressed or implied in the letters— even in this brief selection of them—are many of the questions that have been bothering a great many commentators on our civilization and a great many plain citizens as well. Does college, with its emphasis on good books and Bach fugues, make women unhappy and uncomfortable when confronted with such routine implements as a floor mop? To put it another way, does the college woman consider herself a little too good for housework—and does the average man find her no good as a wife at all?

Is the college woman who marries doomed perhaps to eternal frustration—always wishing, while doing the dishes, that she had used her degree to become a career woman? Or is the career woman, for all her independence from domestic chores, just a frustrated housewife?

Does the college woman who marries find that she has tossed her diploma away, and has no more time or opportunity to act like an educated woman than the girl who enters marriage from the eighth grade? Or does she, as some of our letter writers suggest, manage to bring an added dimension to her family and her community?

It is already obvious, just from the letters, that the answers can never be a simple yes or no. Our graduates, having all the infinite variety of human nature, react and respond in different ways. But our data do afford some rather unexpected glimpses into the relative positions of the college wife and the college career woman—and also of the woman who tries to work both sides of the street as wife and jobholder too. For the remainder of this part of the book, we shall be comparing, contrasting, and otherwise trying to understand the college graduate housewife, the unmarried career woman, and the working wife.

CHAPTER 7

Home Versus a Career

Among our women graduates, at the time of the survey, 42 out of 100 were housewives, devoting full time to their families. Another 19 out of 100 were working wives, combining a family or at least a husband with a job outside the home. And 31 were career women: the unmarried jobholders among our graduates. (The great majority of the career women had never been married; a fairly substantial minority were widows, and a few were divorcees.) The other eight graduates of 100 constituted a special case fitting into none of the three main categories. Some were graduate students, or young women still living at home and not holding jobs. A few were women who had been working but were retired or unemployed, and a few were divorcees presumably living on their alimony. The majority, however, were older women who had been widowed too late in life to start on a job of their own, or had been so well·provided for that they did not have to work.

This miscellaneous group of eight in 100 defies any kind of classification or analysis and we shall have to ignore it in our discussion—except to note here its connection with what might be called the life cycle of the Former Coed. When the figures on the graduates are broken down into age groups, the proportion of housewives, working wives, career women, and "miscellaneous" fluctuates quite rapidly. Unfortunately the pattern is greatly obscured by the tendency, mentioned in Chapter 5, for the older groups to produce more spinsters than the younger groups; and there is no point in trying to set up any sort of clear-cut table. But there seems to be a definite trend, which we can describe if not illustrate, that goes something as follows:

Among the youngest graduates, those under 30, the proportion of career women is quite high, and even among those who have married about one in three is a working wife. It is not until the thirties that the graduates have really established their family lives; the thirties are the years for marriage, child-bearing, and the rearing of the children. The proportion of career women drops to its lowest point, and so does the proportion of working wives among the married women. But starting in the forties the role of the coed as a full-time family woman begins to decline. With her children fairly well grown, she is likely to think once more in terms of a career, and to become a working wife on at least a part-time basis. Divorce is also more common among the graduates over 40, and widowhood begins to become an important factor. After 50, the proportion of housewives is the smallest of all—only 31 in 100—and fully 18 of 100 have entered the miscellaneous group, chiefly through widowhood and secondarily through divorce.

Our letter writers, although they have never studied this pattern statistically, show an intuitive awareness of it. There is this comment, for example, by a woman who is stymied by a problem which our figures indicate is common among graduates whose children have grown up:

I wish, even more, that I had equipped myself for a career which could have been combined with homemaking wherever I was. I have moved a great deal—and now that I want some challenging work, I am in those dreadful forties and far from before-marriage employment contacts.

The fear of widowhood comes up even more frequently—as perhaps is only to be expected in view of the wide publicity that has been given to the edge in life span which women enjoy over men. There is this comment by a woman who now recognizes, late in life, how ever-present that fear once was:

As I look back, I think I would take specific courses which would train me for a career, rather than general cultural courses. Many times, during my early married life, I was concerned as to how I would earn a living for myself and two children, should the need arise. Fortunately, that need never came to me, but I might have had more peace of mind had I been trained to some specific way of earning a living.

Even more common among the letter writers is the exact opposite—a spontaneous mention of a feeling of financial independence, and therefore of ability to meet almost any contingency, resulting from college education. These brief excerpts offer a quick summary of the attitude:

I am prepared to teach if the necessity to do so should arise. I feel that gives me some security.

Although I am not now working, I still feel I have a profession to which I could turn if necessity demanded.

Again I would take specific courses in training for a career, even though I am now married and am not working. I feel more secure knowing that, in case something happened to my husband and I would have to return to work, I am equipped to take a position.

All in all, I am most satisfied with my college education. To date it has been of no help to me as far as a career is concerned, except for a short period of working in a bookshop and rental library. But in later years it will be there to rely on should the necessity arise.

My college training has helped me in my enjoyment of life in that I have a definite feeling of security in knowing I'm equipped to support myself should anything happen to my husband, and am able to contribute should anything arise that would require my working to help out in a financial difficulty for us. It's a grand feeling not to feel completely dependent!

For all the fluctuations of time and the graduates' attitudes toward them, however, the fact remains that as of any moment the housewives make up the largest group of women graduates (42 %) and the unmarried career women the next largest (31%). And since there is some suspicion that each of these may at times envy the other, our purpose in this chapter is to examine how well the two groups are doing. Indeed it is actually impossible to understand the situation of the coed who has become a housewife without having some clues as to what she would be doing had she not married. The housewife misses a career and the career woman misses a family, and perhaps the real question here is which misses the more.

To see what the housewife has missed, let us first examine what the career woman has. On the matter of her title in life, as can be seen in Chart 16, she has quite a bit. Even by comparison with the highly successful male graduate, whose job profile is reproduced in Chart 16 from the data we have already noted in Chapter 3, the college graduate career woman is certainly holding her own. In job prestige, she ranks among the upper crust in overwhelming numbers. Naturally, in this still predominantly masculine society, she does not include nearly so many proprietors, managers and executives—only 12% compared with 34% among the men graduates. But when it comes to professional jobs of all types, she scores even higher—70% compared with 50% for the men.

CHART 16

The brighter side of being a career woman: The Title

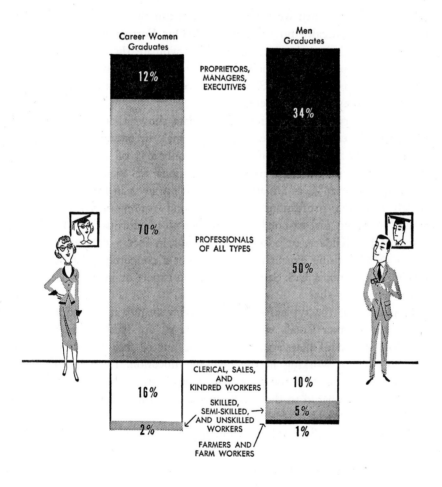

Career Women
Graduates

Men
Graduates

PROPRIETORS,
MANAGERS,
EXECUTIVES

12%

34%

70%

PROFESSIONALS
OF ALL TYPES

50%

CLERICAL, SALES,
AND
KINDRED WORKERS

16%

10%

SKILLED,
SEMI-SKILLED,
AND UNSKILLED
WORKERS

5%

2%

1%

FARMERS AND
FARM WORKERS

In all the types of work below the line that divides the important posts from the small-fry jobs—i.e., from such routine tasks as clerical, sales, and manual—the Former Coed is nearly as scarce as the man graduate.

At this point, however, all resemblance between the economic success of the career woman and her male colleague comes to an abrupt end. As we discovered in Chapter 3, the median earned income for all Old Grads at the time of the study was $4,689. The median income for the career women was only $2,689! In fact just about two out of three college career women, as can be seen in Chart 17, were earning less than $3,000 a year—and thus falling into a bracket where only the least wealthy 14% of male graduates were found. In the higher brackets to which most of the men were accustomed, as can also be seen in Chart 17, there were practically no women at all. Our Former Coeds are much more successful than the average working woman; their median income was better than two and a half times the $1,000 median shown by that year's census data for all U.S. working women. But compared with the Old Grads, they were nowhere.

Indeed a further examination of our data shows that college women are not really challenging the top-ranking male breadwinner on his own ground at all. At the time of our study, only 6% of all college career women were in the high-paying professions of medicine, law, and dentistry. Only 26%, as a matter of fact, were even in the business field which runs the professions a close second for money-making. Our typical working girl ex-coed was nothing so glamorous as a Portia, or a female Dr. Kildare, or a lady dentist, nor in fact a department store buyer or advertising executive. She was not a concert pianist or author or chorus girl, nor a U.S. Senator or fashion expert or interior decorator. Then what was she?

In plain fact, the typical college career woman was a schoolteacher. Of all the Former Coeds who at the time of our study were working at a job instead of marriage, nearly three out of five—the exact figure was 59%—were working in the field of education. Even in this field, they tended to occupy the poorer paid positions. (Their median salary was $2,610, compared to the $3,584 median we found for men graduates in the teaching field.)

The affinity of the working woman graduate for schoolteaching has one rather peculiar aspect. As we have just seen, the graduates working in the field of education not only outnumber any other type of career

CHART 17

The darker side of being
a career woman: The Pay

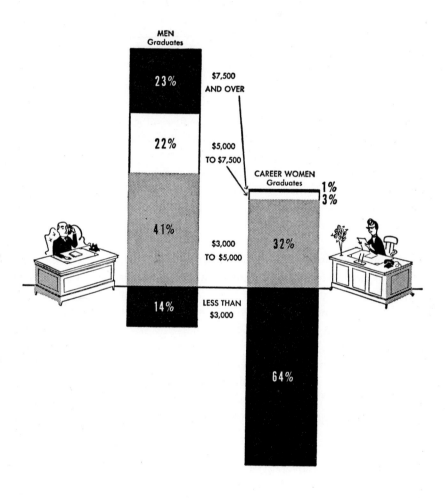

woman but actually outnumber all other types of career woman combined. This is a fact we derive from the actual job status of our graduates at the time of the study. Now if we go at the figures from the other direction, we find we can predict that the student who trains herself to be a teacher is by far the most likely of all graduates to wind up as a career woman for the rest of her life—i.e., as a permanent spinster. And here we arrive at a matter which we have thus far ignored in the chapter—the fact that the term "career woman," as we have been using it, covers a very great deal of ground.

Among the youngest "career women," we can safely assume, most regard their jobs as an interlude before marriage. Even if they have no specific plans for marriage in the near future, even if they think of their jobs as their most intense interest at the moment, they must be looking forward toward marriage at least out of the corners of their eyes. Presumably a small minority are already confirmed career women in the permanent sense, more interested in a job than in marriage. Others are probably on the border-line; they can be dissuaded from their careers only by an exceptional man, if any. But certainly the majority of the youngest working women, say those under 30, must be thinking of their jobs as a temporary thing. They may work at their jobs very hard or only with their left hands, but they can hardly regard the jobs as a lifetime matter.

The unmarried working woman in her thirties is probably a somewhat different type. In general, she holds a more responsible position and makes more money. On the one hand she may well have become more interested in the thought of a permanent career; on the other hand she may have become less hopeful about marriage. And by the time the unmarried working woman reaches the forties, she is pretty well confirmed in the lifetime pattern of spinsterhood and a job. True, women do marry after 40. But by that time they have fewer opportunities, and less inducement. Of the unmarried women graduates of 40 or over, fully 91% had attained positions as executives or professionals, and only 9% held rank-and-file jobs. This is considerably better than the over-all record of working graduates, as can be seen by comparing the figures with Chart 16. Moreover, 47% of them had moved into the $3,000-$5,000 salary bracket, and another 8% were earning $5,000 or better—which again is much better than the total over-all financial record of the working women graduates as shown in Chart 17.

Thinking only of the permanent career women in our sample—whom we shall roughly define as all unmarried working women over 40—we find a definite relation to the type of college training. Of all the graduates over 40 who studied home economics, only 21% were still career women. The proportion then rises to 30% of those who studied the humanities, 36% in business administration, 41% in the sciences—and 49% in the field of education. In other words the chances that these older college women would remain unmarried career women, or on the other hand would marry, seem to have been pretty well set the minute they decided to specialize in education courses as preparation for teaching. Once the student had made this decision, the chances were about one in two that she would remain an old maid teacher the rest of her days. The probability of spinsterhood was higher than for the specialists in any other type of college course—indeed more than twice as high as for the girls who decided on home economics. In fact the figures show that there has been as great a correlation between spinsterhood and training for schoolteaching as we found earlier between spinsterhood and Catholicism, or spinsterhood and working one's way through school.

This is another of those chicken-and-egg situations. It may be that the girls who are least likely to marry are the ones who gravitate toward teaching. Or there may be something about the training and the professional life of the teacher that militates against marriage. Along the lines of this latter possibility, two conflicting theories suggest themselves. Perhaps the teacher becomes so dedicated to her job, despite the poor pay, that she is reluctant to give it up even for marriage. Or perhaps she is forced by her job and the community into such an inhibited social life that she never meets the right kind of men under circumstances conducive to romance. Oddly, since this whole problem affects the lives of so many of our graduates, the letter writers offer very few clues. Of all our letters, only one comments specifically along this line, and a single expression from all our thousands of subjects cannot be taken as in any way typical or significant. We offer it here only as one teacher's very positive opinion:

The only "minus" relative to my position, as I see it, is the horror of living alone. And so many teachers, feared by the public 'cause they neither split their infinitives nor dangle their participles, are so dreadfully "alone." They spend their best years helping some Univ. keep its doors open in the *summer!*

They should be off dancing, cooking, gossiping ('n' not about Pithecanthropic Man and the exact measurements of his jaw when found!).

All of which leads us to our next consideration, namely what the permanent career women in our group have missed. What they have missed, of course, is just one thing—marriage and children—so that it now becomes pertinent to inquire how successful the marriages of our women graduates have been.

We found in Chapter 4 that the male college graduate, besides being more likely to marry than the average man, is also much more likely to stay married; he is not nearly so prone to be separated, divorced, or widowed. It turns out that the pattern is much the same for the women graduates. They are not nearly so likely as the average woman to get married—but once married they tend to stay that way. As Chart 18 shows, nine out of ten graduates who ever were married were living with their husbands at the time of the survey, compared with about eight of ten wives in the population at large.

True, about the same percentage as in the population at large were living alone as divorcees—but the combined total of divorcees and wives living alone through separation was only 4% for the college women as compared with 7% for all women. Without much question, the marriage of a college woman appears to be less likely to founder than the average—even though the college woman, if her marriage does fail, is more likely to get a divorce (probably because she can better afford the cost), and thus write a formal finis to the whole unhappy affair, than to remain in the dubious status of informal separation.

One of the remarkable things about Chart 18—the fact that the ratio of widows among our graduates is only a third of the ratio among all women—is reminiscent of something else we discovered in Chapter 4. Just as the Old Grads are seldom widowers, our Former Coeds are seldom widows. Their spouses, too, seem to be notable for longevity.

The college wives, for all their favorable comparison with the average woman, do not do quite so well as the college husband. Due to the difference in the male and female life span, the percentage of widows is 5, whereas in Chapter 4 we found that the percentage of widowers among Old Grads is only 2. The 4% who are separated or divorced contrast with 2% among the men. Moreover, the Former Coeds have fewer children than the Old Grads. Among the married college women

CHART 18

The college wife
stays married

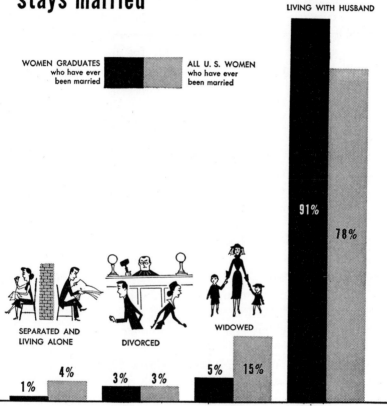

LIVING WITH HUSBAND

WOMEN GRADUATES
who have ever
been married

ALL U. S. WOMEN
who have ever
been married

91%

78%

SEPARATED AND
LIVING ALONE

DIVORCED

WIDOWED

1%

4%

3%

3%

5%

15%

31% are childless, compared with only 21% of the married college men. Among the graduates who do have children, the average for the women is only 1.88 compared with 2.03 for the men. These differences hold for all age brackets: at whatever age, the women tend to have slightly more divorces and slightly fewer children than the men.

In all these figures, however, the working wife—who represents a peculiar special case—plays a significant role, which will be discussed in the next chapter. By and large the Former Coed seems to be doing pretty well at marriage—and in every respect except number of children has a more stable married life than the average woman. Any theoretical fears that college might make a woman unfit for matrimony seem to be thoroughly dispelled by the facts; indeed the so-called "dissatisfied house-wife" certainly does not seem to be dissatisfied enough to leave home.

In some respects she may be even better off than she realizes. Let us take, for example, the old adage, which housewives have quoted for years when feeling sorry for themselves, that "woman's work is never done." On the face of it, this seems quite reasonable. Babies do refuse to pay any heed to the normal nighttime sleeping habits of mothers, and even after the most restless night tend to pop awake at the dawn. Meals—even normal adult meals—come three times a day, on a schedule lengthening into hours, say 7 A.M. to 8 P.M., that no self-respecting union would think of permitting. And even after the coffee is served at night, there are still the dishes to be washed. There are bound to be times when the average housewife, leaving the luncheon dishes to rush out and rescue the wash from a thunderstorm, praying that the baby won't wake up until the last sheet is off the line, wondering if she will have time to wash her hair in the brief interval between ironing and getting the dinner ready—and all this while still dead tired from being up three times to give the second oldest his medicine at night—there are bound to be times when the housewife thinks about her unmarried sister's 9 to 5 office hours and starts to hate her husband.

For some light on this whole subject, the graduates were asked to report how many hours of pure and unadulterated leisure—time all their own to do the things they really wanted—they had enjoyed on the last weekday before answering the questionnaire. The answers were not quite what one might have expected. It turned out that one housewife out of four reported only two hours or less, which is hardly any leisure to speak of—but so did one career woman of every five. On the other hand a third of the housewives—exactly the same ratio as among career women —reported five free hours or more, which does not exactly constitute slavery. A few of our graduate housewives have maids; some have other types of help, and of the remainder a substantial number must deserve great credit for efficiency. In one way or another, they find almost as many free hours on the average day as the career woman.

Many of the younger housewives who read this book will probably look at that last paragraph with cynical disbelief. But these readers can cheer up; their day is coming. It is the younger wife, with small children and a husband not sufficiently established at his job to afford household help, who is the busiest. Our statistics show that of graduate housewives in their thirties, only 27% have as much as five hours free time a day. But among the housewives in their fifties, fully 44% do. In other words the housewife, if nothing else, can look forward to an increasing amount of leisure as she grows older. One of our letter writers was being more prophetic than she realized when she commented:

I am greatly pleased that my 8-year-old son shows an inclination for things mechanical for maybe, in a few years, he can take over some of the menacing mechanical details of "HOUSE" and I can go back to enjoying the fruits of my liberal education.

The career women, on the other hand, seem to have less and less leisure as they grow older. Of those who were just starting their careers, and perhaps not taking them too seriously, 40% reported five or more hours of leisure. But of the confirmed and permanent career women over 50, only 22%—just half the proportion among housewives of that age—could claim five hours.

This discussion of leisure prepares the way for another finding that would otherwise have been quite unexpected. The housewives turned out to have read just as many current books and the same type of books as the career women; and an even greater percentage of wives than career women were regular readers of at least three magazines, although the career women tended to read more "serious magazines." The wives did not belong to so many civic or social organizations as the career women, but were more regular attendants at those to which they did belong, perhaps because they had more time. Neither group of women proved to be very active politically; the most surprising development along all these lines, perhaps, is the very small extent to which college career women participate in political organizations or any of the formal groups which really make community policy. On one big test of political responsibility, the matter of voting, both types of college women scored well. Of both career women and housewives over 40, 94% had voted in the last election. On the number of other political activities, the career women were slightly ahead.

All in all, throughout these comparisons, the college housewife comes off pretty well. The evidence is that the college career woman does not lead nearly so glamorous, wealthy, or influential a life as is sometimes supposed—and that the college housewife, on the matters we have been able to measure, is not nearly so harried in fact as she is sometimes made to appear in fiction.

CHAPTER 8

Home Plus a Career

Our great-grandfathers would doubtless be shocked by the thought, but there are quite a number of socially acceptable reasons, in the middle of the twentieth century, for a married woman to hold a job as well as keep a home. She may merely be marking time, and incidentally contributing to the family savings account, while waiting for the children to start arriving. She may, without any stigma, be helping a struggling young husband to keep up the payments on an automobile—or actually even helping him through law school. Knowing that she can never have children, or having decided against them, she may prefer a permanent career to staying home and cooking the meals. (The "business couple" is a familiar family group in the newspaper want ads, well known to all people who manage apartments or seek jobs as housekeepers.)

The reasons range between two extremes. At the one end there is the woman who is so interested in or dedicated to her chosen field of work that she insists on following it even if her husband is so wealthy that practically all her earnings go for income taxes. At the other end there is the woman who has to work to keep the family income up to what she considers a respectable, or (probably in some cases) even a non-starvation level. There presumably are many wives who forego motherhood and work all their lives to support an invalid husband, or a husband who simply has proved a failure as a breadwinner. There are undoubtedly others who would rather work than let the family income drop even a little bit below the Jones's.

Among our Former Coeds the number of working wives is just about one out of five, or 19% to be exact. Nothing that we know about their backgrounds—their type of college, the courses they took, their religion, or anything else—helps explain how they happened to become working wives, except for just one thing. There does seem to be a steady correla-

83

tion between working one's way through school and ending up as a working wife. Of the Former Coeds who were completely supported by their parents during college days, only 17% were working wives at the time of our survey. But among the girls who had earned up to half their own college expenses, 22% were working wives. And among those who had earned from half to all their expenses, 26% were working wives. These are not particularly large differences, but they do follow a consistent pattern. The girls from families wealthy enough to send them through college do not become working wives so often as the girls whose families were only able to pay part of the expenses; and the most likely of all to become working wives are the girls from families able to afford none or only a small part of the college expenses.

Why? One reason may be that many coeds from well-off families never think very seriously about getting a job after college; they feel either that they will soon be married, to boys wealthy enough to support them, or that if they remain spinsters they will not have to worry about finances anyway. In sociological terms, they are not job-oriented. True, they may later on become career women or even working wives— but only more or less by accident and upon second thought. Their primary aim in college is not to prepare for or otherwise anticipate a job. They do not want to work and do not expect to. Often, indeed, they go through a very difficult period in the years after college. Perhaps marriage does not occur so quickly as they had expected, and they get bored doing nothing while waiting. Or perhaps they fall in love, contrary to the script, with a young man who hasn't a nickel and is desperately struggling to finish medical school or establish his own business. Then they start looking for jobs—but without any real psychological or educational training for them. The girl from the poorer family, on the other hand, has been thinking of a career all along; in fact she has actually been working at some kind of job either after school or during the summers. She is used to the idea of winning at least part of the bread—and may like the process so well that she is inclined to continue it even if she marries a man whose income can give her a life of ease amidst servants and luxury. A job, as all working people know, can get to be a habit.

On the other hand, a better reason may be that girls from poorer families tend to meet poorer boys—in other words, that they less often find husbands who are able to support them even in accustomed style, much less in luxury. Certainly our working wives are not distinguished for wealth in their own present families any more than in their family backgrounds. As Chart 19 shows, the combined incomes of the working wives and their husbands, by and large, are just about the same as the family incomes of the housewives. Without the working wife's salary, the incomes would be much lower. Chart 19 leaves little doubt that many of the working wives hold jobs because of financial necessity— either unquestionable, starvation-avoiding necessity by anybody's lights, or what constitutes necessity by their own lights.

As for the jobs our working wives hold, their position in life can scarcely be distinguished from that of the career women; they fall into the same pattern of jobs as has been shown for the unmarried women in Chart 16, give or take a few percentage points. (Usually, in fact, just fractions of percentage points.) And just about the same high proportion of professional people among them turns out to be teaching. In rank and title, the working wives have equal stature. Their pay, however, is considerably lower. The median income for the single career women among our subjects, as has been noted, was $2,689. For the working wives, it is only $2,466. Indeed nearly a third of the working wives—31% to be exact—were earning under $2,000 a year. This poor showing, undoubtedly, is partly accounted for by wives who work only part time, and also by women who went to work late in life without any experience or after years of letting their economic skills rust. But we are also probably entitled by the statistics to assume that a single woman, whose life more or less revolves around her job, is likely to earn more money than a housewife who has to be thinking what to cook for dinner when she gets home.

Except for the matter of pay, the working wives seem to resemble the career women more than the housewives. This is certainly true as regards the important factor of motherhood—which is denied to our unmarried career women and which the working wives seem to deny to themselves. It is chiefly the working wife who pulls down the birthrate among married women graduates. Taking just those under 40, less than a third of the working wives have any children. The exact ratio is 30%, whereas among housewives of the same age fully 82% have borne children. It is true that many of the young working wives state that they *plan* to have children—but even their plans in this regard are less ambitious

CHART 19

Two breadwinners are equal to one

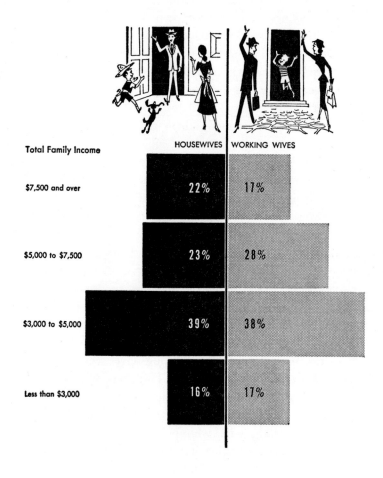

Total Family Income	HOUSEWIVES	WORKING WIVES
$7,500 and over	22%	17%
$5,000 to $7,500	23%	28%
$3,000 to $5,000	39%	38%
Less than $3,000	16%	17%

than those of the housewives, and judging from the experience of our graduates it seems doubtful that the plans will actually materialize.

Of the working wives under 30, only 3% say they do not plan to have any children, while 37% expect to have one or two and the other 60% actually expect to have three or more. But among the working wives who have reached their thirties, these ambitious plans have already dwindled quite substantially; in this age group 17% have decided not to have any children at all, while 48% still plan one or two children and only 35% plan three or more. And the actual experience of the women who have been working wives right along indicates not only that the plans dwindle but also that reality seldom lives up to the plans. Among the working wives over 40—most of whom would have had a child by this time if they were ever going to—40% are still childless.

All our figures seem to indicate, as a matter of fact, that some of the most vital decisions in our Former Coeds' lives are made in the early years of marriage. If the Former Coed decides to spend a year or so as a working wife, the chances are pretty good that she will remain a jobholder forever, and will never have children. The pattern seems to be that the year of childless jobholding lengthens to two years, and then to four, and then to ten, until at some point the working wife finally decides she is too old to start a family anyway. At any given moment the job seems like more fun than housework, or the extra income seems too important to give up; the working wife, even though she may plan all along to quit the job some day and start rearing a family, tends never to make the break. One might even speculate here that the working wife's husband may tend to take advantage of the situation. As long as his wife is working, he does not have to take full responsibility for the family finances; and this is a situation which many men, being only human, might relish. This is only a guess, of course—but it may be that the husbands of working wives earn less money than the husbands of housewives because they are never forced to make the extra effort.

All guessing aside, the general rule seems to be: once a working wife, always a working wife. And also: once a working wife, seldom a mother.

On the other hand the Former Coed who has a child early in her marriage is unlikely ever to go back to work. She may be the type of graduate who is full of career ambitions; she may want to have a child or several children very quickly, see them through the difficult period

of infancy, get them safely off to school, and then pick up her career at
the point where she left it. But somehow these plans—like the plans
of the working wives to retire and have a family some day—do not seem
to materialize. Of the married women graduates who have had children,
only 9% are found as jobholders in our under-30 group, and only 16%
among the graduates in their thirties. Of the childless wives in this age
bracket, 64% are working.

Even in later years of life, when the women who have had children
have seen the babies grow into independence, and are now fully free to
do anything they like in the way of careers, the mothers among our
graduates are still typically housewives. Among the mothers 40 and
older, only 27% have become working wives. Of the wives of this age
who have never borne children, 55% are working.

Not only does the fact of bearing a child militate against a Former
Coed's ever having or resuming a career, but every additional child re-
duces the chances still further. The moment she becomes pregnant the
first time, the Former Coed becomes overwhelmingly likely never again
to hold a job. With each succeeding child, the chances of jobholding
decrease still further. Motherhood and careers, among our graduates,
prove to be quite incompatible. Motherhood militates against the career—
and a job militates against motherhood.

Since children are a well-known factor in stability of marriage, or vice
versa—and since our working wives prove to have very few children—it
becomes pertinent to ask about the success of the working wife's marriage. But the survey was conceived as a study of college graduates at
a definite moment in time; the questionnaire was concerned with what
the graduates were doing on that very day rather than with what they
had done in the past, or with the highly nebulous possibilities of what
they might be doing in the future. Thus we did not inquire—as we now
wish we had—how many of the Former Coeds had divorced themselves
from marriages in which they were working wives. Nor did we inquire—
which would have been statistically dubious anyway—how many of the
working wives at that moment felt their marriages were nearing the
rocks. We do not, therefore, have any direct measurement of how well
the working wife's marriage stands up in comparison to the housewife's.
We can only make the best of some circumstantial evidence.

We do know this: of our Former Coeds who were married and
living with their husbands at the time of the survey, some had been

through the divorce courts in the past. Of this group of twice-married women, the working wives outnumbered housewives by nearly two to one. Among the graduates who classed themselves as working wives at the time of the survey, 3.4% had been divorced in the past. Among the graduates who were plain housewives, only 1.8% had ever been divorced. Assuming that a woman who is now a working wife tends to have been a working wife in the past, we have one hint that the marriage of the working wife is more likely to be unsuccessful.

For our second hint, we have this fact: among all the women graduates who were holding jobs at the time of the survey, 6.8% had been divorced, while among the women not holding jobs the proportion was only 2.6%. (Naturally these statistics are influenced by the fact that many divorcees have to go to work to make a living, or go to work anyway to relieve their boredom.)

For the third hint, we are forced reluctantly into what may sound like a lawyer's brief, or even an exercise in theoretical geometry. We discovered, earlier in this chapter, that the working wives are not so well off financially as the housewives; the working wife and her husband together do not earn any more than the housewife's husband earns all by himself. We concluded that some or many working wives must hold their jobs chiefly from financial necessity. Now it so happens among college women that the divorce ratio is extremely dependent on income; the less the income, the greater by far are the chances of divorce. For example, if we take married women graduates over 40— to confine the statistics to marriages which have had ample time to succeed or fail—our figures show that only 5% of the graduates with a family income of over $7,500 a year have ever been divorced, whereas among those with a family income under $3,000 a year a full 20% have been divorced.* The working wife is poorer; the poorer women graduates have much more tendency to divorce. The *ergo* seems inescapable.

All these clues point in the same direction, and there is nothing in our statistical evidence to indicate in any way that they might be misleading us. It seems perfectly safe to assume that it is the working wife among

* Strangely, income does not make nearly so much difference among our Old Grads. In the same age group, 9% of male graduates with a family income over $7,500 have been divorced, compared with 12% who have incomes under $3,000. It may be that the girls the Old Grads marry—who are frequently not college girls—are more tolerant of relative financial failure than the Former Coeds.

our Former Coeds who not only holds down the birthrate but also builds up the rate of divorce and separation. Even among the working wives, a large majority manage to keep their marriages going—but obviously their marriages are subject to a lot more strain.

We concluded our previous chapter, in which we compared housewives and unmarried career women, with a discussion of leisure time, some cultural activities, and political effectiveness. To bring these statistics up to date now, with the working wife included, we can summarize briefly as follows:

The working wife has less leisure time than either of the other types of Former Coed. Among the graduates reporting only two free hours or less on a typical day were 20% of the career women, 25% of the housewives, and 37% of the working wives. Reporting five free hours or more were a third of all career women and housewives, but only 17% of the working wives.

Despite her lack of leisure time, the working wife manages to read as many current books as the other graduates. In magazine reading, she falls about halfway between the career woman and the housewife. Among the graduates who were regular readers of at least three magazines, there were 67% of the housewives, 62% of the working wives, and 59% of the career women.

The working wives belong to slightly fewer social, civic, or political organizations than either the housewives or the career women—and also are less regular attendants at meetings of the organizations to which they do belong. On the matter of voting, however, the number of graduates who had cast ballots in the last election was 89% for both working wives and housewives and 92% for career women.

In some respects—notably in following cultural pursuits and fulfilling her political obligations as a voter—the working wife seems to be doing remarkably well despite her busy life and lack of leisure time. But she does not score high at motherhood, and there is every reason to believe that her marriage is more likely to end in failure. Coupling all this with the fact that she does not make nearly so much money at her job as the unmarried career woman, we are forced to conclude that the working wife occupies a rather ambiguous twilight zone. By and large she does not combine the advantages of marriage with the advantages of a career—rather, she seems to be in the unhappy position of being neither fish nor fowl, not quite a wife and not quite a career woman either. There are undoubtedly many exceptions—and perhaps many intangible factors, not measured in the survey, that give the working wife a great deal of satisfaction. But in general, and on the basis of what we have measured, it appears that the average graduate who tries to be both wife and career woman is not fully successful either way.

PART FOUR

The Group Portrait

9

Six Million Opinions

Since men and women play such different economic roles in our society, we have thus far considered our graduates as two separate groups: the Old Grads and the Ex-Coeds. Now it is time to attempt a group portrait, for despite their varying careers college men and women play an almost equal part as citizens. There are no sex barriers when it comes to holding a political opinion or casting a ballot, or helping to mold the social and religious life of the community. Our graduates, men and women alike, have their notions of how our government should be run, how our society should be organized, and how the United States should deal with the rest of the world. Their thoughts are important for two reasons: in the first place the six million college graduates constitute an important bloc of public opinion, and in the second place the graduates are presumably in a more advantageous position than the average person to influence the opinions of others.

Are the graduates for or against the New Deal? Are they isolationalists or internationalists? How do they stand on civil rights? Are they Republicans, Democrats, or Independents (or perchance even Socialists or Communists)? Do they support the churches or have they all become atheists? And what, incidentally, do they think of the colleges that helped make them what they are today?

Naturally these are difficult questions. But our survey does seem to cast at least a little light into this area—and while in some cases the beam may be flickering and untrustworthy, in other cases it seems to make the facts clear beyond doubt. Some of the answers we get are quite surprising—especially in contrast to the folklore—and this section of the book will be devoted to them.

Point 1: Such Conservative Young Radicals!

Part of the folklore about college people stems from the fact that over the years college students have had a great propensity for shocking their elders. The college set always seems to go about twenty dangerous steps farther than its parents ever did—or at least than the parents can remember doing, the capacity of the older people to forget that they were ever young and foolish being quite notorious. From time to time in recent memory college students have taken up such outlandish fads as rolled stockings, slacks, raccoon coats, convertibles, blanket parties, and the consumption of live goldfish. They have made the nights horrible with their bonfires, snake dances, and fraternity initiations; they have torn down goalposts and deposited cows in the chapel belfry.

All this is really none of our business here; we would only be getting into the propagation of folklore if we attempted to speculate on whether this type of social behavior is actually as common on the campus as some people think or is only over-publicized, or indeed whether college students behave any differently from their contemporaries of equal youth and exuberance. But many critics of the American college have tended to make two charges more or less in the same breath: they have said that college people were both "wild" and "radical." Some of the same newspapers that have delighted in publicizing the more boisterous campus incidents have also maintained that all college professors are Communists and that the students are being led to perdition. Many parents have had two worries inextricably blended in their minds: the first that their children might get out of hand socially on the campus, the second that the children might simultaneously acquire a whole set of radical and un-American notions.

It is easy to see how the college could acquire a reputation in the folklore as radical. Indeed it is perhaps a minor miracle that the college has not been the subject of even more widespread and more heated argument. In many ways the campus is the center of American intellectual life, and therefore the center of a kind of mass debate among all kinds of ideas and viewpoints. It is the business of higher education, as a matter of fact, not to bow down before the icons but to examine them, question them, and where necessary destroy them. In this process it is inevitable that occasionally a student taking a course in the history of zoology will horrify his fundamentalist parents, or that an economics student will lean toward Keynes rather than toward Adam Smith and therefore send his self-made businessman father's blood pressure boiling, or that a young woman intrigued by the behavioristic school of psychology will shock a mother brought up in a view of human nature tending more toward sweetness and light.

In the last two decades, during the conflict of the 1930's between laissez-faire economics and the big-government theories of Franklin Roosevelt—and still more recently the conflict between American democracy and Russian Communism—the word radicalism has been narrowed and sharpened in meaning. Nobody could hope to define precisely what the word means to most people as of this moment, much less what it has meant at various times during the turbulent political debates of our recent past; indeed radicalism is a word like liberalism or conservatism, with a different meaning for almost every person who utters it, and even for that person a different meaning in July from the meaning it had in June. But in general the word has come to mean just one thing—a Communist, or a sympathizer with either the present Russian regime or with the general objectives of theoretical Communism. Short of open sympathy with Communism, it has been possible to propound the most drastic kind of government powers and controls without necessarily being considered a radical. Bernard M. Baruch, for example, has been an ardent advocate of complete and total government control over prices, wages, and indeed the whole economy, not only in a world war but also in a period of limited mobilization such as the nation undertook upon the outbreak of the war in Korea. Yet nobody has ever accused Mr. Baruch of radicalism. He has been known as a capitalist, a free-enterpriser, and a foe of Communism, and therefore he has completely escaped any charges of deviation. The same thing has been true, in a somewhat different way, of Harry S. Truman. Many of the laws advocated by Mr. Truman would have greatly increased the power and influence of the government and curtailed individual freedom of action, at least by the definition that individual freedom of action had in the United States in the past. Yet few critics have talked of Mr. Truman as a radical, whatever other names they might have called him. In other words, the United States has come to accept with scarcely a quiver of excitement some ideas that would have horrified previous generations.

If our graduates turn out to be "a little bit radical"—in a manner of speaking—we should therefore not be at all surprised. The real surprise would come if they turned out to be quite conservative: if they seemed to have the same sort of viewpoint, say, that would have been considered anti-radical in the 1920's or earlier.

One thing that would have been considered quite radical by most Americans in the 1920's, but was the prevailing majority philosophy of government by the time of the survey, is the New Deal—and we have a pretty accurate notion of how the graduates feel about the New Deal. As part of the survey they were asked to agree or disagree with a number of statements of opinion, on a good many subjects, and from the list we can pick four statements that bear very strongly on feelings about government. As can be seen from examining the four statements in Chart 20, they are in no sense an exact measurement of pro- or anti-New Deal sentiments, such a thing being impossible anyway. But in general a strong anti-New Dealer would be inclined to agree and a strong pro-New Dealer to disagree, while a person who was on the fence might agree with some of the statements, disagree with others, or take refuge in the no-opinion column.

If the graduates should develop to be pro-New Deal by the standards of Chart 20, we should hardly be entitled to call them radicals—for any theory of government which had won a majority vote in so many con-secutive presidential elections was certainly not radical by the lights of current political thinking. But if they turn out to be anti-New Deal, we can be absolutely sure that they are *not* radical. The majorities piled up on the yes side of the column in Chart 20, therefore, are significant in themselves. And it is even more noteworthy that only 6% of the gradu-ates disagreed on all four questions, another 5% on three out of four, and 25% on two out of four, making a total of 36% who cast what we shall roughly call a pro-New Deal vote. On the other hand 37% agreed on all four and another 27% agreed on three out of four, making a total of 64% who can be classed as anti-New Deal.

There is, however, a great difference in the voting by age groups. Among graduates under 30 years old the proportion of anti-New Dealers is only 49%. In the thirties the proportion rises to 62%, in the forties to 71%, and after 50 to 80%. (This is not merely a matter of the gradu-ates' growing wealthier as they grow older; the same pattern holds re-

CHART 20 **Opinions on government**

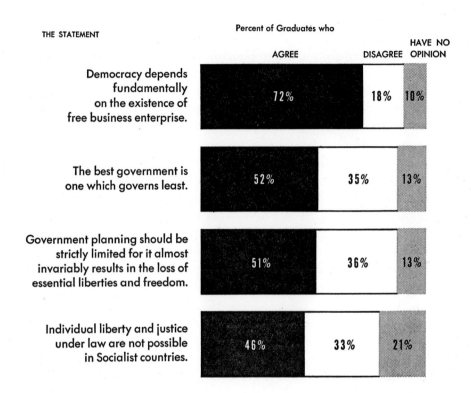

THE STATEMENT

Percent of Graduates who

	AGREE	DISAGREE	HAVE NO OPINION
Democracy depends fundamentally on the existence of free business enterprise.	72%	18%	10%
The best government is one which governs least.	52%	35%	13%
Government planning should be strictly limited for it almost invariably results in the loss of essential liberties and freedom.	51%	36%	13%
Individual liberty and justice under law are not possible in Socialist countries.	46%	33%	21%

gardless of income.) The older the graduate, in other words, the less likely he is to be a radical by any kind of definition. Perhaps the graduates change as they get older; after all, conservatism is supposed to be the province of older people, and radicalism the province of youth. Or perhaps the statistics merely reflect the changing intellectual climate of our recent history. Our 50-and-over graduates were at least 35 years old and probably well set in their political thinking before Franklin Roosevelt and the New Deal came along. Our under-30 graduates, and many of the graduates in their thirties, grew up under Franklin Roosevelt.

However provocative the age differences may be, they should not be permitted to obscure the basic point. On the whole, and in every age group except the under-30's, our graduates are sharply anti-New Deal. For people considered in the folklore to be suspect of radicalism, our graduates are very conservative folk indeed.

Point 2: The Internationalist versus the Isolationist

Chart 21 explores the graduates' position on another important issue of the day: the question of the United States' role in world affairs. Grouped here are six statements * that can be taken as a rough measure of internationalist or isolationist sentiments. They are by no means a perfect criterion and indeed any single statement in the list could be debated almost endlessly. It was quite possible, for example, for a person of strongly internationalist sentiments in 1947 to feel that the United Nations as then constituted was unsafe to trust with binding decisions. Statements numbers five and six also contain a vast amount of room for difference of opinion; certainly not all internationalists would agree. But the fact is that while a disagreement on any of these statements might not necessarily indicate isolationist leanings, an agreement definitely indicates internationalist sentiments; so that the large proportion shown in the yes column of Chart 21 is a significant measure of how the graduates feel about world affairs.

As another way of looking at the same set of responses—a way that makes up in convenience what it lacks in complete accuracy—let us say that a graduate who agrees with five or with all six of the statements in Chart 21 is an internationalist. A graduate who agrees with three or four is an in-betweener, and a graduate who agrees with none of the statements, or with only one or two of the six, is an isolationist. By this standard 37% are internationalists; 40% are in between, and only 23% are isolationists. Thus no matter how the responses are tabulated, it is clear that the weight of graduate opinion is quite heavily on the side of internationalism.

Age again plays a prominent part in the graduates' sentiments. Among

* Naturally the survey questions were not worded exactly as shown here—the questions were always put as positive statements, and a strong interventionist graduate would agree with some and disagree with others. For convenience in presenting the statistics, we have reworded the statements here so that an agreement always means an interventionist response, and a disagreement an isolationist response. The same procedure has been followed in the charts to come in this chapter.

CHART 21

Opinions on international affairs

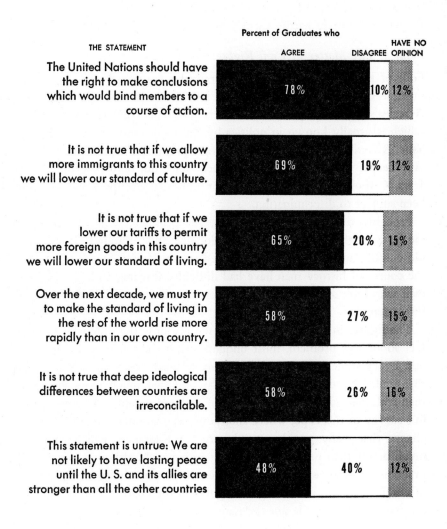

Percent of Graduates who

THE STATEMENT | AGREE | DISAGREE | HAVE NO OPINION

The United Nations should have the right to make conclusions which would bind members to a course of action.
78%   10% 12%

It is not true that if we allow more immigrants to this country we will lower our standard of culture.
69%   19%   12%

It is not true that if we lower our tariffs to permit more foreign goods in this country we will lower our standard of living.
65%   20%   15%

Over the next decade, we must try to make the standard of living in the rest of the world rise more rapidly than in our own country.
58%   27%   15%

It is not true that deep ideological differences between countries are irreconcilable.
58%   26%   16%

This statement is untrue: We are not likely to have lasting peace until the U. S. and its allies are stronger than all the other countries
48%   40%   12%

graduates 50 and over the proportion who qualify as isolationists on our scale is 31%. The figure drops to 24% among the 40-year-olds, 20% among the 30-year-olds, and 18% among those under 30. In view of the great sea-change in American opinion in general in our recent history, from the violent isolationism of the 1920's and early 1930's to the broader world outlook that began with the rise of Hitler and with World War II, these figures are hardly surprising.

Point 3: The Matter of Civil Rights

Four of the statements put to the graduates for agreement or disagreement, as can be seen in Chart 22, fell into a pattern that relates to one of America's most difficult and touchiest problems: the unsolved dilemma which is usually known in politics by the euphemism of the civil rights issue. A franker phrase, of course, is race prejudice. Indeed the issue goes even deeper than a mere matter of race—since not only Negroes but also Jews, Catholics, Mexicans, and other minority groups have sometimes been subject to discrimination.

Probably the best way to describe the problem, which has so many facets, is as the conflict between tolerance and prejudice. It is a very old conflict and by no means confined to the United States; all through the course of history men have had difficulty learning to live with other men who look different, speak a different language, or worship at a different temple.

The figures in Chart 22, which show only how the graduates *say* they feel about this problem, must unquestionably be taken with a grain of salt. Every student of the American scene knows that this whole issue is surrounded by considerable hypocrisy, and that much more lip service than real homage is paid to the ideal of real and complete tolerance. Even in a survey of this type, where anonymity is guaranteed, there is a strong chance that many people would vote for tolerance, which sounds so much better than prejudice when put into words, although not actually practicing tolerance in their daily lives. In all probability many students of ethnic relations, examining the figures in the chart, will conclude that the remarkable thing is not the majorities in favor of tolerance, but the relatively large number of people who were frank enough to disagree. On the other hand, the figures show at the very least that prejudice is not considered respectable or popular among graduates.

CHART 22 **Opinions on minorities**

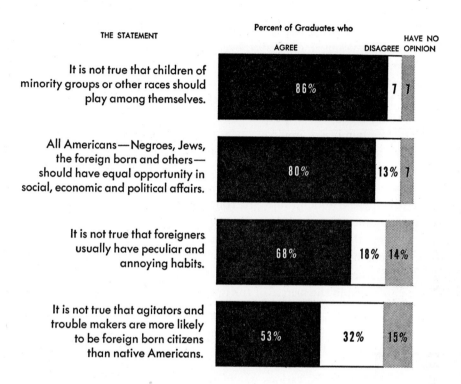

THE STATEMENT — Percent of Graduates who — AGREE — DISAGREE — HAVE NO OPINION

It is not true that children of minority groups or other races should play among themselves. — 86% — 7 — 7

All Americans—Negroes, Jews, the foreign born and others—should have equal opportunity in social, economic and political affairs. — 80% — 13% — 7

It is not true that foreigners usually have peculiar and annoying habits. — 68% — 18% — 14%

It is not true that agitators and trouble makers are more likely to be foreign born citizens than native Americans. — 53% — 32% — 15%

Once again the figures in the chart can be rearranged, as was done in the cases of New Dealism and anti-New Dealism and internationalism versus isolationism. In this case we can set up our standards as follows: a graduate who agrees with all four statements is tolerant; a graduate who agrees with three is an in-betweener, and a graduate who agrees with two or less must be considered as frankly prejudiced. On this scale 38% of the graduates qualify as tolerant, 30% as in-betweeners, and 32% as prejudiced—a remarkably even division which is an interesting reflection of the deep and disturbing nature of the problem.

In this case the age differences are especially notable. Of the graduates 50 and over, 47% rate on our scale as prejudiced. But this proportion drops rapidly to 34% among the 40-year-olds, 29% among the 30-year-olds, and a mere 24% among the under-30 group. Of the newest crop of graduates, in other words, only about half as many are "prejudiced" as in the oldest crop. Here is a case where opinion among the graduates has obviously been changing sharply over the years. To the finding that prejudice is not considered respectable among our graduates as a whole, we can now add that what respectability it does have is among the older generations. The younger graduates, even regardless of their own religious backgrounds, have moved strongly in the other direction.

There is another very provocative comparison that can be made here. As will be explained in detail in Chapter 20, college graduates tend to be a fairly migratory sort of people. Among the graduates in the survey we have quite a number of graduates who were born and reared in the South but have moved away, and also quite a few who were reared elsewhere but now live in the South. In addition, of course, we have a great many who have spent all their lives either below or above the Mason-Dixon line. When these four groups are compared on the matter of tolerance versus prejudice, we get the peculiar pattern shown in Chart 23.

It appears that Southern graduates who have moved "north" (i.e., to any of the non-Southern states) have substantially less prejudiced views— but Northerners who have moved to the South are, if anything, only more confirmed in the matter of tolerance.

Point 4: Religion and Atheism

On the matter of how religious the college graduates are—or how irreligious—one question asked in the survey seems to go right to the heart of the matter. Among the various statements put to the graduates, for agreement or disagreement, was this one: "Religion has little to offer intelligent, scientific people today." Naturally a religious person would immediately disagree, without a moment's hesitation. A militant atheist would be just as quick to agree. The agnostics and doubting Thomases would either agree or put down "no opinion," probably depending in part on whether they interpreted the statement as applying to organized religion or to religion as a philosophic concept.

In tabulating the graduates' response, it is necessary to divide them into the groups brought up as Catholics, Protestants, and Jews. Of the Catholic graduates, 91% flatly disagreed—thereby expressing full faith in their religion. Among Protestants the ratio dropped to 84%. And among Jews only 56%, hardly more than half, gave this affirmation of religious belief.

When we examine the actual churchgoing habits of the graduates, as has been done in Chart 24, the differences among Catholics, Protestants,

CHART 23

Mobility and opinions on minorities

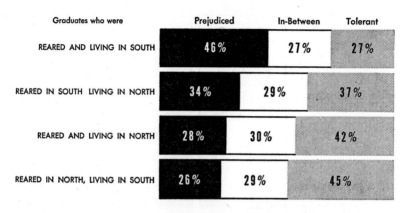

Percent whose attitudes on minorities are

Graduates who were	Prejudiced	In-Between	Tolerant
REARED AND LIVING IN SOUTH	46%	27%	27%
REARED IN SOUTH LIVING IN NORTH	34%	29%	37%
REARED AND LIVING IN NORTH	28%	30%	42%
REARED IN NORTH, LIVING IN SOUTH	26%	29%	45%

and Jews take on an even sharper pattern. About four of five Catholic men and nine of ten Catholic women attend church regularly—every week or nearly every week—and the number who do not attend church at all is very small. Among Protestants the number who attend regularly is notably smaller, and the number who rarely or never attend goes up to three men of ten and one woman of five. Among the Jews only about one person of eight attends regularly, and nearly half do not attend at all. (It is noteworthy that among Catholics and Protestants the women are more regular churchgoers than the men, but this difference between the sexes does not apply to the Jewish group.)

Unfortunately we do not have any figures for the population as a whole to compare with this information about the graduates. We have no way of telling whether our graduates are more or less religious-minded than non-college people of the same age and background; nor do we know how their churchgoing habits compare. All we know, from the *Christian Herald's* annual reports on church memberships, is that out of 153 million Americans, in 1950, about 50 million belonged to Protestant churches, 29 million to Catholic churches, 5 million to Jewish congregations, and 2 million to other churches—leaving 67 million who were not active members of any church. How many of these last millions avoid the churches

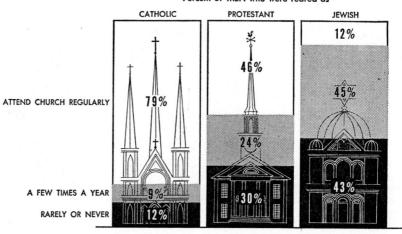

CHART 24 Graduates as churchgoers

Percent of MEN who were reared as

	CATHOLIC	PROTESTANT	JEWISH
ATTEND CHURCH REGULARLY	79%	46% / 24%	12% / 45%
A FEW TIMES A YEAR	9%	30%	43%
RARELY OR NEVER	12%		

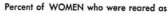

Percent of WOMEN who were reared as

	CATHOLIC	PROTESTANT	JEWISH
ATTEND CHURCH REGULARLY	89%	59% / 22%	12% / 41%
A FEW TIMES A YEAR	5%	19%	47%
RARELY OR NEVER	6%		

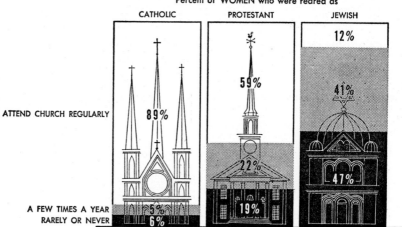

for reasons of agnosticism, and how many simply have neglected to go through the formalities of church membership, is not recorded.

About all we can do is make a guess. Among Catholics and Protestants, especially the Catholics, there seems to be little evidence that college training undercuts religious beliefs. Among our Jewish graduates, however, the proportion who have broken with religion is quite high, and the proportion of active participants in the religious congregation is notably small. Whether college has anything to do with this phenomenon among the Jews, we cannot say.

10

In the Voting Booth

At the time of the survey the Democratic Party had won four straight presidential elections and was about to win another one; it had controlled the White House and with one exception the Congress for 15 years. Most political experts, looking at 1947 with the added wisdom of hindsight, agree that in that year the Democrats were without question the majority party. True, they had lost the Congressional elections of 1946, but in view of their 1948 victory that turned out to be merely a temporary setback, due probably to the meat shortage and high prices of the time.

From the end of the Civil War until 1932, the United States had been predominantly Republican, and Democratic presidents not only rare but also somewhat accidental. Even the election of Franklin Roosevelt in 1932 would hardly have come about except for the business depression. But Roosevelt was one of the most magnetic political figures of our history (even though he repelled some people as strongly as he attracted others), and he brought about a tremendous shift in American political thinking. During his 13 years as President whole new crops of American voters grew up, attained their majority, and seemed to become Democrats almost as a matter of course. It should be pointed out that there were a good many politicians, including even some of the wisest ones on the Democratic side, who if pressed for their honest opinion would have said in 1947 that the country was still predominantly Republican, and that the long string of Democratic successes was due only to Roosevelt's personal attraction coupled with the reluctance of voters to change horses during the war years of 1940, 1942, and 1944. But in retrospect, following the election of Harry Truman in 1948, even these politicians now concede that they were wrong and that the temper of the nation in the late 1940's was thoroughly Democratic.

The United States was Democratic—but our college graduates were not. In the election of 1944, even in wartime, 51% of the graduates favored Dewey and only 47% favored Roosevelt. (The other 2% favored one or another of the minor parties.) Looking forward to the 1948 election, at a time when nobody could be sure who the candidates might be, 41% of the graduates were undecided how they would vote—but another 40% intended to vote Republican and only 19% were fairly sure they would vote Democratic.

Another gauge of the graduates' political sentiments, perhaps better because it is uncomplicated by the personalities of the candidates in any given election or by any temporary feelings of exasperation or gratitude, is the way they classify themselves by party affiliation. The figures are shown in Chart 25, which further bears out the picture of the graduates as predominantly Republican.

Putting together the information in the chart with the actual voting records and plans of the graduates, we can reach a number of conclusions about our graduate sample:

Among the graduates who definitely give themselves a party label, the Republicans outnumber the Democrats about 3 to 2.

The number of Democrats among women graduates is definitely higher than among the men.

A large number of graduates—nearly four out of ten men and about three out of ten women—list themselves as Independents.

The Independents were voting, at the time, about half for the Democrats and half for the Republicans.

Although there are more women graduates than men who call themselves Democrats, there are just as many women Republicans as men Republicans. The explanation is that fewer women call themselves Independents.

The number of graduates who belong to any of the minor parties—Socialist, Communist, Prohibition, Farmer-Labor, American Labor, Liberal, etc.—is only 1 out of 200.

In evaluating the Republican trend shown by all these figures, it must be remembered that in most of the Southern states Republicans are traditionally so scarce that they are sometimes exhibited at county fairs. In these states, except under very exceptional circumstances, there is no quarrel between Democrats and Republicans; by and large everybody is a Democrat and all the debating of issues takes place in the primaries. It

CHART 25

Graduates are Republican

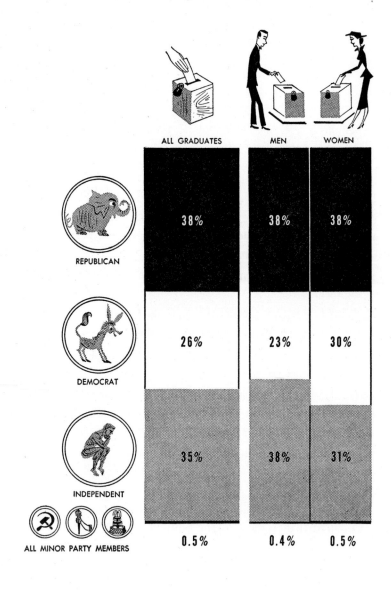

	ALL GRADUATES	MEN	WOMEN
REPUBLICAN	38%	38%	38%
DEMOCRAT	26%	23%	30%
INDEPENDENT	35%	38%	31%
ALL MINOR PARTY MEMBERS	0.5%	0.4%	0.5%

so happens that about 22% of our graduates were living in the South, and most of the 22% had also been reared there. If it were not for the sectional politics of these graduates, the Republican slant would be much more pronounced. Indeed we had better take a look right now—since the Southern states affect all the statistics in this chapter—at the politics of the South as opposed to the politics of the rest of the nation, which for convenience here we shall again call the North.

Chart 26, which tells the full story, is a quite fascinating commentary on the relationship between politics and geography. Reading from the top down, it is first of all clear that the graduates who were born, reared and are still living in the South follow the traditional Southern voting pattern. Only an insignificant number—nine out of 100—are Republicans. Only about one out of four calls himself an Independent. The vast majority—nearly seven out of 10—are Democrats. But when Southern-born college people migrate north after graduation, they turn out to be not nearly so devoted to the Democratic Party. The proportion who class themselves as Democrats drops well below the 50% mark; the proportion of Republicans and Independents rises sharply.

The Northerners who go South after graduation are much more stubborn in their voting habits. Of all these migrants expressing a party preference, the majority are Republicans, even though voting in a lost cause. The proportion calling themselves Democrats is not much greater than among Northern-born graduates who have stayed on their original side of the line.

By far the most significant figure in Chart 26 concerns the graduates who were born and reared in the North and have remained there after graduation. This is our largest single group of graduates; in fact it makes up 71%, or nearly three-fourths, of our total sample. Among this big group, who attained their majority and now cast their ballots in states where there is a real contest between the two parties, 45 out of 100 are Republicans, only 18 out of 100 are Democrats, and 37 out of 100 call themselves Independents.

Eliminating the effect of the one-party system in the South, our graduates have proved to be strongly Republican—and this at a time when majority opinion in the U.S. was definitely Democratic.

CHART 26 **Mobility and politics**

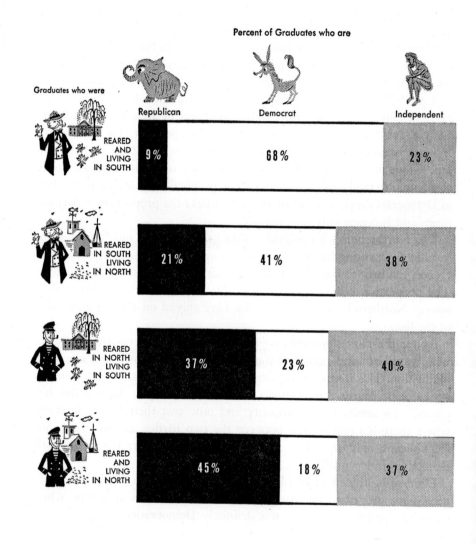

Percent of Graduates who are

Graduates who were

Republican — Democrat — Independent

REARED AND LIVING IN SOUTH: 9% | 68% | 23%

REARED IN SOUTH LIVING IN NORTH: 21% | 41% | 38%

REARED IN NORTH LIVING IN SOUTH: 37% | 23% | 40%

REARED AND LIVING IN NORTH: 45% | 18% | 37%

Politics by Age and Income

It was a political axiom at the time of the survey that the Republicans were the party of the rich, relatively speaking, and the Democrats the party of the poor. Perhaps it is only to be expected, therefore, that our graduates should turn out to be mostly Republicans—since we have already seen that they are a notably successful group by financial standards. On the other hand, it was also a political axiom at the time that the Democrats were the party of the young—which creates a paradox because our graduates are distinguished for their youth as well as for their wealth. By the premises of the day's politics, the graduates were pulled one way by their salaries and another way by their age—and this is obviously a place where it will be interesting to divide and subdivide the statistics for some further enlightenment.

On the matter of income alone, it quickly becomes clear, as shown in Chart 27, that the proportion of Republicans among the graduates does rise in direct relation to income, while the proportion of Democrats declines. The differences, however, are less than one might have expected. The men in every income bracket, even under $3,000 a year, are more Republican than Democrat. Only among the women with family incomes of less than $3,000 a year are the Democrats in the lead, and even there by only a small degree. The matter of wealth certainly does not tell the whole story.

The types of jobs held by the graduates seem to offer a better clue. Leaving out the women, who are not so likely to be employed and are more difficult to classify even when they are working, we find that among men graduates the greatest proportion of Republicans is furnished by the business proprietors, executives, and administrators. In this group the confirmed Republicans total 43%. The proportion among professional men excluding teachers is 42%—and then it drops off rather sharply to 35% among white collar workers, 29% among teachers, and 23% among skilled and semi-skilled workers. Thus the jobs of greatest economic prestige—those capable of providing the largest incomes—produce more Republicans than the jobs which are routine by nature or carry a definite income ceiling. Within the various job categories actual income does not seem to make nearly so much difference as the potentials of the job; an executive earning under $5,000 a year is almost as likely to be a Republican as one earning more than $5,000 a year, and among teachers and workmen the salary seems to have practically no effect whatever.

CHART 27 # Income and the ballot box

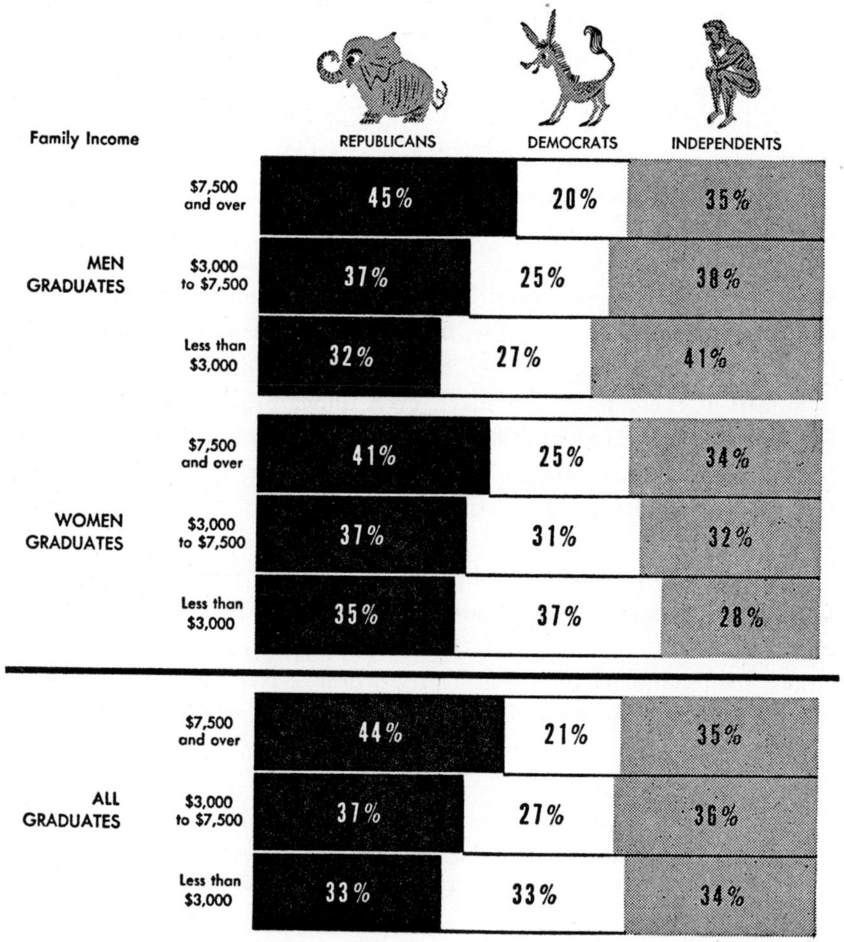

Family Income		REPUBLICANS	DEMOCRATS	INDEPENDENTS
MEN GRADUATES	$7,500 and over	45%	20%	35%
	$3,000 to $7,500	37%	25%	38%
	Less than $3,000	32%	27%	41%
WOMEN GRADUATES	$7,500 and over	41%	25%	34%
	$3,000 to $7,500	37%	31%	32%
	Less than $3,000	35%	37%	28%
ALL GRADUATES	$7,500 and over	44%	21%	35%
	$3,000 to $7,500	37%	27%	36%
	Less than $3,000	33%	33%	34%

This is a point on which politicians could have some heated debates. A good New Deal or Fair Deal Democrat would doubtless argue that the graduates often are dazzled by their high-sounding jobs into identifying themselves with the party of special privilege—whereas their real economic interests, if judged by their salaries instead of their titles, lie with the Democrats. On the other hand a good free-enterprising Republican would doubtless argue that the people to be found running their own businesses, holding down administrative jobs, or working on their own as professionals are simply more likely to have a love of risk and initiative—and therefore to be Republicans—than the more security-minded people in the less responsible jobs or in such relatively risk-proof professions as teaching.

The effect of age on voting habits follows a sharp and definite pattern. The best way to show it is Chart 28, in which we have again confined the figures to men graduates and have taken only the "richest" and "poorest" graduates who fall into the over-50 or under-30 age brackets. Given the same income status, the over-50 graduates are much more Republican than the younger men. In fact the older graduates are strongly Republican even when earning less than $3,000 a year, while the very youngest graduates do not have any pronounced majority of Republicans even when they are in the top income bracket.

Many other statistical tables could be drawn up along this same line, but there is no point in doing it here because the results are always the same. With a very few exceptions, the Republicans have the lead, or at least a 50-50 basis, no matter how the figures are broken up. But the ratio of Republicanism is always in direct proportion to age. The older the graduate, the more likely he is to be a Republican. The younger he is, the more likely he is to be a Democrat. Age, in fact, makes much more difference than wealth. We have no way of determining from our data, of course, whether the graduates actually tend to switch from the Democratic to the Republican Party as they get older—or whether the figures simply reflect the fact that the older graduates grew up at a time when the whole country was predominantly Republican, and the younger graduates at a time when it was predominantly Democrat. Nor do we have any way of knowing what if anything has happened to the graduates' sentiments as a result of the changing tides of U.S. politics since the survey was made.

CHART 28

Age
even more than income
affects the vote

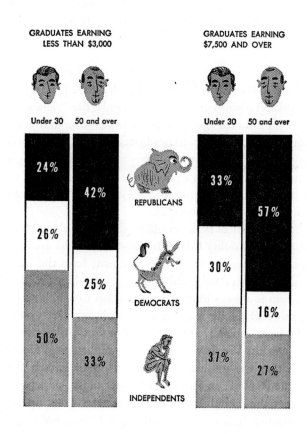

GRADUATES EARNING
LESS THAN $3,000

Under 30   50 and over

GRADUATES EARNING
$7,500 AND OVER

Under 30   50 and over

24%   42%

26%

50%   25%

33%

REPUBLICANS

DEMOCRATS

INDEPENDENTS

33%   57%

30%

16%

37%   27%

Father's Influence

In politics the traditional rule is: like father, like son. There has always been a tendency for politics to be a family matter, for wives to favor the party of their husbands and for children to follow the politics of their elders. Some of the more cynical politicians, as a matter of fact, believe that heredity plays a greater part in elections than all the political issues and speeches put together.

The question is: Do our graduates follow the traditional pattern, or are they an exception to the rule? And we can get a pretty solid answer, since most graduates—about seven out of eight—knew and were able to tell us how their fathers usually voted. It turns out that of the fathers whose views are known, 56% usually voted Republican and 44% usually voted Democrat—which means that our predominantly Republican graduates also have, or had, predominantly Republican parents. Indeed the figures show that 58% of the graduates belong to the same party as dad. And only 10% have actually switched to the other party—with the remaining 32% calling themselves Independents. If we disregard the Independents, and consider only the graduates who definitely consider themselves Republicans or Democrats, we find that 85% follow the politics of their fathers and that only 15% have switched!

The small amount of switching that has taken place, however, has done so in a most extraordinary manner, as can be seen in Charts 29 and 30. In Chart 29 we consider only the graduates who had Republican fathers, and in Chart 30 those who had Democrat fathers. In both cases the figures for the graduates are broken down by income and also are divided into two age groups, over and under 40, to allow for the known effect of income and age on political views. What emerges, with all these factors taken into account, is a great contrast between the Republicans and the Democrats. The Republican fathers have lost very few of their graduate sons and daughters to the Democrats and the number lost is extremely constant regardless of the age or income of the children. Indeed the figures in all columns are a study in consistency, never varying more than a few percentage points. The Democrat fathers, on the other hand, have lost considerably more of their children to the Republicans—the losses being greatly affected by the age and even more by the income of the graduates. Especially for the over-40 group of graduates from Democrat families, the proportion of Democrats declines and the proportion of Republicans increases with almost perfect regularity as income goes up. In

CHART 29

The politics of Graduates from Republican  families

Percent who are now

Graduates Present Income	REPUBLICANS	INDEPENDENTS	DEMOCRATS
40 AND OVER			
$7,500 AND OVER	66%	28%	6%
$5,000 TO $7,500	62%	29%	9%
$3,000 TO $5,000	62%	31%	7%
LESS THAN $3,000	69%	24%	7%
UNDER 40			
$7,500 AND OVER	60%	33%	7%
$5,000 TO $7,500	57%	36%	7%
$3,000 TO $5,000	63%	31%	6%
LESS THAN $3,000	55%	37%	8%

CHART 30

The politics of Graduates  from Democratic families

Percent who are now

DEMOCRATS

INDEPENDENTS

REPUBLICANS

Graduates
Present
Income

40 AND OVER

DEMOCRATS	INDEPENDENTS	REPUBLICANS	
39%	34%	27%	$7,500 AND OVER
46%	34%	20%	$5,000 TO $7,500
53%	27%	20%	$3,000 TO $5,000
67%	21%	12%	LESS THAN $3,000

UNDER 40

DEMOCRATS	INDEPENDENTS	REPUBLICANS	
40%	50%	10%	$7,500 AND OVER
54%	35%	11%	$5,000 TO $7,500
55%	35%	10%	$3,000 TO $5,000
61%	30%	9%	LESS THAN $3,000

the under-40 group, the number of Democrats again goes down steadily as income increases. In this group, however, the losses to the Republican Party are much smaller, and not appreciably affected by income. As the under-40 graduates from Democratic homes get wealthier, they simply become more Independent in their voting habits.

To sum up: the graduates from Republican families have remained very stubbornly Republican. Only a tiny fraction have switched to the Democrats. While a considerable number have become Independents, the majority have continued to call themselves out-and-out Republicans. Their tendency to remain Republican is not affected very much if at all by the income bracket in which they wind up, and is just about as pronounced among graduates under 40 as among older ones.

The graduates from Democrat families are considerably less Democrat than their fathers. Among the over-40 graduates, a substantial number have switched to Republican, the proportion of deserters rising consistently by the size of their incomes. Even under 40, there are fewer sons and daughters of Democratic fathers who call themselves Democrats than there are graduates from Republican families who call themselves Republicans. But here the difference is accounted for mostly by graduates who have become Independents, rather than by any great defection to Republican ranks. It is still noticeable, however, that even among the under-40 graduates from Democrat families, the strength of Democrat sentiment goes down as income goes up.

By and large the graduates do follow the traditional pattern; the sons do tend to vote like their fathers. But whatever effect college has is to the benefit of the Republican Party and to the detriment of the Democrats. It is rather ironic, in the light of our findings, that the Democratic Party should have been the great advocate in recent years of more Federal aid to higher education!

The Independent Voter

No discussion of the political affiliations of our graduates would be complete without special mention of the Independents, who comprise such a large group—about one out of three—and crop up with such regularity among graduates of all ages, family backgrounds, and income groups. In fact the big number of Independents is perhaps the outstanding political phenomenon among the graduates; it is highly unlikely that a census of the non-graduate population would produce anything like such a proportion of men and women who disclaimed favoritism to either party.

One remarkable thing about the Independents is that it is very difficult to correlate their political stand with anything else that we know about them. They occur with about equal frequency in all income brackets; they come with about equal frequency from all types of colleges; and they voted about half Republican and half Democratic the last time they went to the polls. We get one possible clue if we consider men graduates only and rank them by year of graduation; doing this we find that the proportion of Independents declines steadily as we go back from the Class of '47 to the Class of 1878. Among graduates of the past ten years, 45% call themselves Independents. The proportion declines to 41% between 10 years and 20, to 37% between 20 years and 30, and to 30% among those who left the campus more than 30 years ago. But these years of graduation differences do not hold, at least not to any significant degree, for the women graduates. One logical explanation seems to be that the men get more and more involved in practical politics, either in their communities or among their working associates, and thus less and less able to remain aloof from the political parties as they grow older. We can probably assume that the newest group of graduates will also number fewer Independents as the years go by.

That leaves us very close to where we started. In fact the only correlation that seems to hold up at all is with college grades. If we divide the graduates into three groups by scholastic standing, we find that 42% of students who made mostly A's call themselves Independents, and that the proportion declines to 35% among the mostly-B students and to 31% among those who report making mostly C's and D's. This pattern, furthermore, seems to hold up even when we control the three scholastic groups by age or by present income. There seems to be no doubt that the best students have the greatest propensity for political independence, and that the poorest students have the least. But even among the poorest students the proportion of Independents is still so high as to be a cause for considerable wonder. In other words the good students have the strongest leanings toward political independence—but they certainly do not have a monopoly on it.

Abandoning the attempt to discover from our figures what turns so many graduates into Independents—an attempt which turns out to be largely futile—we can enter a slightly more fruitful field of inquiry. There are some very definite differences in the opinions held by the Independents—as compared with Republicans or Democrats—on the subjects we discussed in the previous chapter. In that chapter we tried to draw up a set of standards for graduates who were outstandingly internationalist in their world outlook; outstandingly tolerant of other races, religions, and nations; and pro-New Deal or anti-New Deal in their attitude toward government. If we now compare the Independents, the Republicans, and the Democrats by those standards, we get the figures shown in Chart 31.

There are a number of notable features about Chart 31. In the first place, the Republicans and Democrats turn out to have only one real ideological quarrel among the three attitudes we are measuring here. When it comes to being internationalist or tolerant, they vary by only six percentage points, and even that difference is somewhat deceptive. It is accounted for almost entirely by the older graduates; among our over-50's the Democrats prove to be considerably more international-minded and more tolerant, but among younger graduates there are practically no differences at all. The only real bone of contention is the very thing that has been the center of the nation's political debate since the mid-1930's—the quarrel between the New Dealers and the anti-New Dealers.

The Independent group, on the matter of government planning, falls into about the same pattern as the Democrats. But its most notable feature is that it contains by far the highest proportion of all graduates who qualify as internationalist and tolerant by our quite strict standards. The Independent, then, tended at the time of the survey to be a man or woman who more or less approved of the New Deal theory of government, was strongly opposed to isolationism, and was a fervent advocate of the political program known as civil rights. The rich Independents as well as the poorer ones held these views, and so did the older Independents as well as the younger ones.

At this point our figures on the Independents run out. It would be interesting to know—and perhaps someone will make a new survey to find out—whether the Independents have changed any of their opinions in the meantime. The big group of graduate Independents must number well over two million influential voters if our sample is at all typical—and anyone who knew their present sentiments would be in a fine position to make a name for himself as an election prophet.

There is one other point, completely lacking in any statistical evidence, that must be made here. In fact the reader, if ever exposed to the college atmosphere, has probably already made it for himself. With very rare

CHART 31 Politics and opinions

Graduates who are

Percent whose opinions on World Affairs are

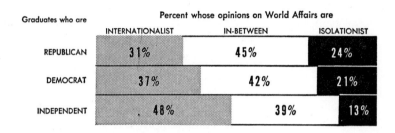

	INTERNATIONALIST	IN-BETWEEN	ISOLATIONIST
REPUBLICAN	31%	45%	24%
DEMOCRAT	37%	42%	21%
INDEPENDENT	48%	39%	13%

Percent whose opinions on Minorities are

	TOLERANT	IN-BETWEEN	PREJUDICED
REPUBLICAN	31%	32%	37%
DEMOCRAT	37%	27%	36%
INDEPENDENT	48%	29%	23%

Percent whose opinions on Government are

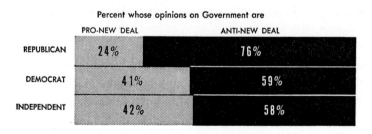

	PRO-NEW DEAL	ANTI-NEW DEAL
REPUBLICAN	24%	76%
DEMOCRAT	41%	59%
INDEPENDENT	42%	58%

exceptions, the members of college faculties present a completely non-partisan façade. It is their job to be critics of history and current events, rather than participants. Moreover, if they do have any strong leanings toward one party or another, it is part of their code to hide their feelings, at least in the classroom. Very few college people have ever heard a faculty lecture in favor of the Democrats or in favor of the Republicans. On the other hand almost every college student who ever took a course remotely bearing on current events has almost surely heard attacks, delivered with the utmost impartiality, on the political demagogues who unfortunately inhabit both parties from time to time. The academic viewpoint, in other words, is to abhor political chicanery, dishonesty, or demagogy wherever found, and to praise honesty and ability regardless of party. Presumably this attitude rubs off on a good many students, and it may be the only explanation we need for the large number of graduates who remain Independent in their post-campus life. Just as college ordinarily teaches its students to keep an open mind between literary romanticism and literary realism, or between the philosophies of Nietzsche and Plato, so it probably teaches a good many of its students to avoid the label of Republican or Democrat—and to decide on the basis of the candidates and the issues in any particular election. The political Independent, indeed, is probably the ideal citizen from the academic point of view.

Whether the Independents are very effective politically is something else again. A strong case can be made—one expert practical politician who has made it is the famous Ed Flynn, Democrat "Boss of the Bronx," in his book called *You're the Boss*—that by and large the Independent is a self-created political eunuch. Taking no part in the workday affairs of a political party, having nothing to do with the platform it chooses or the candidates it puts up for office, he is reduced to merely casting a vote of approval or disapproval on election day. By that time, the argument goes, he is too late; often he can only choose between the lesser of two evils. Thus perhaps two million Independent voters whom the colleges seem to have produced are a political question mark. From one point of view they constitute a good, big, impartial jury which acts as a check and a challenge to both parties. From another point of view, however, they represent a great waste of talent and brains.

Insofar as our survey was able to measure the political activity of the graduates—by such conventional standards as following current political events, voting in elections and primaries, signing petitions or writing to

Congressmen, etc.—there are no discernible differences between the Independents and the graduates who call themselves Republicans or Democrats. Indeed in the kind of activities that probably count the most, our graduates are all somewhat derelict. Only 17% had contributed money within the past year to a political cause or organization, and only 3% had done any fund-raising work for such a purpose. Moreover only 6% had held an elective office, or even unsuccessfully tried for one, within the past four years. In overwhelming majorities, the graduates of all shades of political coloration go out to vote; they follow political events in the newspapers and magazines and discuss them with their friends. But very few of them, even the staunch Democrats and the staunch Republicans, do much actual work for their parties.

It may be, of course, that the mere fact of belonging to one party or the other, and being as ready and eager to vote in primaries as in elections, gives the Democrats and Republicans a greater political voice than the Independents. But perhaps the ultimate political fact about our graduates is this: while they are an unusually well-informed and alert group of citizens, and conscientious about going to the polls, neither the Republicans, Democrats, nor Independents among them carry as much political weight as their position in life would justify. Like most non-graduates, most graduates seem to leave politics to the professionals. The tragedy of U.S. politics may be akin to that of the weather—while everybody complains about it, nobody including those best qualified does much about it.

CHAPTER 11

What College Graduates Think
About College

In the business world, one good measure of a firm's success is its number
of satisfied customers. In the world of education, the same measure must
have at least a certain amount of validity. If the great majority of all graduates are glad they went, we have to chalk up a mark in favor of the
colleges. On the other hand if the majority of graduates consider the
whole thing a waste of time, money, and effort, we should be moved to
some serious doubts.

This does not mean that the testimonials or complaints of former students can be taken as the final verdict on the value of higher education
as practiced in the United States. A testimonial might mean only that the
graduate was taught in college to be smug about his own learning and
accomplishments, not that he was really well educated or taught any real
accomplishments. A complaint might mean only that the graduate is a
chronic misfit and misanthrope who dislikes everything he has seen of the
world and of himself. But even considering these objections, it seems
profitable to examine what college graduates think of their college experience. A person undecided whether to go to Kennebunkport, Maine,
for his vacation could probably best make up his mind by finding as
many people as possible who had been there and asking them what they
thought of the place. A high school student debating whether to go to
college, or parents undecided whether or not to send the children, could
certainly do worse than seek the advice of as many people as possible
who have themselves been to college.

It turns out that our graduates, if they had it all to do over again, would
go back to the campus almost to the man. Out of every 100 graduates, 98
say they would return, with the men and women voting alike to within a

fraction of a percentage point. Indeed the great majority, or 84%, would go right back to the same college where they got their degrees. A few, 14%, would go back to college but to a different campus. Only two out of a hundred would stay away from college and take some different type of training.

In fact the graduates have remarkably few regrets of any kind about their college careers. One might suppose, for example, that many graduates would prefer in retrospect to take a different type of course. After all a college student has to make the decision on his "major" field of study while still quite young; often there is a certain amount of whim or accident about the courses taken, and tastes and interests change as the years go by. Yet even here three out of four students say they are satisfied, and only one out of four wishes that he had taken a different course of study. The proportion varies considerably depending on the type of major studied, as shown in Chart 32. But even the pharmacists, who are at the bottom of the list, still cast a heavy majority in favor of the field they chose.

The only significant doubt that the graduates seem to express is on the matter of generalized education versus specific. Educators have been debating this question on a high policy level for many years, of course; and the sentiment of the graduates indicates that it is often a matter of great personal and practical as well as theoretical concern. Only 44% feel that they made a wise choice on this matter—that is, that they were correct in choosing a curriculum that was mostly general, or mostly specific training for an occupation, or a 50-50 mixture of the two as the case may have been. Of the remaining 56%, it so happens that 35% wish they had taken more specific training, while 21% wish they had received a more generalized education. In the next chapter we shall go into detail on this conflict, and on the relative success or failure of the students who have generalized and the students who have specialized. In the meantime we can simply make the observation that of all the possible sources of regret which we have examined, this one seems to produce the most actual dissatisfaction. Perhaps the advantages of both types of education are so great that the students—as well as the educators who set the policies of the colleges—have a hard time making a decision. The pattern of our statistics—35 out of 100 wishing they had specialized more, 21 out of 100 wishing they had followed a more generalized curriculum—looks in some ways like a matter of the greener grass on the other side of the fence. Perhaps its ultimate

CHART 32

On second thought—
the grass is sometimes greener

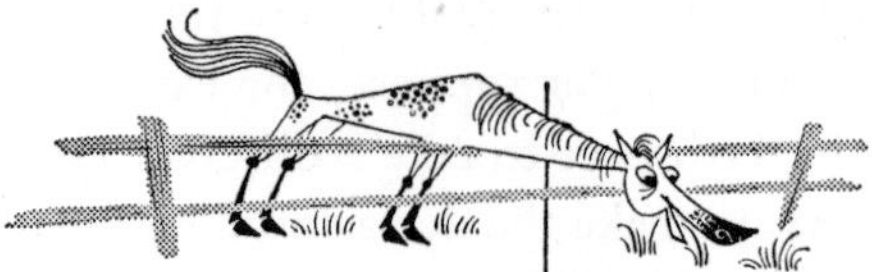

The field they majored in	Percent who wish they had done otherwise	The field they most frequently mention as a better choice
PRE-MEDICAL	9%	A DIFFERENT PROFESSION
PRE-LAW	14	MEDICINE
HOME ECONOMICS	14	THE HUMANITIES
PRE-DENTAL	18	A DIFFERENT PROFESSION
ENGINEERING	19	A DIFFERENT BRANCH OF ENGINEERING
FINE ARTS, MUSIC	22	THE SOCIAL SCIENCES
PHILOSOPHY, RELIGION	24	THE SOCIAL SCIENCES
SCIENCES, MATHEMATICS	24	A DIFFERENT BRANCH OF SCIENCE
AVERAGE FOR ALL GRADUATES	25	
AGRICULTURE, FORESTRY	27	MEDICINE
EDUCATION	28	BUSINESS ADMINISTRATION
SOCIAL SCIENCES	30	BUSINESS ADMINISTRATION
BUSINESS ADMINISTRATION	30	ENGINEERING
HISTORY, LITERATURE, LANGUAGES, ETC.	33	MEDICINE
PHARMACY	33	MEDICINE

meaning is that the colleges have not yet found the happy medium between the two types of education.

Despite the problem of general and specific education, if we add up all the answers of the graduates on matters relating to doing it over again, we get an impressive picture of satisfied customers. Just about a third of the graduates—33%—would do exactly as before: they would choose the same college, follow the same major course of study, and take whatever ratio they did of specialized and general training. Another 37% would change only one of these three factors. Only 22% regret two of their three decisions; a mere 8% regret all three. And perhaps the greatest testimonial of all is the fact that even of this somewhat disgruntled 8%—who feel that they went to the wrong college, took the wrong course, and chose unwisely between generalization and specialization, in other words practically went down on three straight strikes—most would go back to college if they had another chance. Although everything else went wrong, they at least feel that they were wise to matriculate.

Apparently this overwhelming vote of confidence does not have a purely materialistic origin. For on another group of questions, as can be seen in Chart 33, the graduates were not nearly so unanimously convinced that their college education had proved of great value in their occupations. True, the statistics in Chart 33 do constitute their own type of endorsement of college. A majority of graduates—not only the men and women with jobs, but even the coeds turned housewife—credited college with being of substantial value as training for what they were doing. Only a tiny fraction felt that college was no help at all in this regard. But taken as a whole, Chart 33 is not so favorable to the colleges as the figures we have just been examining. Of all the graduates, just seven out of ten feel that college "helped a lot," to use the words of the questionnaire, in their present occupations. The others believe only that college "helped some," or not at all. Now of course phrases like "helped a lot" and "helped some" are highly subjective and can be interpreted in almost any fashion one chooses; this is an area in which really accurate measurements are impossible. But it does seem noteworthy that any large percentage of graduates, after voting so fervently in favor of college and indeed in favor of most aspects of their own college careers, should be at all begrudging in the amount of practical occupational help they attribute to college.

CHART 33

Opinions on the
occupational benefits of college

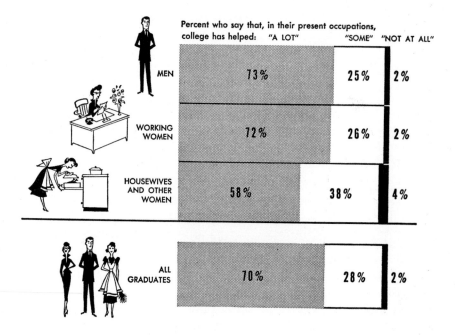

Percent who say that, in their present occupations,
college has helped: "A LOT"   "SOME"   "NOT AT ALL"

	"A LOT"	"SOME"	"NOT AT ALL"
MEN	73%	25%	2%
WORKING WOMEN	72%	26%	2%
HOUSEWIVES AND OTHER WOMEN	58%	38%	4%
ALL GRADUATES	70%	28%	2%

Chart 34 casts some additional light on this point. When the graduates are divided into groups by the courses they majored in, and then are examined as to whether they feel college has helped them "a lot" or just "some" or not at all in their occupations, some very sharp differences appear. In the professions of medicine and dentistry, practically all the graduates credit college with helping "a lot." But from these fields down the percentages drop rather quickly, until at the very bottom only a bare majority of the social science students, or 54%, feel that their training helped "a lot." Yet we have seen how thoroughly the graduates approve of college in general; evidently their approval does not depend entirely on the occupational boost they feel it has given them.

This supposition gains further credence from the graduates' letters. To be sure, many of the letter writers are critical of college; and we shall

CHART 34

The more specialized the training, the more college helps in an occupation

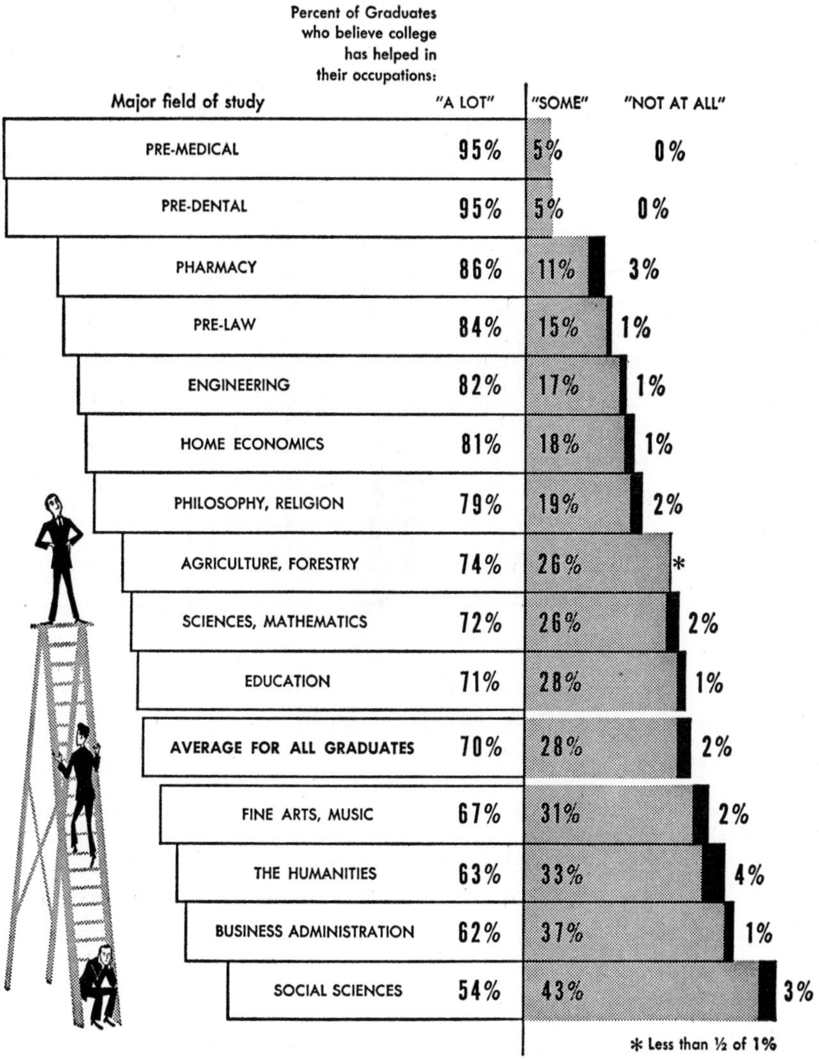

Percent of Graduates
who believe college
has helped in
their occupations:

Major field of study	"A LOT"	"SOME"	"NOT AT ALL"
PRE-MEDICAL	95%	5%	0%
PRE-DENTAL	95%	5%	0%
PHARMACY	86%	11%	3%
PRE-LAW	84%	15%	1%
ENGINEERING	82%	17%	1%
HOME ECONOMICS	81%	18%	1%
PHILOSOPHY, RELIGION	79%	19%	2%
AGRICULTURE, FORESTRY	74%	26%	*
SCIENCES, MATHEMATICS	72%	26%	2%
EDUCATION	71%	28%	1%
AVERAGE FOR ALL GRADUATES	70%	28%	2%
FINE ARTS, MUSIC	67%	31%	2%
THE HUMANITIES	63%	33%	4%
BUSINESS ADMINISTRATION	62%	37%	1%
SOCIAL SCIENCES	54%	43%	3%

* Less than ½ of 1%

consider their complaints, both general and specific, in Part Seven of the book. But the majority of letters are highly favorable, and it is quite remarkable how few of them mention the cash value of a diploma as a reason for going to college. Take this excerpt from the letter of a successful Virginia attorney:

I am thoroughly convinced that college training has made it possible for me to enjoy life to a much greater extent than would have been true if I had not gone to college. There is no doubt in my mind that I am a better citizen for this reason. As a lawyer, I come into contact with all classes and kinds of people, and I am reasonably certain that college trained people are more aware of their responsibilities to their fellow citizens and, with rare exceptions, provide local leadership in worthwhile activities.

Whatever the weaknesses in the American educational system are, and I presume there are many, I do not have any doubts at all as to the value of a college education.

Of course one might argue that this graduate's financial success is actually an important factor, implied if not expressed, in his high regard for college. And it is quite true that the younger graduates, who have not had time to get used to success, do seem somewhat more preoccupied with it. There is this letter, for example, from a rising young automotive engineer in Detroit:

What I would have been without my college education I cannot even conjecture. I feel it to have been the key which opened up life for me, without which I believe I would have had, to put it bluntly, "a much tougher row to hoe."

But then what is one to make of the following letter, from a successful Pennsylvania attorney who goes out of his way to stress the non-financial benefits of college?

One of the great pleasures and advantages of college in my own life was that it gave me leisure to pursue my own private interests. At the time these were bound up largely with literature and history. Both of these subjects, or rather the reading that I did independently or in connection with courses, have markedly increased my enjoyment of life and have fortunately helped me in my career. . . .

The chief benefit that I received, I believe, was the result of a period of comparative irresponsibility set in a studious atmosphere. It has always seemed to me that the mental stimulation which is possible in college is much more important than the actual courses which are studied.

There are also a number of letters from men who did not gain very much financial success from college, but nevertheless give it their hearty endorsement. This letter from a graduate in Massachusetts is a case in point:

Because of unavoidable circumstances I was unable to follow the career for which I trained. However, my college training has helped me to enjoy life and be a good citizen by giving me a philosophical outlook on life, an appreciation of spiritual values, and a guiding line to keep me from going out of bounds in this game of life.

And so is this one from a North Carolina newspaperman:

My college training has helped me in my enjoyment of life. . . . I suppose it has helped in my career, although I believe I could have done as well (with probably more work) without it. I did get a feeling of community responsibility that I believe would have been missing without a college background. I believe a college background does (or should) make one realize that he has more of an obligation of citizenship because one has had more opportunities.

My college education is not a disappointment—definitely. I am the sort of person who can enjoy knowledge for knowledge's sake and not feel cheated because some Joe without knowledge can make more money than I do.

Or this from a St. Louisan:

It has enabled me to obtain employment of a type which is more interesting and enjoyable than would otherwise have been probable. . . .

Financially, I may be earning somewhat more now. However, in eleven years I have not yet "made up" for the time and money invested in the college training. Prospects for progress may be better.

College training has given me a much broader understanding of this world (and universe) and of the basic principles which govern it. Consequently, I believe I am better able to recognize true values in many phases of life on personal, local, and world levels, and therefore am able to be a better citizen.

So much for the letters from men. We move on now to the career women, who, as we have seen, very seldom gain any spectacular financial returns from their education. Yet the career women write even more enthusiastically than the men. This letter is from a woman, now holding an administrative post in a Pennsylvania high school, who got her college degree the hard way—working on it piecemeal and finally obtaining it 18 years after her high school diploma:

College training has enabled me to work and live with those who are mentally active and inquisitive. It has helped me in my career for without this training I would have been unable to qualify for the various positions I have held. The courses taken in college opened entirely new avenues of thoughts and cultural development. The associations formed have materially added to my happiness. I cannot conceive that a college education could be a disappointment to anyone. If the individual believes himself to be disappointed it may be not because of the college or the courses taken but that the cause may be found within himself. He may not be college material, have chosen the wrong professional field, or be emotionally undeveloped.

Along similar lines is another letter from a schoolteacher, this time in New York:

Without college training, I expect that I should be something of a misanthrope or a perpetually disgruntled person, always seeking knowledge but never being quite satisfied or secure about what I gathered. It has made a tremendous impression on my life—one that I am grateful for. I don't mean to sound smug, for I don't feel that because I have been to college I am automatically a better person than my neighbor. All I know is that the academic life suits my nature, and I am glad that I was able to recognize my needs and fulfill them. That is what I believe makes me a better citizen and one who is willing to take responsibility in my community.

College showed me the way to develop my special talents more quickly and completely than a mere high school education would have. College, however, never can make a person what he isn't. It can help the individual to broaden his potentialities, but it can't implant seed on barren ground and expect to reap a full harvest solely because the seed was sown.

The following is from a woman who also trained to be a teacher, and now holds a government job in the field of education:

As to the enrichment and enjoyment of life, my college training has given me priceless treasure. I was born and reared in a small village. My parents had more education than the average parents of their day. My father was a high school superintendent, and at one time taught preparatory classes in a small college. Nevertheless, opportunities were limited by the period and the locale.

It was at college that I began to appreciate beautiful art and music. In my mind there stands out my first notice of the statue of Winged Victory that stood in the wide hall of our Administration Building. I began to wonder and to ask questions. We had the best musicians and lecturers of our day—"Star

Courses," they were called. I chose all my electives in English literature. I studied Shakespeare and loved him. I still do. Each year we saw the Coburn and Ben Greet Open Air Players on our beautiful campus, and in the spring we prepared and presented an Elizabethan pageant. . . . Those years are green in my memory.

And we have this from a woman who has wound up working for the Red Cross in a Massachusetts hospital:

A book perhaps could be written on what extent college training has helped in one's enjoyment of life, in a career and in making one a good citizen. The mere learning of new subject matter is of course of tremendous value to one in later life; the large fields of human thought—philosophy, religion, science, few are the persons who would in any way be acquainted with these subjects without college study. In addition to learning, as such, the development that comes to one from living away from home, making oneself stand for something and be somebody without the help of family reputation, developing self-assurance, poise, and a mature point of view all contribute to a person's later effectiveness whether in marriage or a career.

The next is from a young woman in Connecticut:

I know that Mount Holyoke had a broadening influence on me and many of my friends. Silly prejudices passed on to us by parents and less enlightened teaching, against races, religions, class and so on, were gradually erased as we lived with all types of people, and grew to understand and like them. The attitude of the faculty and staff also helped to make us realize that some of our ideas were pretty old-fashioned!

And this from a career woman in Seattle:

I think college is a privilege that no one should forego if he or she has the mentality for it. Maybe what a person learns is not so important, but the contacts, the sociability, the extra-curricular activities are. Where else can people meet on such an equal footing and with so many common interests as in college—certainly not in the humdrum office. . . .

Or this even more succinct tribute from a Michigan librarian:

My education has been a great enjoyment to me and I am grateful it has provided me with a pleasant way of life though not a particularly lucrative one.

And these two which come from career women in Florida and in Missouri:

College taught me how to enjoy living with other people outside of my faith and appreciate their religion and views on life and politics. I learned independence and self-assurance.

In my own family of seven children, five had A.B. degrees. . . . I feel that the degreed members are much more tolerant, one-world minded and self-directed.

Perhaps the most objective letters of all are from the married women graduates, who are making no materialistic use whatever of their diplomas, and therefore are completely free from any suspicion of financial bias. Indeed the supreme test of a college education—insofar as its spiritual values are concerned—would seem to lie with these women, whose daily routine of housekeeping and child-rearing is much the same in all physical aspects as for non-college housewives.

To see how well the college education meets this test, we can begin with one of the most extreme cases imaginable. The following is a letter from a Virginia woman who spent all the long college years required for a medical education, earned her M.D.—and then chose to become a housewife instead of practicing medicine. One might suppose that she would regret all those years of study, from which she has extracted no economic or practical gain of any kind, but instead she writes:

My college training has given me a sense of accomplishment, a broadening of viewpoint, a feeling of being able to evaluate situations that arise and material that may come to my attention.

I don't know how college could have helped me more.

And for some other typical comments we can take brief excerpts from the letters, in order, of college wives in Connecticut, Michigan, Connecticut again, and South Carolina:

The sense of responsibility I gained because of being privileged to go to college has made me feel I had to make whatever contribution I could to the life of my community. This was heightened, perhaps, by the fact that my grandparents were immigrants and that I was the first member of my family to attend college.

It seems to me that most of the experiences I was ready for, I had. My days were full of interesting new experiences, some good—some not so good, but all valuable in helping me develop better judgment, know more about the world and myself. The people I met, both students and faculty, were grand to know tho' of course not all were grand people.

College gives you a broader outlook on life. A smattering of this and that makes one realize how much a person doesn't know—gives one an open mind.

At least I can be contented when by myself, and this is a skill.

The letters speak for themselves—and often, although they were not intended as literary compositions, with a great eloquence. There are all kinds of reasons, not necessarily connected with money, that our graduates are almost unanimously glad they went.

12

The A.B. and the Specialist

All cultural and spiritual considerations aside, the college diploma does have a considerable cash value. As we have discovered, the men graduates greatly surpass the average man as breadwinners. The college women who hold jobs are handicapped by the fact that in the economic sense this is still a man's world—but still they do much better than the average working woman. Our survey gives ample proof that college is what so many practical parents hope it will be for their children: the road to financial success.

Yet college, as we have also seen, is not just one road but many roads. On the day he enters, the student is confronted by an almost bewildering array of signposts. He can take any number of courses; he can train for any number of careers. And while he is on the campus he can elect to keep his nose in his books, to engage in a big variety of extra-curricular activities, or to concentrate on a purely social life. No matter what he decides to study or how hard he decides to study it, the chances are that he will outstrip the average man in later life; this was the moral of the chapters in which we considered the general statistics on the financial success of our Old Grads and our Former Coeds. But now it becomes pertinent to talk in specific terms. What kind of students, taking what kind of courses, have done the best after leaving the campus? Of all the roads that college offers, which are the surest paths to financial success?

We can begin with the most publicized crossroad of all—that point of grave decision where the student must commit himself to a specific education which will train him for a definite career, or to a general education which will help him become the old traditional ideal of the well-rounded citizen, versed in many fields of knowledge. (And in the economic sense, theoretically capable of growing into and adapting himself to more jobs than the specialist.) To the long argument which has raged over specific versus general education our survey can at least offer the answer to one important question: Who is the more successful—the A.B. or the specialist?

I. THE GRADUATES' OPINIONS

In the previous chapter we noted that this whole subject is the most frequent source of post-graduate regrets; 35% of our graduates wish they had taken more specialized training and 21% wish they had taken more generalized training, leaving less than half who are satisfied with the choice they made. If we examine their letters, we get a pretty clear picture of their reasons. There is this comment, for example, from an Old Grad in Maryland who ardently wishes that he had specialized:

Courses pointing to a technical or professional career are more preferable than a generalized education. This is an opinion based on my own experience. After I got out of college, I still didn't know what my future would be.

And this succinct one-sentence summary from a Birmingham merchant who wishes the same:

I would take more specific courses because today the world is highly competitive and a specialist is better equipped.

Plus the complaint of an Arizona woman who is now a housewife but once had to find a job, with considerable difficulty:

I most certainly would take specific courses which would train me for a career, inasmuch my first year out of college was spent attending a business school in order to learn something useful and practical. At the home town university I probably would have mastered the art of pounding a typewriter or taking shorthand notes—but at Stanford University my major was psychology, which *could* help me understand my young son but which *did not* bring in a salary after college years.

A sales executive in Baltimore adds this note:

I took a cultural course while at Princeton, and while I have nothing to say against this program, if I had it to do over again I would take a more specific course that would train me for a career. Not that this specific training, say for example in engineering, would necessarily mean that I would want to be an engineer, but this specific training as an engineer would better prepare me for any business enterprise.

On the other hand there is an equal amount of conviction in the letters from graduates who took specialized courses and wish they had obtained a more general education instead. Their regrets take many forms. One is the feeling of having missed something, of never really having been educated at all in many of the fields of human knowledge. A Chicago public relations expert writes:

As a school of journalism major, I received some sort of introduction into the field of public relations about which my work at present is centered. I do regret, however, the heavy concentration of work in journalism to the point where I was unable to take more work in philosophy, economics, history, the arts, etc.

A St. Louis lawyer, who seems to start out with this same general feeling, expresses himself along somewhat different lines which emphasize human relations rather than textbook culture:

I have the opinion that a college education should supply a person a little knowledge about a great many things, sufficient to give the student enough knowledge about each subject so that he will at least know what the subject is about generally and where he can get further knowledge on it if and when he wishes. I think the result to be attained is to impart a little culture, a rather broad knowledge of people and the humanities, and give him some idea of how to best get along with people—any people with whom he may come in contact. In other words a college education should do three things: a) it should teach a person to think, reason, and express himself in a logical and understandable fashion; b) it should supply enough interesting thoughts and avenues to keep one fairly contented the rest of life; c)—and probably most important of all—it should impart poise and make a person readily adaptable.

Some of the graduates who specialized feel that this type of training does not really have nearly so much vocational value as is popularly believed—or at least that it has not had this value in their own particular cases. The letters of this type come from people in a remarkable variety of occupations. Although we do not wish to weight the argument here, or to make it seem that more graduates are dissatisfied with specialized than with general education—which would indeed be directly contrary to the facts—we believe that it is pertinent to present enough of the letters here to give an idea of the range. We start with perhaps the most unexpected of all, from a Connecticut doctor who seriously questions the value of his specialized pre-medical training:

If I learned anything in college that actually helped me in medical school I am unable to recall it at present. Perhaps one year of physics and one of a combination of organic and inorganic chemistry is essential, but the much-touted pre-medical courses are only another hurdle. The literary, history, and political courses . . . give one a much broader and more substantial base on which to stand.

Along similar lines from a Kentucky banker:

I would take general cultural courses. Many boys just out of high school do not know what they want to do as a business for the rest of their lives. They may prepare for something that later becomes distasteful.

I think the best specific training is received by working in the business itself. I have in mind my own experience. I received a B.S. degree in Commerce and Business Administration, which was supposed to train me to be an executive. However, my real training in this field came after I graduated and started working, and it was a good many years before I was capable of being an executive.

From a woman college teacher:

I should take general cultural courses rather than specific courses to train for a career, because I believe that life is richer by the familiarity with different fields of knowledge rather than by confining oneself to his own trade. For instance, I had many courses in education; few of them have been of any practical value; instead I might have taken courses in art, which I enjoy, or more courses in literature.

And from a young woman whose letter explains her position:

I majored in home economics, which is a field requiring many specific courses. I felt that quite a number of these were unnecessary and useless and only served to block a student's interest in other courses unless she could afford to spend more than the usual four years in meeting the requirements for a degree in home economics. I don't regret my major but I still wish I had been allowed a much wider choice in English courses, languages, art, psychology, etc. It's the general cultural courses that round out an individual's point of view and develop his thinking. A great many of the details in specialized courses can be learned very easily on the job.

Perhaps the best argument of all along these lines comes from a man who had had the opportunity to study a great many other careers besides his own—a man who was working at the time as a vocational counselor for the Veterans Administration. He writes:

Most of the narrow, specific "vocational" courses are either too thin or are given in a vacuum not suitable to the degree of vocational orientation of students. My experience in industrial personnel work, occupational analysis, and vocational counseling also confirms the impression that specific courses do *not* train the student for a career, but merely create a desire for one. In the long run, depth and breadth of understanding are the factors that make for a successful career. Since the motivation factor is important, some courses of vocational significance are helpful in the formation of vocational aims; but the chief value of college education does not reside in such "training" . . . "Trade" courses have been unrealistically advertised.

So much for the graduates who, if they had it to do over again, would switch from general education to specialized, or from specialized to general. But before we go into the statistical facts disclosed by our survey we had better consider the remarks of another big group of graduates, the 44% who have no regrets whatever on this score and instead are glad that they specialized or that they took general courses. The letters from this group are also full of conviction, and they also cover a wide ground of practical and theoretical argument. In fact the letters can be shuffled into what sounds like a town hall debate on the whole question. Let us start with this proposition from a Cincinnati engineer who believes sincerely in a specialized education:

I should take mechanical engineering, just as I did, because I was impatient to get to work. You can get your culture as you go along, even if you study technical subjects, if you are inclined that way.

And the rebuttal from a New York stock broker who is glad he took a generalized curriculum:

I would take general cultural courses. Why? Because there is time enough for business later.

A woman in Ithaca, N. Y., who favors specialization writes:

I do feel that whatever one's ability, one should be equipped to earn a living after college—not just a clerking or filing job.

And a male graduate in Washington, D. C., taking the other side of the argument, answers:

A good job and great riches should be the by-product and never the end of a college education; these should not be the grounds on which the success of a liberal education is judged.

A Wisconsin manufacturer, who is doing his best to persuade his young acquaintances along the lines of the liberal education, makes a point:

I have advised many young people who were going to college to take as many courses as possible in subjects in which they were *not* interested, subjects which they would probably never learn about in later life but which are certain to turn up useful at some time or other. I have even pointed out that going to college to learn about things they want to know about was almost a waste of time, because if they were really interested they would find out about these things whether they went to college or not.

The rebuttal comes from a Philadelphia physician who has become convinced, apparently somewhat against his own original hopes, that culture does not even have any avocational value in our modern society:

Culture courses are no longer needed to occupy a parlor or drawing room chair. Conversations over the tables of night clubs, beer gardens, baseball games, and trolley car seats do not smack of French, Gothic architecture, or why the Greek oratory was superior to our own.

A graduate who has become a Canadian forest ranger, is not too happy with his pay, but otherwise has nothing but gratitude for what college did to him, rises to argue the case of liberal education:

No matter what college I attended, I would definitely not want to reduce the number of general cultural courses I took. In fact I regard them as the most worthwhile of all. I am convinced that I am more tolerant, broader-minded, and a better citizen in every respect than I would have been had I confined myself to a strictly technical program in school.

To which a California engineer, happy that he himself had a specialized education, gives a polite Bronx cheer:

It is regrettable, but culture is inedible!

On the side of specialized education, a woman graduate in Oklahoma, married but working as a secretary, makes this point:

If one has no need for making a living, general cultural courses are all right. But since my need was to earn a living, I felt specific training was better.

A young man from Milwaukee answers:

Specific training is soon forgotten and outdated. It is never specific enough.

And a Philadelphia printer adds:

In the present-day world of specialization specific training has its good points, but the individual who has the benefit of general cultural courses is better equipped to adapt himself to changing economic conditions.

But a Massachusetts manufacturer, while recognizing the value of general education, still favors the specific:

Whereas a few general cultural courses may be advisable and even necessary, too many would prevent the specific training which is badly needed for any specialized career.

To which a male schoolteacher replies:

Relative to courses, I think that for the average kid an A.B. in liberal arts is best. He is too young to seriously settle on one technical line of thought and bury himself. Give him the cultural background first. . . . We're part of an extremely technical world getting more technical, but God help us if we don't polish our brutality some!

Perhaps we should leave the last word in the debate to the women, to whom the last word traditionally belongs. A Texas housewife introduces a new argument in favor of liberal education for women students, the majority of whom are bound to become wives:

Anything which broadens your knowledge and enjoyment of literature, history, music, and the other arts enriches your whole life. Particularly in the case of a woman who marries and discontinues her career, as I did, the cultural courses are the ones which mean the most over the period of her whole life.

On the other side a housewife in California introduces a novel argument in favor of specialized education—even for women who wind up keeping house:

I would take specific courses because a person who attends a university should have a definite goal. There is not the incentive when taking just cultural courses.

And at this point we leave the letters, which cast so many new lights on how graduates themselves, from a layman's point of view, feel about the academic argument that has been waged over their heads by the education experts, and turn to the statistical facts.

II. THE ACTUAL FACTS

The generally educated graduates are those who took a broad training in the humanities (philosophy, the fine arts, literature, languages, or history), or who majored in the physical or social sciences while also taking a wide variety of humanities courses. The specialists are the doctors, lawyers, dentists, and the engineers, or the graduates who concentrated on one of the physical sciences to the exclusion of practically all else. But even a humanities major may have concentrated so intently on one field of knowledge—say the Greek language and Greek literature—as to consider himself a product of specialized rather than of general education. And a number of doctors and lawyers have taken their A.B.'s, in a considerable range of general courses, before entering their professional schools. What the survey questionnaire did, therefore, was actually ask the graduates whether they felt they had received a general or a specialized education during their college days, as a check against making any gratuitous assumptions from the subjects in which they majored.

If we now confine our figures to men only, and list the most important fields of college study in the order of how much specialization they involved—in the opinions of the graduates who majored in them—we get the pattern of earnings shown in Chart 35. In general, the more specialized the college course, the more graduates it produces in the $5,000-and-over bracket.

There is only one exception to this rule: the education majors whom we have already noted as an exception to most rules. The men who specialize at college in training for schoolteaching jobs do not make more money than the generally educated men; in fact they make less. But in every other field, specialization and financial success are closely correlated. The student who decides to specialize has a much better chance to make a high salary than the student who decides to take an A.B.; he also runs far less risk of winding up in the low income brackets. On the simple materialistic scale of post-graduate finances, specialized education has general education beat hollow.

This is only true, it must be remembered, for men graduates. Indeed all the facts in this whole section of the book relate only to men. For women graduates the situation is entirely dissimilar. To them it makes absolutely no difference at all in earnings to have specialized or to have taken a general course. Nor do most of the other factors discussed in the

CHART 35

Major field of study
and earnings

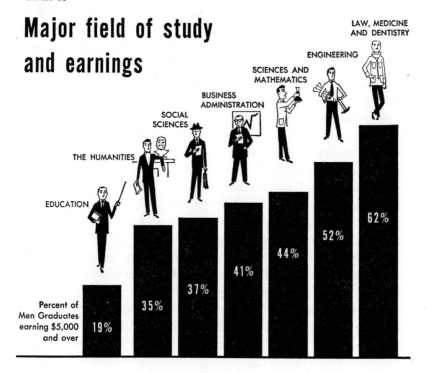

LAW, MEDICINE
AND DENTISTRY

ENGINEERING

SCIENCES AND
MATHEMATICS

BUSINESS
ADMINISTRATION

SOCIAL
SCIENCES

THE HUMANITIES

EDUCATION

Percent of
Men Graduates
earning $5,000
and over   19%

35%   37%   41%   44%   52%   62%

next few chapters make any difference. The women graduates are equal in their unequal pay; college helps them rise well above the earnings of the average woman, but nothing they can do or study in college makes them rise nearly so high as the men. There simply seems to be a ceiling on women's earnings—and the graduates of all types, of all family backgrounds, of all schools, and of all kinds of courses seem to run into it. It can be said here for once and all that the matters we are discussing in this section, because of the effect they have on the earnings of men graduates, have no effect whatever on the women. (There is a single exception, which we shall note when we get to it.)

Getting back to the men, on whom we shall now concentrate for this and the next three chapters, the survey offers some clues which certainly explain in part, if not *in toto*, why the specialists earn more than the A.B.'s.

In the first place, a great many of the humanities graduates have gone into types of work which are notoriously poorly paid. The figures show that 27% of them have become teachers; another 15% have gone into the clergy, and 1% into the arts. This makes a total of 43%, or nearly half, who have chosen a life work in which the financial rewards are limited by the very nature of the job. Reason number one for the low pay of humanities graduates is that many of the students who elect this course are men who have ignored the economic factor in deciding what type of career would suit them best.

Not all the humanities graduates, however, wind up where they do as a matter of choice. In this respect they differ greatly from such specialists as the doctors, lawyers, dentists, and engineers. Among graduates who started out studying for law, medicine, or dentistry, eight out of ten have ended up practicing their chosen professions; one in 100 has gone into some other profession, and two out of ten hold a business or government job. But among humanities graduates, only four out of ten have actually gone into the type of career they planned; roughly one out of ten has gone into some other type of professional work, and five out of ten have taken jobs in business or government. The humanities graduates, with their more general and more nebulous training, seem to have a harder time getting started in their careers, and many of them end up in fields which they had never contemplated. Even among the 27% who have become teachers, we can presume, many have settled for this sort of work because nothing else seemed to offer itself.

Even in the learned professions, the humanities graduates do not hold their own with graduates who have had more specialized training. If we compare them, for example, with the teachers, clergymen, and artists in our group who majored in the more specialized field of the physical sciences, we find that the proportions earning under $3,000 a year are 36% for the humanities majors and only 21% for the science majors. And among the humanities graduates who wind up in business jobs, the composite record is very poor indeed. The best measure that our survey provides is this: of the humanities graduates in the business field, fully 24% have had to settle for the rank-and-file jobs, as either white collar or manual workers. This is far above the proportion of all men graduates in such jobs, as we saw in Chapter 3. And it is in even more startling contrast to the record of such specialists as the engineers in the business field— only 6% of whom have wound up in the less desirable jobs.

Reason number two for the low pay of humanities graduates is that

many of them never get started in the careers they planned, but instead
turn to other work which represents their second or third choice, or
sometimes even a case of grasping at any job opportunity that came along.
And particularly in the business field, the humanities graduates do not
appear to be nearly so well suited—either as a matter of training or as
a matter of temperament—for the more responsible and better-paying
positions.

The social science graduates, who represent another big field of general education, show a little different pattern. Even fewer of them—less
than four out of ten—wind up doing what they had hoped and expected
to do. Not nearly so many of them, however, are found in teaching, the
clergy, or the arts: only 18% of them altogether. What happens to the
great majority is that they end up in business jobs; a full 65% of all men
graduates who had majored in the social sciences were working in the
business field at the time of the survey. And at these business jobs their
composite record was not even up to the record of the humanities graduates. We noted before that 24% of humanities graduates in the business
field were holding down rank-and-file jobs, as compared with only 6%
of such specialists as the engineers. Now we can add that of the social
science majors who had entered the business field, the proportion with
rank-and-file jobs was 31%!

All the evidence points in the same direction. The young men who
enter college to become lawyers, doctors, dentists, and engineers are the
ones who know exactly where they are going—and have the best chance
to get there and to be well paid for being there. Among the young men
who go to college for A.B.'s, in either the humanities or the social sciences, fewer seem to have a definite goal—and even when they have and
reach the goal, it is usually in teaching or the clergy where the financial rewards are anything but spectacular. Many of the A.B.'s seem to
arrive at graduation day without any very clear idea of the next step,
and to settle for whatever kind of job they can find. When they wind
up in the field of business, which after all provides most of the available
jobs, they do not do nearly so well as the specially trained graduates—
perhaps because they never planned it that way and are never fully
satisfied with the jobs.

As to whether their failure to attain the same financial success as the
specialists really bothers them, we cannot be sure. We can only hark
back to the letters in the early part of this chapter, which would indicate

that some of the men with general education would gladly trade it for a greater economic reward, while others feel they have gained something far more precious than money. And we can add that the generally educated graduates, especially when compared job for job with the specialists to allow for different occupational habits, seem to read substantially more books and to engage in more community and political activities—which are perhaps among the measurements of personal satisfaction as well as of "good citizenship."

As a matter of fact, the generally educated graduate seems to be almost a different sort of citizen altogether from the man who has been a specialist all his life. For the most dramatic proof, we can look to our high-paid professional men, the doctors, lawyers, and dentists. Some of these men, as we have mentioned, have taken their A.B.'s before entering their professional schools; they have been trained in the humanities or the social sciences as well as in their professions. Others have had a much more specialized education; before embarking on their actual professional courses they have taken the standard pre-medical, pre-legal, or pre-dental curriculum. The subjects they studied before becoming professionals, as can be seen by the following figures, make a considerable difference in their civic lives:

The Number of Doctors, Lawyers, and Dentists
Reporting Seven or More Civic Activities

Those who majored in the humanities or social sciences	42%
Those who majored in pre-professional courses	30%

The same drop in interest, from the generally educated professional men to those who had specialized training, occurs for political activities insofar as we can measure them. And the difference persists among older graduates as well as among the young ones who are closer to the campus influence. It is quite clear that the generally educated graduates are the most active and interested citizens of their communities and their nation. They are much less likely to be "narrow specialists" in their private lives. They play a more active and varied role in society, and perhaps a more useful and rewarding one as well.

They also differ, quite noticeably, in their opinions on world affairs, on races and religions, and on government. To use the doctors, lawyers, and dentists as an example again, only 18% of those with a general educational background are isolationists by the scale we have been using in the book, compared with 37% of those whose training was specialized from the beginning. The proportions qualifying as tolerant on our scale are 37% for the generally-educated and 27% for the specialists. The pro-New Dealers number 42% among the generally-educated and 27% among the specialists. The same trends, toward a greater degree of internationalism, tolerance, and pro-New Dealism, also hold for the generally-educated men in the fields of business and the learned professions.

We have already noted in Chapter 11 that of all graduates the humanities and social science majors are among the most dissatisfied with their choice of college courses. But if we analyze the figures, we see that they do not mean quite what appears on the surface. For example, the humanities and social science majors who subsequently went into law, medicine or dentistry are not at all dissatisfied with their general education; they vote in about the same proportions as members of those professions who had more specialized training before entering their fields. Now, a cynic might explain away this fact on purely financial grounds; after all, lawyers, doctors, and dentists make a lot of money, regardless of which route they chose toward their professions. But it is also a fact that the humanities graduates who have become teachers, clergymen, or practitioners of the fine arts—and have thereby entered the worst paid fields of all—are equally happy with their college choice. In fact they cast a slightly higher vote. Among this group 81% would again choose the same major if they had it to do over again, while among the humanities students who went into the high-paid professions the figure is 78%.

The facts, obviously, are these: the graduates who had a general education are quite satisfied if they have gone on to take specialized training and have ended up in a high-paid profession. They are also satisfied, despite finances, if they have gone into one of the low-paid "learned" professions where a general education provides a suitable and useful background. The large proportion of generally-educated graduates who regret their college choice is accounted for almost entirely by those who have wound up in business jobs. The business field is not what the generally educated graduates foresaw, and in it they have little opportunity to use their knowledge of literature, history, sociology, or Latin conjugations. Moreover they find themselves, by and large, passed by men who have had more technical training. Some of them console themselves with the thought that college taught them how to enjoy living, even though they are somewhat dislocated jobwise and have less financial success than their college competitors from the specialized fields. But a great many come to the conclusion that a broad cultural background is simply not worth the price that it seems to exact in terms of workaday failure. ("Failure," of course, is a very relative term; we have seen that all college graduates, generally speaking, far surpass non-college men. But in this section of the book we are examining the fact that some college graduates do less surpassing than others, and that they will sometimes be inclined to make invidious comparisons.) Among the generally educated graduates who now hold business jobs, fully half wish that they had taken more specialized training.

There is a strong temptation here to moralize. Until recently, the great debate in educational circles has been couched mostly in either-or terms; the idea has been that we must offer students either a broad, general education or a very specialized one. And most of our graduates feel that they have, in actual practice, had either one or the other; only 2% state that their education has been both general in some ways and specific in others. The question that arises is whether the colleges should not be trying to combine both types of training—rather than arguing which to favor.

The same question has occurred to a number of our letter writers. A woman graduate who is married but is also a college instructor in home economics writes:

> My first two years were taken up by cultural courses, such as English composition and literature, history and languages, even including classical Greek. But thereafter I studied only scientific subjects, particularly chemistry and physics.
>
> Perhaps the early unspecialized so-called cultural instruction diluted the narrow specialization in the later years, but whatever the cause, I cannot help feeling satisfied with the whole experiment. The scientific courses have been the basis of my professional life and I think a satisfactory one, and the cultural courses have offered me much enlightenment and understanding in my private life.

Another woman who is combining marriage with a career (this time as a social worker) writes along similar lines:

> I feel very definitely that, where it is possible, it is greatly to the advantage of any student to take a cultural college course and then go on to specific work. This I did myself attending the New York School of Social Work.

One gets far more from one's professional training when one is a little older, and the background of a cultural college education keeps one from becoming narrow. This tendency to narrowness, to a special training with no broad outlook, no appreciation of other fields, of history, of general knowledge, is all too prevalent. Young people are trained for one specific line of work, but they are not educated.

From the men graduates we have two letters which bear very strongly on this point. The first is from an engineer who was graduated from Louisiana State University:

I owe my job as a design engineer to my college training. It was purely technical and only slightly cultural because of the time element. Anything cultural or helpful in my enjoyment of life I had to obtain rather hastily. Because I like engineering so much, I have received quite a bit of pleasure out of a very fine job.

College could have helped me more by having a longer course, say another year, and being very general for the first two years so that I could take a great variety of subjects and then begin to specialize in the third, fourth and fifth years.

The second is from a Detroit musician who has reached a similar conclusion from a quite different direction:

I would take issue with Dr. Hutchins of Chicago and other educators who favor, exclusively, the classic curriculum and the broad general education. I have found that college arouses the student's desire to become expert in at least one field—generally a practical field. He is associated with well-educated professors (specialists). He sees the value, the confidence, and the plaudits that accrue to those who know the answers. He sees that military specialists win wars, that economic specialists make the financial policy of the nation, that political specialists govern, that scientific specialists add to the total civilization, and that medical specialists save lives.

The student cannot be satisfied with Latin and literature alone when the world demands (and his self-respect demands) that the individual exploit his line of talent to the full. On the other hand he cannot know only one field, say chemistry, and nothing more—else he will never be able to live with himself.

The answer seems to be that four years of college cannot give the many-faceted and yet specialized education that living in the present world demands. It seems now that the Liberal Arts (cultural) course plus at least a year of specialization is the minimum of college preparation with which the college student can be satisfied.

Perhaps the great question which all statistics and letters from our survey pose, on the matter we are considering in this chapter, is just this: In our tremendously complicated modern world, and for a student who must both learn to earn a living and learn to live with his conscience, can either the general or the special education be enough by itself?

13

Phi Beta Kappa and Big Man on Campus

There are two completely opposite theories about how to get the most out of a college career. Educators, and most parents, like to hold up the Phi Beta Kappa as the good example: if you study hard you are sure to go to heaven, and incidentally have the happiest and most profitable life en route. But a good many students have the notion that grades are mostly nonsense; they figure that an A in philosophy sells no insurance policies, and that the way to get ahead in life is to be a campus leader and make a lot of friends. Thus the Phi Beta Kappa, a bookish fellow, and the Big Man on Campus, a hail fellow well met, are generally considered to be two antithetical types.

Actually they are not so far apart as commonly thought. The all-A students, by and large, are not so unsociable and retiring as pictured. Indeed they are more likely than anyone else to be the campus leaders. Among our group of graduates it turns out that 29% of the A students held at least two campus offices, as opposed to 22% of the B students and only 16% of the C and D students. The better a student's grades, in other words, the more likely he is to "get around" on the campus. And, conversely, the students who accumulate a long list of extra-curricular activities and offices are more likely to be the better students than the poorer ones. The Phi Beta Kappa usually has a lot of interests, of which grades are only one.

The question remains, however: Are A's the key to a career, or are they just a waste of effort? A part of the answer will be found in Chart 36. Grades certainly seem to bear a direct relation to the types of jobs the graduates hold after college. The A students tend to wind up in the professions. Fewer B students are found in the professions, and more of them in business. Among C and D students, the professional men are fewest of all and the businessmen the most numerous.

CHART 36

Grades make a difference
in type of career

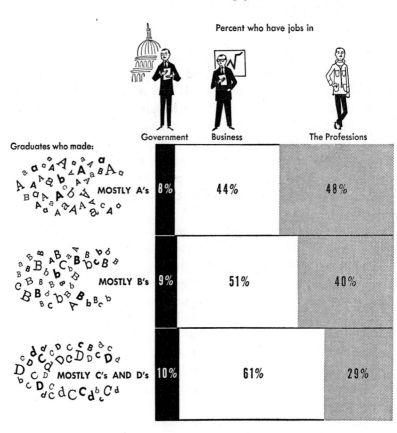

Percent who have jobs in

Government   Business   The Professions

Graduates who made:

MOSTLY A's   8%   44%   48%

MOSTLY B's   9%   51%   40%

MOSTLY C's AND D's   10%   61%   29%

Another part of the answer is contained in these figures: at the time of the survey 50% of the male A students were making $5,000 a year or more, compared with 41% of the C and D students. To carry the income bracket a step higher, 27% of the A students were making $7,500 a year or more, compared with 21% of the C and D students. In general, therefore, the best students were doing better financially than the poorest students—but hardly enough better to inspire anyone to burn the midnight oil for a Phi Beta Kappa key, or to strike terror to the heart of the student who is just hanging on by the skin of his teeth.

But these salary figures do not tell the full story. Included among the professions, which the A students enter in such notable numbers, are teaching and the clergy—the lowest paid of all U.S. professional fields. In fact 38% of all the A graduates were in the low-paid professions, in contrast to only 23% of the C and D graduates. Thus in substantial numbers, the better students have chosen a life work which almost never provides entree to the highest income brackets. To get the full picture of how grades affect earnings, we shall have to divide the graduates into occupational groups.

This has been done in Chart 37. In every occupational field, it develops, the A graduates have the best earnings record. Their advantage is most pronounced in the learned (and low-paid) professions. Despite the difficulty of attaining a high salary in this field, a total of 31% of the A graduates has managed to hit the $5,000 mark, compared with only 16% of the C and D students. In the high-paid professions, mostly law, medicine, and dentistry, they also have a clear advantage. Even in government jobs, they reach the top more frequently.

In the field of business, however, the advantage of the A student, while still fairly clear-cut, is much more tenuous. The A graduates have done only slightly better than the B graduates, and the B students only slightly better than the C and D students. For all practical purposes, and thinking only of income, the man who plans to enter the business world can well argue that grades mean nothing at all. The college diploma, as we saw in Chapter 3, has a great financial value in business as well as in other fields. But a degree *summa cum laude* is not much more valuable than a degree that was in jeopardy until the last examination grade was in. It appears that in all truth an A in philosophy does not sell many insurance policies— or make a man a much better factory foreman, file clerk, junior executive, merchant, or manufacturer.

CHART 37

Grades and earnings for men

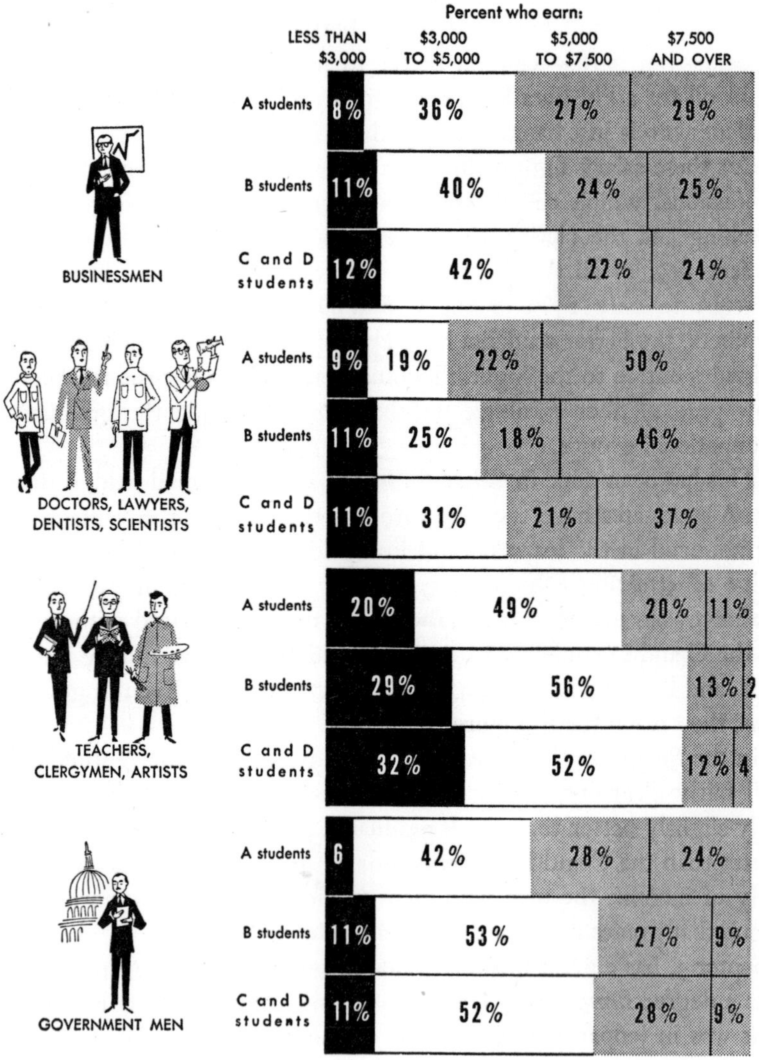

Percent who earn:

	LESS THAN $3,000	$3,000 TO $5,000	$5,000 TO $7,500	$7,500 AND OVER
BUSINESSMEN				
A students	8%	36%	27%	29%
B students	11%	40%	24%	25%
C and D students	12%	42%	22%	24%
DOCTORS, LAWYERS, DENTISTS, SCIENTISTS				
A students	9%	19%	22%	50%
B students	11%	25%	18%	46%
C and D students	11%	31%	21%	37%
TEACHERS, CLERGYMEN, ARTISTS				
A students	20%	49%	20%	11%
B students	29%	56%	13%	2
C and D students	32%	52%	12%	4
GOVERNMENT MEN				
A students	6	42%	28%	24%
B students	11%	53%	27%	9%
C and D students	11%	52%	28%	9%

CHART 38

Grades and earnings for working women

Percent who earn

LESS THAN $3,000	$3,000 TO $5,000	$5,000 AND OVER	
61%	27%	12%	A students
72%	18%	10%	B students
63%	27%	10%	C and D students

BUSINESSWOMEN

48%	24%	28%	A students
60%	26%	14%	B students
50%	35%	15%	C and D students

DOCTORS, LAWYERS, DENTISTS, SCIENTISTS

55%	34%	11%	A students
65%	30%	5	B students
73%	22%	5	C and D students

TEACHERS, ARTISTS

41%	48%	11%	A students
55%	33%	12%	B students
63%	33%	4	C and D students

GOVERNMENT WOMEN

This matter of grades is one thing that seems to affect the earnings of women in much the same way that it affects the earnings of men, and therefore the figures for women have been broken down in Chart 38 exactly as they were in Chart 37 for men. The chart has to be presented with considerable apology, for it does not include enough cases for statistical reliability, and therefore contains some erratic zigs and zags. There are not so many women graduates as men to begin with, and many of the women are housewives and therefore out of the job market. Of the women who work, most are concentrated in the teaching field, as has been noted, and very few have entered the high-paid professions. More-over, as is inevitable in a survey of this kind, we do not know the college grades of all the working women. The upshot is that, while the sample of A, B, and C and D students in the learned professions is adequate, we have only 70 cases of businesswomen who made A grades, only 25 cases of A women in law, medicine, or dentistry, and only 20 cases of C and D women in the high-paid professions. Thus the chart must be read for interest only, and with many grains of salt.

Yet even with these reservations, the chart does seem to contain enough clues to justify some generalizations. In the field of the learned profes-sions, where the total sample involves 1,136 women, earnings rise in direct proportion to grades. In the high-paid professions and in government, although the small sampling produces some freaks, we are entitled to assume that the same pattern exists. In business, on the other hand, one is immediately struck by the remarkably similar records of the A women and the women who made C's and D's. We can probably take for granted that, just as for men, grades make a difference in a woman's financial suc-cess in every field except business. And it should be pointed out again here that of all the factors in this section of the book that affect the earn-ings of men, this is the only one that seems to matter for the women.

At the point where we left off discussing the men graduates, to whom we must now return after noting this single exception to the general rule that women have no place in this part of the book, we had just discovered that grades play a much smaller role in business success than in any other field. If grades do not, then perhaps extra-curricular activities do? Perhaps there is something to the theory of being a campus leader and making a lot of friends?

We throw out the first fact, and with it a large dash of cold water. For the most prominent men on the campus, those who participated in four or more extra-curricular activities, the median income is $4,345. For those who never participated in any extra-curricular activities at all, the median is $5,248! Try to find any justification for the winning-friends-and-influencing-people theory in those figures!

Actually, however, the medians are a little unfair. They seem to indicate that extra-curricular activities are a handicap to later-life earning ability, and such is not really the case. It so happens that the older graduates, who as we have seen make the most money, went to school at a time when extra-curricular activities were less popular than now. It also happens that the graduates in law, medicine, dentistry, engineering, and similar fields of great specialization, who also have a good earnings record, are not so prominent in campus affairs as are other students. (Most of these courses are pretty strenuous; possibly the students do not have much time for anything but study.) If we rule out the matters of age and of occupational field, it turns out that there are practically no differences at all in the earnings of graduates who avoided extra-curricular activities completely or who engaged in one, two, three, or a dozen. Not even the matter of leadership, as measured by the number of campus offices held, seems to have the slightest effect.

These figures hold for the business field, where grades do not seem to matter very much, as well as for other fields where grades seem to make a fairly substantial difference. To cite just one piece of evidence, without going into all the statistical ramifications: among the officers of at least two campus organizations, 19% have had to settle for the routine rank-and-file jobs in business, either as white collar or manual workers. For the men who held one campus office, the proportion is 17%—and for those who never held a campus office the proportion is 19%. It may be that business is more a matter of whom you know than what you know—but obviously you do not meet them through campus activities. Nor does leadership or lack of it in college necessarily imply leadership in the business world.

We started out the chapter by noting that good grades and campus activities are not necessarily incompatible, that indeed they often tend to go together. And in recognition of this fact we have in previous parts of the book divided the students into four groups rather than two: we have spoken of the Greasy Grinds, who make A's but seldom engage in any campus activities outside the library; the All-Around Students, who make A's and at the same time run the clubs and are the life of the party at the dances; the Big Men on Campus, whom we have identified as the students who concentrate on extra-curricular activities while just skinning by on grades, and the Students Who Just Sat There—that is, the men and women who did not make good grades but did not set the campus afire either. Perhaps we should use these categories, rather than the matter of grades alone or extra-curricular activities alone, as a guide to earnings in later life. Certainly this is done in the college yearbooks—where almost invariably an All-Around man is chosen the most likely to succeed.

Dividing the men into these four groups, we get the following pattern of median earnings:

Greasy Grinds	$5,141
All-Around Students	4,775
Big Men on Campus	4,648
Those Who Just Sat There	4,300

When you think about it, the figures are rather strange. The Greasy Grind, often considered by his classmates as hopelessly impractical, sits right on top in the very practical matter of post-graduate finances. The All-Around Student, the cynosure and envy of all eyes, does not surpass everybody else nearly so often as the yearbooks predict. The Big Men on Campus, who probably consider themselves the most practical and down-to-earth of all, come in third in a four-horse race. The Students Who Just Sat There come in last, but their showing is by no means disreputable and entitles them to feel, in retrospect, that the effort of making better grades and going out for more activities would simply not have been worth the trouble.

But again the figures are rather distorted, this time chiefly by the fact that many of the specialists, who usually wind up making high salaries, are too busy or are disinclined to bother with extra-curricular activities. (The Greasy Grind nowadays, as a matter of fact, is less often a long-haired poet than a very pragmatic fellow with a slide rule in his pocket.) If we divide the graduates into the A.B.'s and the specialists, we can probably get a fairer picture. Suppose we make this separation, and then inquire how many of the graduates were earning $5,000 a year or more at the time of the study. Among the graduates of the humanities or other "general" courses, the proportions work out to 39% of the Greasy Grinds, 39% of the All-Around Students, 40% of the Big Men on Campus, and

35% of the Men Who Just Sat There. For the specialists, the proportions are 54% of the Grinds, 59% of the All-Arounders, 57% of the BMOC's, and 48% of the Sitters.

From this point of view, the differences between the Grinds, the All-Arounders, and the BMOC's are negligible. The Students Who Just Sat There, on the other hand, are at a disadvantage, but only a very slight one. Perhaps the most surprising message of all about the figures in this chapter is that the parents, friends, and fiancée of the Student Who is Just Sitting There, barely hanging on from one examination to the next, and meanwhile winning no popularity contests, need not worry so much as they usually do. Even though his college record may be undistinguished in every respect, he is not necessarily doomed.

CHAPTER

14

The Boy Who Worked His Way

As we found very early in this book, the picture of the college campus as the exclusive preserve of rich youngsters is an illusion. The campus is inhabited by a broad cross section of American life, and while some of the youths who stroll its paths never have to give a thought to financial matters, most of them already know what it means to pursue a paycheck. They are full-time students and part-time taxi drivers, table waiters, and timber cruisers—all to help pay for that eventual diploma. Among our own sample of the college-educated population, we saw in Chapter 2, eight out of ten of the men graduates worked their way through school in whole or in part.

What price working one's way? Does the working student make as good grades as the boy who gets his money by just writing home for it? Is he crowded out of campus activities by the student who has more time for them? And when it comes to making a living in later years who will have the economic edge—the young man who waits on tables at a sorority house, as one U.S. President did, or the lad who can drive up to the front door of the sorority house in the convertible his dad gave him for Christmas?

Once again the statistics are going to do violence to the folklore, and even to the fondly held opinions of many of the Old Grads. For through many of the letters from our Old Grads who worked their way there runs an extremely wistful note. The men who worked are a little regretful that they had too little time to study, or too little time to engage in extra-curricular activities, or too little time simply to have fun. For example a Midwestern graduate says:

My college education was very satisfactory—but I didn't do it justice for lack of time to study. Working your way through college is fine if you aren't

166

taking a full schedule of courses at the same time. My time seemed to be spent more in working than in studying.

And a successful lawyer who in his youth was, as he says, "a poor boy who spent a year in a C.C.C. camp," has this complaint:

My only regret and the only thing I would do differently, if possible, is to participate more actively in social activities. When in college I was too poor to take part . . . and thus I will always believe that I missed something important by being forced to be an onlooker rather than a participant in this important part of youth.

A graduate engineer adds:

I have spoken to and known many students in my time, and find that if they do not have money worries they usually participate in extra-curricular activities. I, myself, had a 48-hour job on the outside while attending the Technical School, and did not derive full benefits.

Looking back across an interval of 40 years at his hard-working college days, another Old Grad remarks:

I have little regard for the youngsters who weep about not being able to get to college because their parents cannot afford to send them. *My* time was spent in study—in classes—working in the kitchens of restaurants—and sleep. . . . It was not a matter of how much time I wanted to spend on study or on extra-curricular activity, but what time I *could* spend and make a living.

Yet along with their understandable wistfulness about having so little time, the graduates who worked their way feel a justifiable pride in having earned their college diplomas through their own efforts. A Presbyterian minister comments:

In view of the fact that I worked my way through college, I find myself wishing that I could have had more time for study and also more time for participation in campus activities. Having said this, it may sound paradoxical to add that if I had it to do over again, I would still prefer to work my way. There was definite educational value and disciplinary value in working which gives one a sense of responsibility and independence and also deepens one's appreciation of an education which is earned the hard way, instead of being dished out on a silver platter.

In a way it hardly seems fair to compare the grades or extra-curricular records of these working students with those of collegians who were free to invest their entire time and energy in the pursuit of Phi Beta Kappa keys or athletic letters. Yet when we do make the comparison, the results are not at all what might be expected. Take first the matter of grades. The percentage figures for all graduates, including women as well as men, work out as follows:

. . . 16% of the graduates who earned more than half their own way reported that their grades were mostly A's, as did

. . . 14% of those who earned less than half of their expenses, and

. . . 16% of those who did not work at all. At the other end of the grade scale, about a fourth of each group reported getting mostly C's or mostly D's. The self-help student, it develops, has just as good a scholastic record as anyone else.

Nor do the statistics show that our self-help graduates missed much, as a group, in the campus activities department. If anything the working boy was more likely to "get around" than his family-subsidized classmates. More than a third of the students who worked their way reported that they had taken part in three or more campus activities, compared with only 28% of those who did not work. Somehow the working students even found time to work their way up to positions of leadership in their activities. The figures show that:

. . . 44% of those who earned from half to all their expenses held at least one campus office, as did

. . . 48% of those who earned up to half their way, and

. . . 42% of those who did not work at all.

So in the two highly competitive categories of grades (which, we have found, have some relation to later income) and extra-curricular activities (which do not), the graduates who worked their way and the graduates who were sent by their families were practically all square on commencement day.

The following letter—from a graduate who worked his way through school and is now a Navy training supervisor—is therefore perhaps not so unusual as it first sounds:

Besides making the "Honor Ten" at graduation (which implies a high scholastic record), I was vitally interested in and devoted great amounts of time and effort to: the Art Students' League—class representative, board of directors; chairman of annual costume-masque ball; the Stock Company (dramatic group)—scenic designer, board of directors, director, actor, etc.;

the Gibbons Club (Catholic club); committee to purchase senior class gift; pledged to a fraternity; attended all the social events of the college—dances, proms, teas, smokers, concerts, etc. To top off this seemingly crowded social program, I worked after school and on Saturdays and helped a great deal with the chores at home.

But obviously the working and non-working students, although more even than one might have guessed in grades and activities, do not start life all square in the sum total of what they got out of going to college. Both missed something. The family-supported graduate missed a certain ᵃmount of preparatory wrestling with the cold, cruel world into which he was being catapulted. The self-supported graduate, whose days contained only 24 hours like anyone else's, at least missed some sleep. As a group he kept up in his studies and made a name for himself as well, but something must have had to give. When we ponder the imponderables— the time spent or not spent in taking advantage of the college's cultural assets, the time spent or not spent on the acquisition of social graces, or even on the intelligent waste of leisure time—it seems obvious that the two do not start out on completely even terms.

We can also assume that the self-help and family-supported graduates were unequal, when they began their careers, in another important respect. Some of the working graduates in all probability came from wealthy families who wanted them to pay their way because it would be "a good experience," or "more democratic" to do so. Likewise some of the family-supported graduates must have come from poor families who were determined that the children should enjoy an "unburdened" college life, whatever the sacrifice. But these working rich boys and subsidized poor boys were surely the exceptions. The big majority of graduates who worked their way as door-to-door salesmen, dishwashers, or stockbrokers must have done so because of financial necessity, and the big majority of those who did not work must have come from families well able to support them. In general, there is bound to have been a considerable difference in the family economic backgrounds.

Considering the difference in background, it is not surprising to discover that on the matter of total income—including investments as well as earnings—the family-supported graduates do better. For all the graduates in the sample—women as well as men, and women who work as well as women who are now supported by husbands either rich or poor—the total family incomes work out as follows:

For graduates who earned half to all their own expenses, the median total family income is $4,831.

For those who earned less than half, the median is $4,995.

Among those who did not have to work at all, it is $5,276.

The figures indicate two things. First, the graduates who worked their way have indeed attained an economic level way above the average of the whole population. But, second, they have not entirely closed the gap that presumably separated their own parents from those who were able to pay their children's way. Nor can the financial difference be blamed entirely on such outside income as trusts, gifts of stocks and bonds, inherited real estate, and other sources that have nothing to do with individual earning power. In Chart 39 we begin examining the actual earnings of the men graduates. It develops immediately that the family-supported men have produced the most high-bracket salaries; the men who had to pay all or most of their way have produced the fewest.

The graduates have been divided into age groups in Chart 39 to give a clearer picture of this queer economic footrace. In the early stages of the race, the self-help and family-supported graduates run virtually in a dead heat. But after the age of 30, for some reason, the group that was sent to college begins to pull ahead of those who had to work their way. The gap increases as time goes on, until, after 40, the family-supported men have a significant lead in income. At age 40 and older, 42% of them are making $7,500 a year or more—but only 31% of those who earned most of their way are doing this well. In fact, the more nearly self-supporting a man was in college, the farther behind the family-supported man he has fallen in later life. There are no important differences in the lowest income bracket—but the family-supported men's record in the $7,500-and-over bracket is outstanding.

What all this amounts to is that the student who works his way starts his career under an economic handicap which, although hardly burdensome at all at the beginning, weighs more and more heavily as the race goes on. He, or rather, his group, never does get up to the income level of the students whose way was paid, and indeed lags farther and farther behind as the years go by. The fact may be highly unfair and is certainly subversive to the Horatio Alger doctrine, but there it is.

Why is this? Why should one group be more likely to succeed than the other? Is it that one type plays a better game of golf, or tells a better locker-room story, or dresses better, or mixes a more authoritative mar-

CHART 39

Earnings of self-help
and family-supported graduates

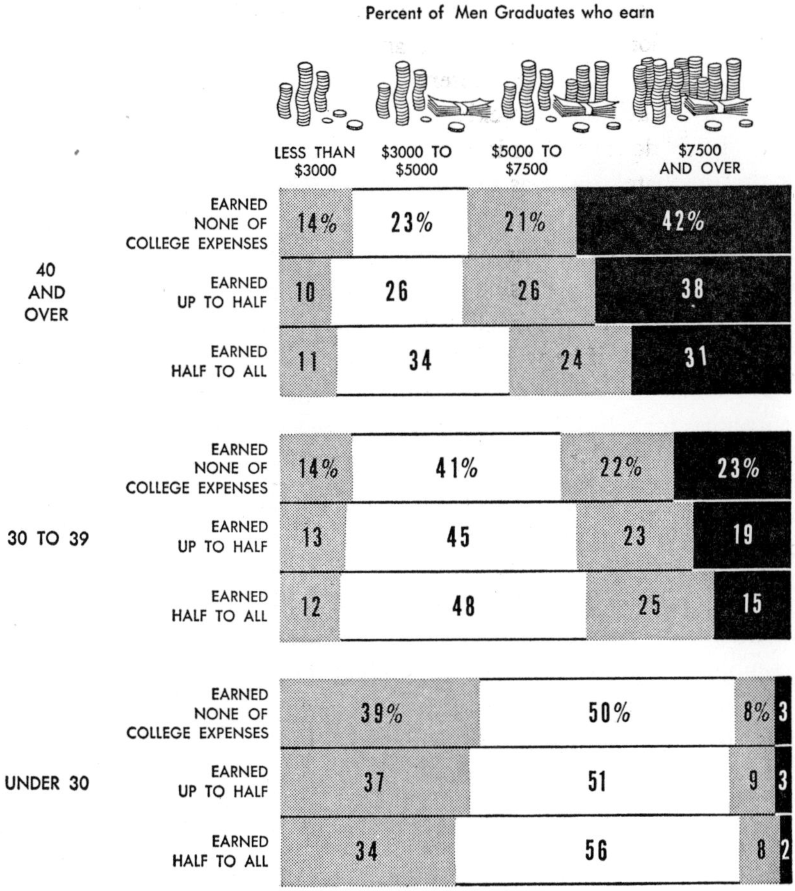

Percent of Men Graduates who earn

	LESS THAN $3000	$3000 TO $5000	$5000 TO $7500	$7500 AND OVER
40 AND OVER				
EARNED NONE OF COLLEGE EXPENSES	14%	23%	21%	42%
EARNED UP TO HALF	10	26	26	38
EARNED HALF TO ALL	11	34	24	31
30 TO 39				
EARNED NONE OF COLLEGE EXPENSES	14%	41%	22%	23%
EARNED UP TO HALF	13	45	23	19
EARNED HALF TO ALL	12	48	25	15
UNDER 30				
EARNED NONE OF COLLEGE EXPENSES	39%	50%	8%	3
EARNED UP TO HALF	37	51	9	3
EARNED HALF TO ALL	34	56	8	2

tini? Perhaps part of the explanation is that family assistance for the supported student does not necessarily end on cap-and-gown day. Thanks to his background or family influence he may start out in jobs with a better chance for advancement. As an over-simplified instance, two young graduates of equal ability, one of whom worked his way and one of whom did not, might begin as clerks for the same railroad; 20 years later the working student by dint of worthy effort might have become head of the accounting department while the other graduate, because social friendships made him a marked man from the start, might be a vice-president about to command a private car. This whole phenomenon is part of the intricate question of what qualities and techniques do get one ahead in the world. This is a matter deserving a separate investigation, and our survey did not attempt to tackle it.

Our figures do show that it is in business, rather than in the professions, that the graduate who was sent to college has the greatest edge on the graduate who sent himself. Chart 40, confined to the 40-and-up group where earning differences are most pronounced, shows that if the self-help student went into a profession—the law, medicine, the clergy, teaching— he is now doing almost as well as the man who was sent through school by his parents. But if he went into business, he is considerably more likely to have fallen behind. It is in the business field—traditionally the great opportunity for self-advancement—where the self-help student, ironically, makes the poorest showing in comparison to the graduate from a wealthier home. Especially at the top jobs, those paying $7,500 and over, he simply fails to keep pace.

We have seen that a technical education is a big help in getting ahead in the business world, but it is not a lack of technical training that handicaps the men who worked their way; 47% of them, as against 42% of the supported students, majored in a technical field and not in the humanities or in other fields which prove less helpful in business careers. The trouble lies somewhere else. One graduate who feels that he has failed to set the world on fire writes, "It's who you know that counts, rather than what you know." Other graduates hold that personality traits, upper-class manners, influential uncles, or "contacts" in general are what count. None of these sounds like a complete and satisfactory answer. But it does appear that other things being equal—including type of college training, grades, and activities—the working student's handicap must lie somewhere in this unexplored area.

CHART 40

The financial gap between self-help and family-supported Graduates

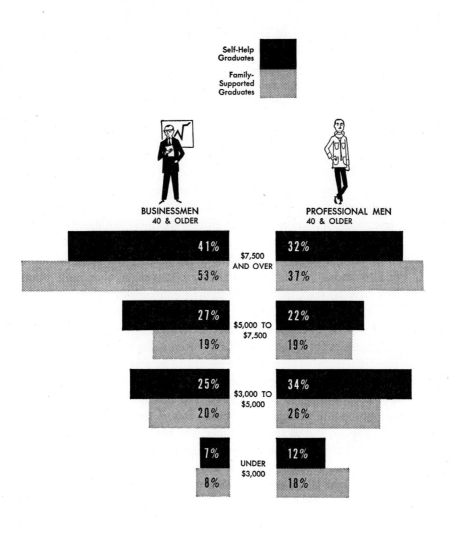

Self-Help
Graduates

Family-
Supported
Graduates

BUSINESSMEN
40 & OLDER

PROFESSIONAL MEN
40 & OLDER

$7,500
AND OVER
41%   32%
53%   37%

$5,000 TO
$7,500
27%   22%
19%   19%

$3,000 TO
$5,000
25%   34%
20%   26%

UNDER
$3,000
7%   12%
8%   18%

None of the foregoing means that anyone need shed a tear, and certainly not pass the hat, for the boy who worked his way. Better than half of his group, once they had reached the maturity of the forties, were earning at least $5,000 a year at the time of the survey and thus doing very nicely indeed compared to the U.S. population as a whole. The boy who worked his way makes relatively less money than the graduates who come from richer families—but he is by no means downtrodden.

In all probability, however, the financial gap between the two groups is getting larger instead of smaller. Having said this, we must quickly explain—for it sounds like a direct contradiction of the figures in Chart 39. In that chart we noted that the gap was biggest among the oldest graduates, smaller in the middle group, and non-existent among the youngest graduates. Taking the figures at their face value, an optimist might argue that all the differences between self-help and family-supported graduates are a thing of the past, being wiped out completely by the new generations of college people in the much more democratic America of the middle twentieth century. But this is a case where the figures cannot stand alone, and must be interpreted in the light of other things that we know about the graduates.

For one thing, we know that the college graduate, unlike the average man, does not reach his earnings peak until late in life; as we saw in Chapter 3, the graduates of 50 and over are making the most money of all. We also know, just from day-to-day observation, that most young graduates have to start quite modestly (in comparison to their ultimate earnings) and that many of those destined to make the most money in the long run—the doctors, the lawyers, the young men learning their fathers' businesses from the ground up—often make the least at the start. Thus the differences in earnings are bound to be smallest among the men just out of school, and to increase year by year as the most successful graduates keep adding to their stature. No matter how one chooses to divide or group the youngest graduates, few if any differences in earning ability appear. But as they get older, and many of them start pushing into the higher brackets, the differences are bound to start cropping up. A young doctor, a young lawyer, a young teacher, and three young businessmen might all be earning $68 a week—which happened to be the median for all men graduates under 30 at the time of the survey. But we know that the doctor and the lawyer are almost sure to go much higher as the years pass, while the teacher is soon likely to hit his ceiling.

Of the three men in business, the first may always remain a white collar worker, the second may become a department head, and the third may wind up as president of General Motors. Today they may rate the same on the charts; 25 years from now they will be widely scattered through the income brackets.

To forecast what will happen to the young self-help graduates and the young family-supported graduates, therefore, it is much more profitable to examine Chart 41. At the time the graduates over 40 were going to school, the chart shows, the poorer college boy was just as likely to enter the high-paid professions as the wealthier boy. But lately, among the men under 40 and especially among those under 30, more and more working students have been going into occupations which are low-paid even at the top. The chart shows that the younger working graduates are under-represented in the high-paid professions of medicine, law, and dentistry, and over-represented in such low-paid professions as teaching and the clergy.

Larger proportions of both groups—in fact two out of three, among self-help and family-supported graduates alike—are going into the business world these days. But in the case of the boys who did not work their way, this represents a switch from the low-paid "liberal" professions to business careers that pay better. In the case of the working students it represents a departure from the high-paid professions in favor of business.

The proportion of graduates who worked their own way to law, medical, or dental degrees has declined steadily, from 27% of the oldest group to only 13% of the youngest. Meanwhile the proportion entering teaching or the clergy has not dropped appreciably. Among the men sent to college by their parents, the exact opposite is true—the proportion entering the low-paid professions has been dropping and is only 9% among the youngest group, while the proportion entering the high-paid professions has remained practically the same.

It may be that the longer courses generally required by colleges nowadays for law and medical degrees—longer and therefore also more expensive—are squeezing more poor boys than rich from these fields. It may also be that the poorer boys have become increasingly discouraged by the length of time it takes to get a career really started in this sort of profession even after the diploma is safely signed—a difficulty that is not nearly so bothersome for the student who can count on his family

CHART 41

Fewer Grads who worked their way are now entering the high paid professions

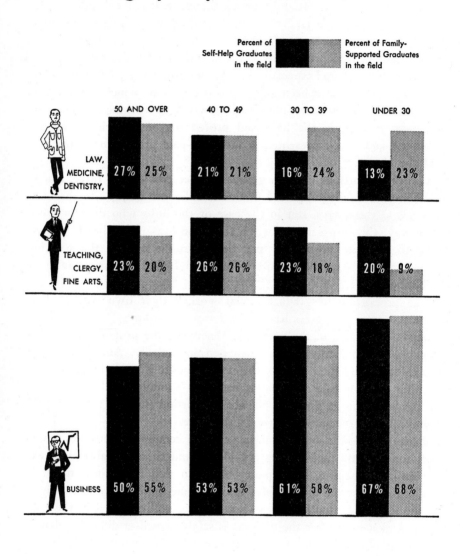

Percent of Self-Help Graduates in the field

Percent of Family-Supported Graduates in the field

	50 AND OVER		40 TO 49		30 TO 39		UNDER 30	
LAW, MEDICINE, DENTISTRY,	27%	25%	21%	21%	16%	24%	13%	23%
TEACHING, CLERGY, FINE ARTS,	23%	20%	26%	26%	23%	18%	20%	9%
BUSINESS	50%	55%	53%	53%	61%	58%	67%	68%

for financial help even after graduation day. At any rate, whatever the cause, the men who have to work their way have recently been staying away from the high-paid professions, and the figures indicate that the trend is still continuing. Meanwhile the flight from the study of the humanities, and from the "learned" but low-paid professions that are so often the end of the road for humanities students—a general trend which we have noted earlier in the book—turns out to be greatest among the wealthier students and almost non-existent among the poorer ones.

By the time our youngest graduates are in their forties—say around 1970—the differences in earnings between the self-help and family-supported graduates will doubtless be even larger than it is today. And if the trends continue, it will grow bigger every year. In the business field, which now attracts two-thirds of the graduates of both types, the self-help man does not keep up with the man who was sent to school by his parents. And while the self-help man manages to hold his own pretty well in the professions, he is increasingly choosing the low-paid professional fields instead of the high-paid ones. Unless something happens to change the pattern, the chances of the self-help students for financial equality will grow progressively smaller.

15

Princeton Versus Podunk

Having just done one form of violence to the Horatio Alger tradition, we are now forced to do another. It would be pleasant to report that the boys from Podunk College, in just as great numbers as the boys from Princeton, go on in later life to become the captains of industry and the professions. As a nation we like to think that all diplomas as well as all men are equal, that the little college at the edge of a small town is as sure an avenue to success as the university in the middle of New York or New Haven. We like to think so—but we are wrong.

When it comes to predicting a graduate's financial success, it develops that the wealth and prestige of his college are the best guide of all. The fact that he went to Princeton instead of Podunk means even more than the fact that he specialized instead of taking a general course, or that he was sent to school by his parents instead of having to work his own way. Our data show that the earnings of the graduates go up steadily as the wealth of their colleges, as measured by their endowment per student, rises from the lowest to the highest brackets. Even among the wealthiest colleges, it is the hallowed Ivy League that produces the richest graduates—and the prestigious "Big Three" of the Ivy League, Harvard, Yale and Princeton, that produce the richest of all. If we divide the men graduates into groups by the type of school attended, we get these sharp differences in median incomes:

THE BIG THREE $7,365
  (Harvard, Yale, Princeton)

OTHER IVY LEAGUE   6,142
  (Columbia, Cornell, Dartmouth, Pennsylvania)

SEVENTEEN TECHNICAL SCHOOLS   5,382
  (California, Carnegie, Case, Detroit, Drexel, Georgia, Illinois, Massachusetts, and Stevens Institutes of Technology; Rensselaer, Rose,

Virginia, and Worcester Polytechnic Institutes; Clarkson College of Technology, Cooper Union, Polytechnic Institute of Brooklyn, Tri-State College)

TWENTY FAMOUS EASTERN COLLEGES $5,287

(Amherst, Bates, Bowdoin, Brown, Clark, Colby, Franklin and Marshall, Hamilton, Haverford, Hobart, Lafayette, Lehigh, Middlebury, Rutgers, Swarthmore, Trinity, Tufts, Union, Wesleyan of Connecticut, Williams)

THE BIG TEN 5,176

(Chicago, Illinois, Indiana, Iowa, Michigan, Minnesota, Northwestern, Ohio State, Purdue, Wisconsin)

ALL OTHER MIDWEST COLLEGES 4,322

ALL OTHER EASTERN COLLEGES 4,235

Why should these wide differences—amounting to over $3,000 from the top to the bottom—exist? One reason for the low figures at the bottom is that the "all other" colleges turn out a disproportionate share of men who go into the low-paid fields of teaching and the clergy, and conversely a smaller share of graduates who enter the high-paid fields of business, law, medicine, and dentistry. But among the other groups of colleges there are no significant differences in the graduates' occupational fields. The Big Three of the Ivy League turn out only a few more doctors and lawyers than the Big Ten Schools, and not nearly so many businessmen as the technical schools with their engineering specialists. The fact is that job for job (as well as age for age) the differences still stand. If we consider only graduates who have entered business and wound up as proprietors and executives of one sort or another, we find that the following proportions were earning $5,000 a year or more at the time of the study:

Of the Ivy Leaguers, 84%.
Of the Big Ten graduates, 68%.
Of the "all other Midwest" graduates, 59%.

At the other extreme, if we consider only graduates who have gone into schoolteaching, we find that these proportions were earning less than $3,000:

Of the Ivy Leaguers, only 7%.
Of the Big Ten graduates, 18%.
Of the "all other Midwest" graduates, 24%.

The moral seems to be that if the Ivy Leaguers go into well-paying jobs they earn even more than any other graduates, while if they go into low-paying jobs they do not do so badly as the others.

Although we have noted that good grades may at least sometimes lead to good incomes, it develops that even the poorest students from the Ivy League share in the general prosperity—and do better than the best students from other schools. Of the Ivy Leaguers who just got by—the C and D students—42% had reached the $7,500 level. Of the A students from the Big Ten only 37% had hit that mark, and only 23% of the A students from the "all other Midwest" colleges. Even the great financial disadvantage of a general education, rather than a specific one, does not seem to hold back the Ivy Leaguers. Of the Ivy League humanities majors, 46% had reached the $7,500 bracket, and of the social scientists 50%. But even among the Big Ten's engineering graduates, with their highly specific training and all the advantages that we found in Chapter 12 go with it, only 23% had reached the $7,500 level.

What all this amounts to is that the differences in earning power between graduates of rich and famous schools and those from small and obscure schools are so great that they override everything else. Earning power rises steadily with each increase in wealth and prestige of the school. At the extremes, the Ivy League graduates do best of all financially even when they make poor grades and take a general rather than specific course, both of which are ordinarily handicaps—while the graduates of the smallest schools do not get up to the averages even when they make fine grades and take the type of specific courses which ordinarily produce the biggest incomes.

As we have already noted from time to time, earnings are by no means an exclusive measure of a college's success or its graduates' feelings of satisfaction. In fact this is one reason there are so many sorts of colleges, catering to young people seeking rewards ranging from a degree in animal husbandry to a husband. But on a simple cash basis, the figures we have been examining here are quite a testimonial to the rich and famous schools, and especially to the Ivy League. It is worth asking whether the figures are perhaps even more of a testimonial to the families of the boys who go there.

Knowing that the rich colleges tend to attract students from wealthy families, and that the wealthy boy tends to earn a bigger income in later life than the boy who works his way, can we write off all the college differences as really just a matter of family backgrounds? From a first glance at Chart 42, one might be inclined to think so. Only one out of five Ivy League graduates had to earn the major part of his college expenses—against one out of two graduates of Midwest colleges. And one in every three Ivy Leaguers did not have to pay a cent toward his education, where only about one out of ten men from most Midwest colleges was so completely subsidized.

But the moral of the chart is not so simple as that. In the Big Ten, mostly comprising state universities with low fees, 86 out of 100 graduates worked their way, wholly or in part. The proportion sent by their parents was just about as low as at other Midwest colleges. Yet as we have seen, Big Ten graduates do better financially than the graduates of our "other Midwest" and "other Eastern" schools. In their case it is definitely not a matter of a son's coasting to success on his father's financial momentum.

Moreover, we know that some poor boys do go to the rich schools; as the chart shows, even in the Ivy League 19% of the graduates have earned more than half their expenses. The question now becomes: what about the relative earning power of graduates who went to different kinds of colleges, but whose economic backgrounds were just about the same? Chart 43 shows the answer: the golden touch of the Ivy League falls on rich and poor alike. By the age of 40, chosen here because it implies a certain financial maturity, 50% of the students who worked their way through Harvard, Yale, Princeton, or some other Ivy League school have risen to the $7,500-or-over income level. This is as many, or more, as among the graduates who were supported by their families while getting degrees at our group of famous Eastern colleges, the Big Ten or the "other" schools.

In general, the different financial rewards of the rich schools versus the obscure ones are just as pronounced even when we separate the graduates by family background. At all types of colleges, the graduates from wealthy family backgrounds wind up making more money than those from poorer family backgrounds, which proves in detail the general rule we found in Chapter 14. But among both the self-help students and the family-supported students, considered separately, the type of college plays a great part in later financial success.

It is not just the family; it must be the school—or the kind of students who go there. There are undoubtedly some factors working here that

CHART 42

How many worked their way?

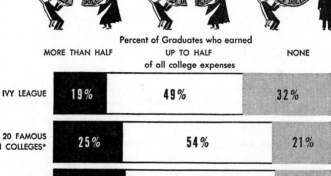

Percent of Graduates who earned

MORE THAN HALF	UP TO HALF	NONE

of all college expenses

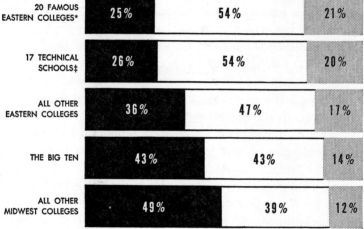

	MORE THAN HALF	UP TO HALF	NONE
IVY LEAGUE	19%	49%	32%
20 FAMOUS EASTERN COLLEGES*	25%	54%	21%
17 TECHNICAL SCHOOLS‡	26%	54%	20%
ALL OTHER EASTERN COLLEGES	36%	47%	17%
THE BIG TEN	43%	43%	14%
ALL OTHER MIDWEST COLLEGES	49%	39%	12%

* Amherst, Bates, Bowdoin, Brown, Clark, Colby, Franklin and Marshall, Hamilton, Haverford, Hobart, Lafayette, Lehigh, Middlebury, Rutgers, Swarthmore, Trinity, Tufts, Union, Wesleyan, Williams

‡ California, Carnegie, Case, Detroit, Drexel, Georgia, Illinois, Massachusetts, and Stevens Institutes of Technology; Rensselaer, Rose, Virginia, and Worcester Polytechnic Institutes; Clarkson College of Technology, Cooper Union, Polytechnic Institute of Brooklyn, Tri-State College

CHART 43

In reaching top income brackets, college makes a difference

Percent of Graduates, 40 and older, now earning $7,500 or more per year

As students, earned more than half
of all college expenses

As students, family paid
all college expenses

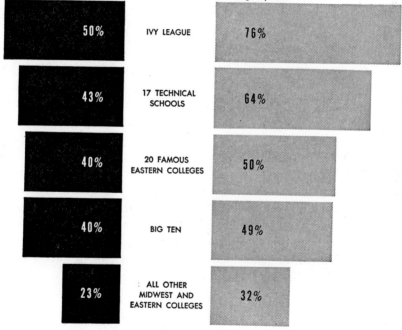

50%	IVY LEAGUE	76%
43%	17 TECHNICAL SCHOOLS	64%
40%	20 FAMOUS EASTERN COLLEGES	50%
40%	BIG TEN	49%
23%	ALL OTHER MIDWEST AND EASTERN COLLEGES	32%

we cannot possibly measure, and many of them must revolve around the personalities, talents, hopes, and ambitions of the students. Although this is necessarily a matter of sheer speculation, we might get the best clue of all by thinking for a moment about some various young men who are leaving high school and faced with making a choice of colleges.

Certainly one type of student who can count on having all expenses paid by his family is the boy from a very rich and socially prominent family, whose parents and grandparents have been college graduates from time immemorial—and from the most famous schools at that. Such a boy might very well be expected, as a matter of course, to follow his father's footsteps at Yale or at Harvard. If he does not go to the Ivy League—but instead chooses some equally wealthy but smaller college, or a state university or a very small and obscure school—there must be a reason. Perhaps he is doubtful of his scholastic ability or his willingness to study, and wants the safety of a school which is considered a little softer touch on the matter of grades. Perhaps he dislikes his family's social life, and all the social implications of the wealthier schools. Perhaps he is an intellectual rebel, and feels that he should go to a more "democratic" school and live a less profitable and more dedicated life than his father. Whichever of these possibilities or any others happens to be the reason, the chances are he is the type of young man who is less able or less interested in making money.

Within the lifetimes of our graduates another very common type of family-supported student has been the son of the self-made man. His father did not go to college; neither did his mother; but the family has made enough money to send the children to college and is eager to do so as a matter of prestige. They live in a small town or a small city; the father is a merchant, a traveling salesman, or a good insurance agent, or perhaps a factory superintendent or the owner of a small manufacturing firm. Although the family has a decent amount of money, it is not among the social elite even in its own community. Such a young man might well prefer a small and unpretentious college, or at the most his state university. If instead he elects to go to one of the famous wealthy campuses, or even to the Ivy League, he too must be something of an exception—motivated by unusual abilities or by extraordinarily high social or career ambitions.

In the case of boys who work their own way through school, it is always easiest to choose colleges where the fees and living expenses are low; and if there happens to be a college right in the home town, that is the easiest of all. For a young man in New Mexico with no means of support except what he can earn with his own hands outside the classroom hours, the thought of traveling all the way to Princeton, finding a job in a strange part of the country, and meeting the higher expenses of an Ivy League education is a pretty frightening thing. The boy who does it must be exceptionally confident, self-reliant, and ambitious to begin with. Moreover he must feel that the college course can give him something well worth straining for.

Very possibly the student bodies at the wealthiest and most famous schools are made up largely of young men who are in a sense the most determined to gain the highest positions in life—or the most likely to inherit them. The smaller and less noted schools possibly have a greater proportion of students who are less ambitious—or who would conceivably not want to have the presidency of a big corporation, and all the trappings that go with it, if it were handed to them on a platter. It may also be that four years of association with rich or ambitious young men on a wealthy campus intensify financial strivings more than four years of the more casual life on a smaller campus. Although we have found that extracurricular activities as such bear no relation to financial success, perhaps personal associations and social contacts on the campus do. Some people believe, and they may be right, that the best way to make your son a financial success is to buy him a dinner jacket and then let him figure out how to pay his way into the places where he can wear it.

16

Church Makes a Difference

The facts in this chapter will undoubtedly shock a great many people. This is because we are about to make a comparison between the college records and the after-campus careers of our white Protestants—the majority group in the U.S.—and such religious and racial minorities as the Catholics, Jews, and Negroes. And it so happens that our data violate the principles of both the two big schools of modern thought on this subject. Some people like to think that the white Protestants are the custodians of all virtues, and that nobody else could possibly have so many brains or so much prestige and success in the community; among college graduates this idea seems to be losing its appeal, as we saw in Chapter 9, but it still exerts considerable influence. On the other hand it is popular among today's intellectuals—and among an increasing number of graduates whether they think of themselves as intellectuals or not—to feel that there are absolutely no differences at all. To this school of thought the idea that a Negro should vote as a Negro, or that a Jew should think as a Jew, is simply anathema.

So goes the thinking, on both sides of this still controversial fence. We now let some facts speak.

In the lives of the various graduates after college there are some wide and unmistakable dissimilarities. The Negro, indeed, has such a low record of economic success as to constitute a special case, which we shall have to discuss by itself a little later. And even among white graduates, religious background has a dramatic relation to financial success after leaving the campus. Just knowing whether a graduate is a Protestant, a Catholic, or a Jew is a better gauge of his present success than anything connected with his college grades, his participation in extra-curricular and social activities, or even the amount of his own expenses that he was forced to earn.

The men graduates as a whole, as we reported early in the book, tend to occupy the jobs of greatest importance and prestige; very few of them have to settle for the routine white collar or manual jobs. But there are some noticeable differences in the proportion of Protestant, Catholic, and Jewish men who attain the prestige positions, and those who are found in rank-and-file jobs. The proportions are as follows:

	Jews	Protestants	Catholics
Proprietors, managers, and executives	33%	34%	26%
Non-teaching professionals	45	34	32
Teachers	6	12	13
All types of white collar and manual workers and farmers	16	20	29

In other words, among the men graduates who took part in the survey, for every four Jews in rank-and-file jobs there were five Protestants and seven Catholics.

Along with the better job status enjoyed by the Jewish graduates goes a higher income. But this is one place where the statistics might fool us, for people in large cities make more money than those in small towns, as we have already pointed out, and it is well known that Jews tend to live in the larger cities. In fact the survey provides some new evidence on how the Jewish graduates gravitate toward the metropolis. In the big cities of 500,000 or more are found 59% of our Jewish graduates, compared with 31% of the Catholic graduates and 19% of the Protestant graduates. And in the smaller cities, towns, and rural areas under 25,000 population live only 12% of all Jewish graduates, compared with 33% of Catholic and 48% of Protestant graduates. So we have drawn up Chart 44 which gives the earnings of our Jewish, Protestant, and Catholic graduates in the big cities and in the small ones. The chart shows that the size of the community makes no real difference. Indeed it could be broken down into additional population brackets, and the fact would still hold that in whatever type of community the Jewish graduates make the most money and the Catholic graduates the least.

Nor do the higher earnings of the Jewish graduates depend upon the fact that so many of them have entered the well-paid professions of law, medicine, and dentistry. The fact is that even within the professions, more Jewish graduates are in the higher income brackets than Protestants or Catholics. The same is true within the field of executive business

CHART 44

Earnings, city size, and religion

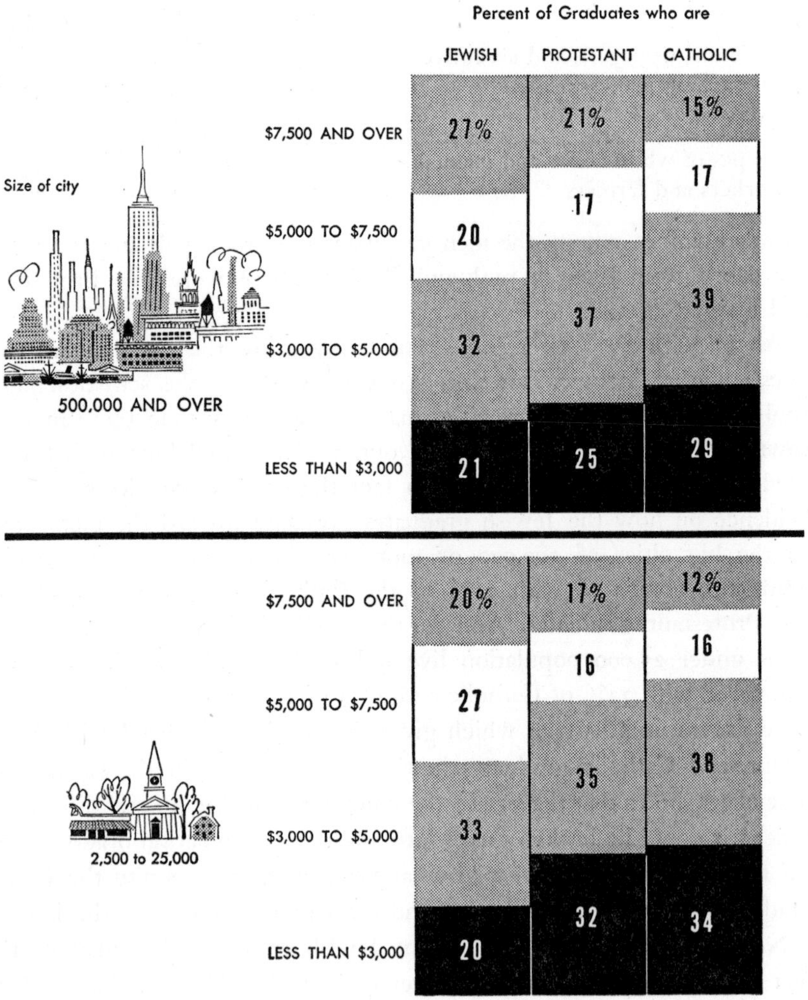

Percent of Graduates who are

	JEWISH	PROTESTANT	CATHOLIC

Size of city

500,000 AND OVER

	JEWISH	PROTESTANT	CATHOLIC
$7,500 AND OVER	27%	21%	15%
$5,000 TO $7,500	20	17	17
$3,000 TO $5,000	32	37	39
LESS THAN $3,000	21	25	29

2,500 to 25,000

	JEWISH	PROTESTANT	CATHOLIC
$7,500 AND OVER	20%	17%	12%
$5,000 TO $7,500	27	16	16
$3,000 TO $5,000	33	35	38
LESS THAN $3,000	20	32	34

jobs. It is not until we get down to the level of the lower-paid positions—teaching, white collar, and manual jobs—that the greater earning power of the Jewish graduate, especially in contrast to that of the Catholic graduate, disappears. In these fields, Jewish, Protestant, and Catholic graduates earn just about the same amount.

Perhaps, harking back to the moral of Chapter 14, which was that men who have to work their way through college never reach the financial level of the men who were sent by their parents, one might assume that the Jewish graduates tend to be the sons of wealthy parents, while the Protestants are more or less in the middle and the Catholics tend to come from poorer families. But this turns out to be untrue, at least so far as we can tell. There is very little difference among the three groups in the matter of being supported through college or working one's own way. Among the Jews, 29% earned more than half their own way; 44% earned part but less than half, and 27% were sent by their parents. For both Protestants and Catholics the comparable figures are 29%, 40%, and 31%. The differences are minute.

College grades do not provide the answer either. The proportions of A students are practically identical—15% for Protestants, 14% for Catholics, and 15% for Jews. And so are the proportions of B students—60% for Protestants, 62% for Catholics, and 63% for Jews.

On the campus, it appears, the three groups start out just about the same. They come from about the same types of economic background, as nearly as this is reflected by the numbers who had to work their way, and they make about the same grades. Yet in life after the campus the Jewish graduates, by and large, wind up in the best jobs and make the most money. The Catholics, by and large, wind up in poorer jobs and make the least money. How can this be explained?

There is no answer anywhere in our figures, but perhaps part of the explanation is obvious. Any minority group which is subject to overt social discrimination is likely to have a strong urge to get ahead in life, to establish some kind of success and equality. The Jewish graduates probably have the greatest motivation to succeed—and of course the most common measure of success in modern society is the paycheck. As to why so many Jews enter the professions where high incomes are almost a matter of course, this too seems fairly elementary. Not only because of discrimination, but also because they were latecomers to the American scene, Jews found many types of business and industry, especially the biggest ones, closed to them. To operate as independent businessmen, they had to get into the smaller fields—like retail stores and clothing manufacture—or into the brand-new ones like the movies. Their better educated sons and grandsons, aware of the limitations upon a Jew in the business world, are likely to turn to the professions as a matter of course. In many small towns where there are only a few Jewish families, the typical thing thirty years ago was for the Jews to be self-taught and self-made men running the clothing stores. Today this older generation has died out—perhaps leaving just one son or two to carry on the retail trade tradition, and sometimes not leaving any—and most of the Jews are now doctors or lawyers.

As to why the Catholics should lag behind in jobs and income, the explanation—if indeed there is any—is far more obscure. Very likely the Catholics have no extraordinary motivation toward financial success as a means of proving their mettle; for while many American Protestants, if hard pressed, would have to concede a prejudice against Catholicism, actual personal discrimination against Catholics has cropped up at only a few times and a few places in our history. But this would only account for the Catholics' not surpassing the Protestants; it does not explain why they should lag behind. It may be that Catholics in the business world meet with a very subtle and unspoken form of obstacle; perhaps many business firms have a sort of quota on the number of Catholic executives, just as political parties are known to set a quota on the number of Catholics who shall appear on the ticket at any given election.

Or perhaps there are some differences in family economic background which are not revealed by the criterion in our survey, which is the matter of working or not having to work one's way through school. We do know that many American Catholics are the descendants of Irish and Italian immigrants who came to this nation fairly recently in our history, and like all immigrants had an uphill financial battle to fight. We also know that the general rule is that the richer the father, the more money the son is likely to make. It may be that the Catholic graduates start under a greater handicap of economic background than can be discerned from counting the number who worked their way through school; it may actually be that Catholic families, with their strong tradition of family loyalty, help send their sons to school to a degree that other families in similar circumstances would never attempt.

Or perhaps the relative lack of financial success among Catholic graduates is simply a spiritual matter. We have noted earlier in the book that the Catholics are the most religious of all the graduates, and by far the most consistent churchgoers. It may be that they simply place less value on worldly success than do Protestants or Jews.

All this, of course, is merely theorizing. The survey shows only that the Jews tend to have somewhat better jobs and make somewhat more money, and that the Catholics are below the average for all graduates in both matters. There is nothing in the statistics to show why. One could speculate endlessly on the reasons—and the whole subject is recommended for round-table discussion.

In their roles as citizens as well as their roles as wage earners, the Protestant, Catholic, and Jewish graduates have some distinguishing traits. Insofar as we were able to measure their participation in community events, the big-city Protestants, Catholics, and Jews play an almost equal role. But in the smaller cities, towns, and rural areas—all communities under 25,000 population—the Protestants lead the Catholics, and the Catholics in turn lead the Jews, by clear margins. (In these communities 62% of Protestants reported five or more civic activities, compared to 53% of Catholics and 47% of Jews.) By our measurement of political activities and interest in national affairs, Protestant and Catholic graduates come out just about even—and the Jewish graduates are well ahead.

Now the question becomes: How, if at all, do the Protestant, Catholic, and Jewish graduates differ in their opinions on major political issues? We do not have the total answer, for a survey of all important political attitudes would be a job in itself, but we do have it for the three very big issues—New Dealism versus anti-New Dealism, internationalism versus isolationism, and prejudice versus tolerance—that were discussed for graduates in general in Chapter 9. Using the same measures that were applied in Chapter 9, and then breaking down the results for the three types of graduates we are discussing here, we get the pattern shown in Chart 45.

The Catholic and Protestant graduates seem to think pretty much alike. There are small percentage differences tending to show that the Catholics are a trifle less internationalist, more tolerant, and more inclined toward the New Deal. But the differences are hardly worth mentioning. There is very little here to indicate any real disparity between the political opinions of Protestant and Catholic graduates—a fact which will become

CHART 45 # Religion and opinions

Graduates who are   **Percent whose opinions on World Affairs are**

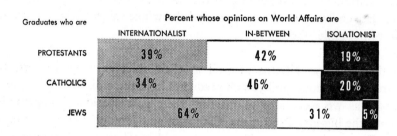

Percent whose opinions on Minorities are

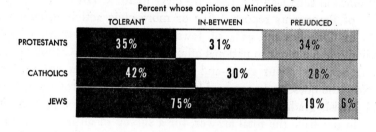

Percent whose opinions on Government are

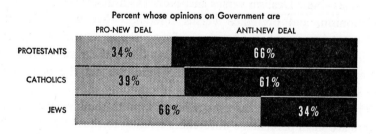

somewhat ironic when we note how different are their actual habits at the polls.

The Jewish graduates, however, are quite another matter. On every one of the three issues, their group vote is markedly different from that of the Protestants and Catholics. They stand out, in sharp contrast, for their internationalism, for their tolerance, and for their New Deal view of government. To translate Chart 45 into some specific political matters, it is obvious that a great majority of Jewish graduates would vote strongly, in any referendum, for full U.S. participation in the United Nations, lower tariffs, and generous immigration laws; for a civil rights bill and a Fair Employment Practices Commission, and indeed for most of the bills that Presidents Roosevelt and Truman have urged upon Congress.

Knowing the opinions of our Jewish graduates—and particularly their feelings about the New Deal type of government—it seems a safe bet that they will not be found on the side of the Republicans in the matter of party politics. Chart 46 bears this out, to an even greater extent than one might have expected. The tiny number of Jewish graduates who call themselves Republicans—only 6 out of 100—is an astonishing thing. Only in Mississippi and South Carolina, the two solidest states of the solid Democratic South, can one find fewer Republicans than among our Jewish graduates!

The Catholics occupy a sort of middle position in Chart 46. They are not so overwhelmingly prone to shun the Republican party as the Jewish graduates, but they are far more Democratic and far less Republican than the Protestant graduates. The reason, as we have seen, can hardly lie in their own feelings about political issues; they have about the same opinions on world affairs and tolerance as the Protestants—and what has been even more important in the matter of political allegiances, they are almost as anti-New Deal. The explanation, of course, is that the Catholics in America have historically voted the Democratic ticket; to be a Catholic has practically always meant to be a Democrat as well. The Catholic graduates follow the tradition—although not, from what is known of the Catholic vote in general, to so great an extent as non-college Catholics. A sizable minority has gone Republican—and an even bigger group is avoiding any definite commitment at all by calling itself Independent.

In fact the large number of Catholic and Jewish graduates who call

CHART 46   Political parties and religion

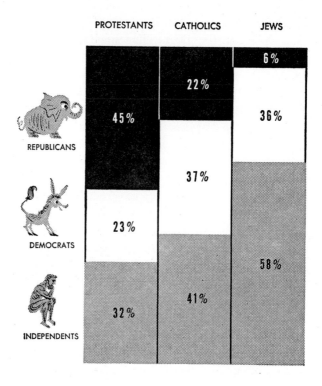

PROTESTANTS   CATHOLICS   JEWS

themselves Independents probably has a special significance. Among our graduates as a whole, as was reported in Chapter 10, the number of Republicans goes up and the number of Democrats goes down with rising incomes. But now it turns out that the effect of income is almost solely confined to the Protestant graduates; among Protestants the proportion of out-and-out Republicans, as opposed to either Democrats or Independents, rises steadily from 37% in the under-$3,000 bracket to 52% in the $7,500-and-over class. But among Catholic graduates the proportion of out-and-out Republicans rises only from 21% in the lowest income bracket to 26% in the highest. And among Jewish graduates the rise is from 3% to 7%—which for all practical purposes amounts to a jump from less than nothing to nothing at all. What we apparently have here is this: the Catholic graduates as a group, and specifically the Catholics in the higher income brackets, are pulled toward the Republican Party by their position in life—and toward the Democratic Party by strong tradition. The Jewish graduates are pulled one way by their incomes and another by their New Dealism. Moreover the whole political question is further complicated by the constantly shifting aspects of the two major parties, as they appear in the public mind from their promises and from the counter-charges of the opposition, as champions or enemies. Buffeted by all these cross-pressures, nearly half of all Catholic graduates and more than half of all Jewish graduates solve the problem by becoming Independents.

On the Negro graduate we can present our figures only for what they are worth. According to a 1947 census study, only about 4% of all U.S. college graduates are non-whites. This means that in any general survey, one would be unlikely to find enough Negro graduates—who make up most but not all of the non-white group—to provide a statistically reliable sample. Moreover, our own graduate sample does not contain even so many Negroes as the census figures would indicate; of the graduates who responded to the questionnaire, only 1.3% in all were non-whites. This may be purely a mathematical accident, of the kind that can easily happen when dealing with small groups. Or it may be that Negro colleges and Negro graduates were somewhat timid about taking part in the survey—as of course they have been forced into timidity about many other undertakings. At any rate we have data on only 102 Negro graduates—too few for any over-all statistical reliability, and far too few to divide and subdivide into the kind of age and income groupings which have proved so profitable in the case of white graduates.

However, what we do have is at least interesting and provocative, if not completely scientific. And with this disclaimer of anything resembling total accuracy, we now present it.

Only a few of our Negro graduates have entered the high-paying professions: 3% are doctors, 2% dentists, and 1% lawyers. Nor have many of them become business executives; in fact less than a quarter of them have any kind of business jobs. The great majority—a full 60%, compared to 29% of all white graduates—have become schoolteachers or are otherwise employed in the educational field. In other words the Negroes do not come anywhere near the record, by our standards of job prestige, of the white graduates. And even when they do have professional status, it is usually in the field of education where we have found salaries to be so uniformly low.

Their record of earnings is naturally quite low by the standards of the white graduates. Comparing all Negro with all white graduates, we find that whereas less than a third of the whites are in the under-$3,000 bracket, nearly two-thirds of the Negroes fall into this category. And while nearly a third of all white graduates earn $5,000 a year or more, only 5% of the Negroes have managed to get that high. The difference is probably due to two factors—first that the Negroes do not get into the same kind of jobs, and second that equal pay for equal work is still an unrealized ideal.

One might assume—and indeed a good many writers on this subject *have* assumed—that the Negro graduates would tend to be a disappointed, frustrated, and embittered group. Perhaps in some ways they are; our survey did not go into their general attitude toward their lives and times. But they are certainly not embittered about their college experience, or what it has meant to them. If they could live their lives over again, 98% would go back to college—which is exactly the same proportion as among white graduates. By the other measure we have used for satisfaction with college—which is the way the graduates feel about the school attended, the subject majored in, and the degree of general versus specialized education—it turns out that 30% of the Negroes are happy with all three choices they made. This is very close to the 33% figure for white graduates.

It is hardly necessary to inquire how the Negro graduates feel on the issue of tolerance versus prejudice. But it is instructive to examine their feelings about internationalism versus isolationism, and about the New Deal philosophy of government. The Negroes in our sample are more isolationist than the whites—37% of them, compared with only 23% of whites, qualify as isolationist rather than interventionist or in-between on the scale we have been using throughout the book. And fully 62% of them fall into the anti-New Deal camp (compared with 66% of Protestants, 61% of Catholics, and 34% of Jews). In the popular political terminology of our day, the Negro graduates constitute a conservative rather than a liberal or radical group.

In the matter of community and political activities, the Negroes rate very high. More of them than white graduates belong to clubs and organizations; more of them take part in community affairs, and fully as many of them as the whites take an active interest in national affairs and national politics. The only place where they fall short is the matter of voting—only 68% of Negro graduates had voted in the last national election compared with 81% of white graduates—but it may be that some of them live in communities where it is still very difficult for a Negro to cast a ballot. When they do vote, 35% of them vote as Democrats, 25% as Republicans, and 40% as Independents. Politicians often talk about "the Negro vote" as if it were a definite and solid thing; it used to be thought that "the Negro vote" always went Republican, in view of the Abraham Lincoln tradition, and since the 1930's it has been assumed that Franklin Roosevelt had won "the Negro vote" to the Democratic side. But at least among our group of Negro graduates, the vote is pretty well split—and it is noteworthy, when the figures are compared to those in Chart 46, that the Negroes turn out to be more Republican than either the Catholics or the Jews.

Perhaps an economic factor does actually operate here, although in a rather hidden and devious way. The Negro graduates, while not at all successful financially in comparison with the white graduates, are quite privileged by contrast to the non-college members of their own race. Their relative financial success and prestige in their own communities may incline them toward both Republicanism and conservatism. But all possible explanation aside, it does seem strange that the Negro graduates, whose earnings are hardly in the same league as those of any other graduates, should turn out to be conservative, anti-New Dealish, and quite divided in their political affiliations—while the Jewish graduates, who earn the most money of all, should turn out to be the militant liberals, the New Dealers, and the most predominantly Democrat.

PART SIX

The Ex-Student Speaks to the Student

CHAPTER 17

Times—and Graduates—Are Changing

At this point our grains of statistical fact on the college graduate have pretty well run through the hourglass; we have recorded just about all that we know from the survey on the matter of what has happened to our graduates. In one way or another we have looked at a great many types—old and young, men and women, A students and D students, students from rich families and those who had to earn their own way. We know from our data something of how well they have done financially, in marriage, and in terms of personal satisfaction and citizenship. Insofar as the past foreshadows the future, we also know something of what is likely to happen to the college graduates of this year and of years to come. Indeed the whole cumulative experience of our group of graduates constitutes an excellent source of guidance and advice to the students now in college and those who are thinking about going to college in the future—as well as to those parents who are wondering whether and how to send the children.

But over and above the statistical evidence, the survey has produced something else which is worth pondering by young people who have not yet been graduated, and by parents of present and potential college students. Besides the averages, the medians, and the percentage charts there are those several hundred letters from graduates of all types and in all walks of life—written with greater frankness and less self-consciousness than might be possible in a face-to-face conversation between a youngster seeking advice and a graduate attempting to offer it. In the letters our graduates have discussed many things—the things they are glad they did, the things they wish they had done, their satisfactions and their regrets, their praises and criticisms of college. Over and over again the letters return to a theme to which a great many graduates seem to have given long and serious thought: the matter of what they would do, and would not do, if they could go back and live their college days all over again. To read the letters is like holding a mass interview, such as no young advice-seeker could possibly arrange, with graduates who have succeeded and graduates who have failed, with some who strongly favor a certain type of school and some who strongly oppose it, with some who advise hard study and some who advocate concentration on extra-curricular activities—in other words, with graduates who run the gamut in experiences, impressions, and opinions.

In this whole section of the book—which is designed especially for the young person thinking about going to college, and that young person's parents—we shall therefore be dealing mostly with the graduates' own comments. We shall include, of course, such additional statistical data as our survey provides to bolster or cast doubt upon the graduates' opinions. But mostly we are here starting on a quite different tack; we have gone about as far as we can in the direction of the facts about graduates of the past, and we now turn toward the sort of opinion and advice which may help the graduates of the future. For the fact-seeker—say the sociologist interested in college graduates as a group force in our civilization—the book is to all intents and purposes finished. For the opinion-seeker —willing to gather and accept random comments of no scientific validity at all, for whatever guidance he can find from them—the book is perhaps just beginning.

To go or not to go? To send the children or not to send them? These, of course, are the first questions and the most important of all. And they are not nearly so easy to answer as educators sometimes think.

The youngster of high school age is often eager for independence, for adulthood, a salary check, possibly even marriage. Moreover the U.S., for all the expansion of higher education that it has witnessed, is not really a scholarly nation at heart. In most communities young children learn very quickly that the accepted grammar school attitude is to hate school, resent the teachers, and get by with as little work as possible. "Teacher's pet," as an epithet for the boy or girl who really seems to enjoy schoolwork, is an old and continuing part of our vocabulary of insult. In high school, particularly in the later years when the boys and girls are beginning to think of themselves as adults, such subjects as history, literature, trigonometry, and Latin seem to have very little to do with life as it is lived in the U.S. During their after-school hours they occupy a world of movies, television, football, and dates; even the adults whom they have an opportunity to observe do not often talk of such matters as are the concern of the classroom. The boys who would like to get started making a living are bound to wonder what Shakespeare can possibly have to do with getting a job; the girls are bound to wonder what Roman history can have to do with romance.

One of the letter writers already quoted in Chapter 12 may have hit the nail on the head. "Culture courses," he said, "are no longer needed to occupy a parlor or drawing room chair. Conversations over the tables of night clubs, beer gardens, baseball games, and trolley car seats do not smack of French, Gothic architecture, or why the Greek oratory was superior to our own."

What he says of the adult world is even more true of the world of the high school student. It is only the rare and exceptional boy or girl, from a particularly scholarly home or attending a high school with an unusually high tradition of scholarship, who hears a single word about his school subjects once the last class bell of the day has rung. And what does college promise, aside from the opportunities for social fun, except more of the same?

The American family—particularly the middle-class family which has accounted for most of the spectacular growth of the colleges in this century—faces an equally grave problem. These are difficult times for the middle classes; the prosperity of the late 1940's and early 1950's has by-passed them almost completely. Their incomes have suffered the constant attrition of higher taxes and higher living costs—and have not gone up nearly fast enough to keep them on an even financial keel. Among us are many middle-class men who, had they held the same kind of jobs 15 or 20 years ago, would never have had to give a second thought to providing funds for their children's college education—and yet today will have to sacrifice to give the children any kind of help at all.

Is college really—to either the youngster or his parents—worth all the struggle? In some cases, to be sure, the answer seems quite easy. If the youngster happens to be exceptionally bright, fond of his high school studies, and eager to become a lawyer or doctor, he himself has no doubts about going to college, and his parents are likely to help him if they possibly can. But not all youngsters have exceptional intellects—the rule of normal distribution of intelligence having not yet been repealed—and many youngsters do not have the faintest idea what they would really like to do for the rest of their lives. The answer whether to go or not to go, to help or not to help, gets progressively more difficult as we move from the scholarly boy or girl with a definite professional aim to the youngsters who dislike high school, are not doing very well at it, and have no idea what if anything to study in college.

The thought is bound to occur, both to some of these youngsters and to some of these parents, that perhaps we are already educating too many young folk. This, as has been mentioned, is also an opinion which has been reached by some educators—although by not nearly so many as believe we should further increase the opportunities for college training— and it turns out to be an opinion common as well among our graduates. A Virginia minister, who himself spent four years getting an A.B. and then three more in a theological seminary, writes as follows:

> I believe in college education only for those who need it and who want it. I feel that much time and money is wasted on college education for youngsters who neither want it or need it. In my opinion, a college education is not an end in itself, but a means to a higher end.

A Vassar graduate who is now married to a Midwestern university professor adds:

> Education in the United States has been idealized as a cure for all troubles: many families are sacrificing to send children to college who are not really college material and would be happier and better adjusted in a shorter course of vocational training.

And a male graduate in Florida who has no current connection with the education field comes to practically the same conclusion:

> I feel that college life is a poor investment for a very considerable number of students. For them business and craft training is more valuable.

Some of the letters along this line come from graduates who are not too happy about their own college experiences, and blame their disappointment in part at least on the ground that the colleges were trying to gear the classwork to inferior students. There is this comment, for example, from a North Carolina physician who explains elsewhere in his letter that he considers most of his pre-medical education to have been an utter waste of time:

> It is my firm conviction that a large number of college educations are wasted on youngsters who, either from laziness or because of precedent, wish to delay

for four more years their going to work. I believe that far too many parents of meager circumstances keep their noses to the grindstone for most of their lives in order to send their boy to college, when all the while the youngster has the capabilities of a good craftsman but could never make a statesman or professional man. I have noticed that this frequently produces a discontented, frustrated clerk instead of a well-qualified, steady, contented manual worker.

But there are also letters of this type from graduates who are great believers in the value of college and have no personal disappointments to sway them. There is this comment, for example, from a New York housewife who thinks so well of her own college that she is sending her daughters there:

The general culture courses are essential and without them one has only a trade-school diploma, in my opinion. That's what's wrong with most American colleges as contrasted to the European university. (Not that I think Europe has a monopoly on it or that there's any good reason we can't have it here. Most of us are in too big a hurry—and too lazy. It's still true there's no royal road to learning.) I think perhaps too many people go to college in this country. For those not suited to it, it can be a ruinous waste of time.

There is this one from an unmarried schoolteacher in Ohio who thought so highly of a college education that she managed, despite financial handicaps, to get one on the installment plan—in bits and pieces whenever she could afford the time and money from the day of her high school graduation until she was past her thirties. Having worked so hard for her own degree, she is perhaps entitled to be somewhat bitter about what the degree means to many modern students:

Being a teacher, I know that many who are attending college now would not have been considered high school caliber twenty-five years ago.

So I says, give 'em an A.B. degree at birth and have it over with. Send only those who are above average mentally to college for an M.A. or Ph.D. Send those who are only average, but studious, to a junior college so that they may be well informed on good literature and the social sciences.

Certainly there are, as has been noted in Chapter 2, a great many more young people going to college today than ever before, in this country or in any other, in modern times or in ancient. In theoretical terms, this can mean one of two things: either 1) the whole institution of college is being democratized, as the proponents of education for everyone so fervently hope, or 2) the college education is being degraded by being geared to inferior students rather than to superior intellects, as some professional educational critics and some of our own layman graduates are inclined to fear.

In practical terms for the modern youngster, however, the whole phenomenon means something quite different. What it means to him, in the simplest materialistic sense, is that if he has any aspirations at all toward white collar, middle-class, or upper-class jobs, he will be competing all his life with people who have had the benefit of college training. One good reason for going to college, in these days when the college education is becoming such a commonplace, is the elementary matter of self-defense.

There was a time when college was largely considered as training for one of the professions. Among our men graduates who are 50 and over, fully 60% planned to become doctors, lawyers, dentists, teachers, clergymen, or scientists. Only 39% planned to have business careers. The other 1% intended to enter the government service. But each succeeding decade of college graduates has seen a steady change in these proportions. Among the graduates under 30, the proportion planning to enter the professions has dropped to less than half—46% to be exact. The proportion planning on business careers has taken the lead, rising to 48%. And this great rise is accounted for not by the engineers, whose proportion has remained fairly constant through the years, but by students who have been training for what are roughly called the "service industries"—such as advertising, public relations, market research, hotel management, and the like. Among graduates over 50, only 5% planned to get into these fields. Among the youngest graduates the proportion has more than tripled, to 16%. Moreover 6% of the youngest graduates planned to enter government service, as compared with only 1% in the old days.

Among women a similar trend has taken place. In thinking of jobs as an alternative to marriage, or as an interlude before it, practically all the women over 50 planned on professional careers. The figures show that 82% planned to become teachers; 12% planned on other professions, and only 6% planned to enter the business field. But among the graduates under 30 the pattern is quite different. Only 52% planned to teach, and 19% planned careers in business. Again it is the "service industries" that account for most of the rise in the proportion of young graduates who foresee a career as businesswomen; 15% of the youngest group of women graduates trained themselves for this general field.

What this means in terms of job competition is a very great deal indeed. Until very recently—certainly as late as the 1920's—U.S. college
graduates were found mostly in a few very special fields. They were in
the "learned professions" of teaching or the clergy, or in such professions as the law and medicine. Even of the minority who had gone into
business, most were in such specialized technical jobs as engineering. The
ambitious non-college man, trying to carve out a business career for himself, was therefore not very likely to bump into college-trained competition. As long as he avoided teaching, which was pretty well closed to
him anyway; or medicine, which was completely closed; or the law office
or jobs in the engineering field, he started his economic life under no particular handicap.

Today the situation is quite different. More young graduates are actually planning to go into business—all types of business, and all phases
of it—than into the professions. The trend toward business careers has
been so steady and so marked that we can presume that it is still on the
rise; we have every reason to think that this year's graduates are more
inclined to a wide variety of business fields than last year's, and that next
year's graduates will be even more so. The young people of today—
including the women, although to a lesser extent than the men—think of
college as preparation for almost everything in the job lexicon from A
to Z. They are marching off the campus, in increasing numbers, into
practically every field imaginable. The non-college man or woman seeking advancement in life will hardly be able to avoid them.

Even nowadays, by no means everybody is going to college; the figure in
the last few years has been about 16% of all young people of college age.
But it is remarkable how, even within the lifetimes of our graduate sample,
college has been brought within range of more and more people who
once would never have thought of going. Whatever else the recent expansion of the college may mean, it certainly has meant a long stride in
the direction of democracy in education.

Among our graduates over 50, 87% are white and Protestant. Only
10% are Catholics; only 2% are Jews. Thus even as recently as the time
of World War I, when the last of our over-50 graduates were getting
their diplomas, college was an experience substantially reserved for the
white, Protestant majority in the U.S. But since that time the minority
groups have caught up. Among our graduates under 30, nearly 25% are

Catholics and 6% are Jews; by the best available measure, Catholics make up 19% and Jews 3% of the total U.S. population. The Negroes are also moving closer to full proportional representation on the campus.

Of our oldest graduates, the majority went to private colleges rather than to state-supported schools—62%. Among the youngest graduates the scale has very nearly been tipped the other way; the proportion of private school graduates has dropped to 53% and the proportion of public school graduates has risen to 47%. The Ivy League has been more or less submerged in the flood; among the oldest graduates there are three Ivy Leaguers for every four from the Big Ten state universities of the Midwest, but among the youngest graduates there are only two for four. At the same time the number of graduates from denominational colleges has remained fairly constant: 18% among the oldest graduates and 22% among the youngest.

In substantial numbers—24%, or about one out of four—the oldest graduates chose their colleges on the basis of family tradition; they went to the school their fathers had attended, and sometimes their grandfathers as well. Among the youngest graduates, this proportion has dropped to 15%. The proportion who mention low cost and an opportunity to work one's way has meanwhile risen from 34% to 44%. More young people have been receiving help in the form of scholarships—a third of the most recent graduates compared to only a fourth of the oldest ones. And more have been working their way. The proportion of men earning at least some of their expenses has always been quite high; it was 75% among the oldest graduates and has risen to 81% among the youngest. Among women, where the figure was much lower to begin with, it has jumped in spectacular fashion; among the oldest graduates it was only 36%, while among the youngest it is 66%.

The details all add up to a pattern of greater democracy on the campus. College is no longer an institution endowed and used by the few; it is now supported and shared by the many. The state-supported college has made great strides even within the lifetimes of our graduates; more students are receiving scholarships; more—especially the women—are helping pay their own way. Catholic and Jewish families are sending their children in as great proportions as other families. The Negroes are gaining. More and more children from modest or underprivileged homes are managing to get their degrees—perhaps not enough to meet the ideal of a higher education for everyone who can use it, but certainly many more than even 30 years ago, and more than 20 years ago or 10 years ago.

The college man and woman of today do not necessarily come from a privileged family; the degree is hardly a guarantee of social background. And more and more students, as their social and economic backgrounds become more varied, are thinking of college more and more as the road to all kinds of occupations in all kinds of fields. To a sociologist conducting this type of survey 20 or 30 years ago the graduates would have been very easy to find—just by looking in the schoolrooms, the doctors' and dentists' offices, the law firms, and the engineering branches of industrial firms, one could have rounded up most of them in a hurry. Today the search is much more difficult—and probably two decades hence one will hardly know where to start looking, much less when to stop.

18

Choosing a College

If you are thinking of going to a big university—or sending your children to one—better listen to these flaming words of warning from a young Californian who went to college under the G.I. Bill of Rights, was graduated a few years ago, and now teaches high school:

I went to the University of California at Berkeley. I wouldn't do it again. It's too big. You get lost in the crowd. Too much machination for me. . . .

In a large school, and especially is this true during the freshman and sophomore years, one has to sit through too many dry lectures. The class is too large for informal discussion; the lecture is often dry because it's a tough job to make day-by-day lecturing sound interesting to an extremely large class.

All you have to do is try to get something done in the administrative building, and you will feel like the cog in a great machine. You sit in the classes, accumulate credits and are duly stamped with an A.B. or B.S. There's a rule for everything. Sometimes you are the exception to the rule, and the rule as applied to you is tommyrot. It burns you up. But, then, there's the machine—eight to five! Education for life through a machine. I often felt that I could learn more in the four years allotted turned loose in a good library.

But then, before you let the letter change your mind, better take note of this Chicago film editor's words:

While I enjoyed my four undergraduate years in a small and sociable institution, I realize now that it was much too provincial, with a very narrow outlook and a completely uninspired faculty.

And this letter from a Wisconsin businessman who also regrets having attended a small school:

I would prefer large schools where I would make broad acquaintances and perhaps get the advantage of having a better staff of professors. In addition there would be more varied extra-curricular activities and less emphasis on "class distinction."

What goes on here? Another great debate among our graduates like the one on general versus specialized education? Is the youngster planning his own college career to get nothing but conflicting advice from his elders—with those who went to big schools urging him to go to small ones, and those who went to small schools urging him to go to big ones?

To a certain extent, yes. There are many graduates of the big universities whose letters agree with the young man from California. Sometimes they feel they were simply lost in the shuffle on a big campus, as does this athletic director in Maine:

I would attend a smaller college because I would get to know more people and because I would get more social life.

Sometimes they feel, not exactly lost, but as if their contacts with the world of education had been far too formal, remote, and cool. As witness this comment by a woman graduate who, intriguingly, is married to a professor at a university just about as large as her own alma mater:

I think I would have received more benefits from a smaller institution. Minnesota was too impersonal.

And sometimes they write quite neat and pithy insults, hitting the big schools in the most sensitive spots. For example a man in Florida comments:

I would not attend a large college unless I felt sure that its faculty loved students more than research.

On the other side of the fence there are numerous small college graduates who wish they had gone to bigger schools. They complain, as did the Chicago film editor, of the provincialism and the lower faculty standards of the small schools. Or, like the Wisconsin businessman, of proscribed social contacts. They wish they had had more famous teachers, better classroom equipment, more varied campus activities, a more cosmopolitan atmosphere. Or sometimes—liking everything else about their college experience—they simply wish they enjoyed the same prestige as graduates from more famous colleges. As one graduate writes:

A big-name college may be better for obtaining higher wages, quicker employment, greater prestige among employees.

But by no means all the letter writers who discuss the large college versus the small believe that they themselves made a mistake. Both types of school have a host of graduates who would defend them to the death. Another woman graduate from the University of Minnesota does not feel at all that the school was "too impersonal." Instead she writes:

I think it is wholesome to learn to find your way in the crowd; to select your friends and group activities. The facilities of the large university are advantageous.

And a Buffalo man who has had a liberal arts education and a quite varied professional career since his college days states:

I would attend the University of Michigan again. Its physical facilities are of the best and the faculty of a generally high caliber. It is a large school—not in the least objectionable to me—and the student body presents a broad cross section of America which I found stimulating.

The satisfied graduates of the small schools are equally positive in their beliefs. One of the older woman graduates writes:

Perhaps the greatest benefit we all received from Southwestern College (Kansas) was the actual living during our attendance. The pattern of life was ideal; most of the students had high aspirations; the college had a good tone. . . . My husband and I both were graduated from the college. Two of our children are university graduates. We do not feel that they secured from the big university what we did from the smaller school.

And a man who is now a business executive in Connecticut writes:

If I had it to do over again I would certainly go to the same small college. I am a firm believer in small colleges where a student can be an individual and not just another number. One of the best things about my college course was that I knew nearly every student and had a fine and intimate relationship with most of the professors.

A nurse in Massachusetts adds:

Since graduating I have seen and visited many other colleges, larger and more "progressive" than my college. I feel, however, that I received excellent training and instruction from my college, and the individual guidance obtained from going to a relatively small college is of far more value to me now as a grown-up person than what I might have received in other ways from going to a large college or university. It seems to me that the college's emphasis on developing well-rounded, open-minded, forward-thinking graduates, with especial stress having been laid on learning to live and work in community life, was more important in the over-all life picture than for a person to have gone to some tremendous well-known university and studied under some big name, where perhaps the development of each student is submerged or overlooked.

This is the sort of advice the prospective student would get if he could interview the gamut of graduates—those who are sorry they went to big schools and those who are glad, those who regret going to small schools and those who are happy about it. The prospective student can select the arguments that seem to have the most personal meaning for *him*—or, if the conflicting arguments leave him confused and unhappy, he can ponder the statistical verdict of our whole group of graduates on this question of the big school versus the small. The only problem with the statistics is a very simple but embarrassing one: who is to say when a college ceases to become small and begins to be large? Just where do you set the dividing line?

There are some substitute figures that will serve the purpose and avoid the embarrassment. A good one is the matter of wealth. The bigger schools usually have more money to spend than the small ones; there are exceptions, of course, especially in the form of very small but wealthy and exclusive colleges, but that is the general rule. Moreover, when debating the question of the big school versus the small, one is usually thinking of the small and not very wealthy college—where the student is not likely to find elaborate physical facilities or a carefully selected and high-paid faculty. Measuring the college's wealth by its endowment per student enrolled, we get the following figures:

The graduates of the wealthiest schools, those with an endowment of $10,000 or more to invest in physical facilities and teaching salaries per student, vote 85% in favor of returning to the same college.

The graduates of colleges endowed from $5,000 to $10,000 per student vote 83% in favor of returning.

Where the college had an endowment of $2,500 to $5,000 per student, the vote of confidence is 85%.

Where the endowment was under $2,500 per student, the proportion of graduates who would go back to the same school is 76%.

We can conclude that the graduates of the very "poorest" colleges (in terms of the money they had to spend on buildings, laboratory equipment, gymnasiums, social buildings, and the like), in other words the graduates of the very smallest and least pretentious colleges, are the least satisfied with their alma maters. But "least satisfied" is a term that means very little in this connection. More than three-quarters of the graduates would go right back to the same school, which is perhaps the utmost in endorsements that a graduate can give to his alma mater. And we might even surmise that of the 24% of graduates who would attend a different school if doing it over, some at least are probably less dissatisfied with their own experiences than bedazzled by what they think they might have had on a larger and wealthier campus.

Once the college endowment has reached $2,500 per student, any additional amount does not seem to add to the vote of confidence it can obtain. There are no significant differences in the number of satisfied customers produced by the intermediate colleges and the wealthiest colleges of all. Just as stone walls and iron bars are said not to make a prison, so our graduates seem to feel that big buildings, Gothic architecture, and a personal 200-power microscope for each freshman do not necessarily make a college. It may be—it is not our purpose in this book to inquire or speculate on such matters—that a college with more than $10,000 endowment per student can do a better educational job than the one with $5,000 to $10,000, and that one in turn a better job than the college with only $2,500 to $5,000. If so, the graduates do not seem to mind. To whatever type of school they went, they would be likely in about equal numbers to return again.

For further light on the question of the big school versus the small, and also the wealthy school versus the not-so-wealthy, we have drawn up Chart 47. Here the same six groups of schools as were examined in Chapter 15 on the matter of post-graduate earnings have been looked at from the viewpoint of how many graduates would return. It will be seen that the Ivy League schools, which we have found to produce the most big incomes, have also produced the greatest proportion of satisfied customers; they get an overwhelming vote of 98% of graduates who would select the same school if they had it to do over. The large Big Ten universities are second, with 84%. The "all other" groups, which include the smallest and least famous schools, come out at the bottom, as they did on the earnings scale. But in no case would more than 28% of the graduates turn thumbs down on their old alma maters if they were choosing all over again. The real moral of all our figures is that the argument over the big school versus the small, or the rich school versus the poor, is largely academic. No matter whether they have gone to big or

CHART 47

A vote of confidence for Alma Mater

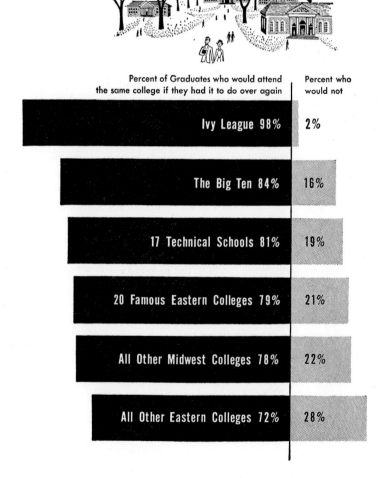

Percent of Graduates who would attend the same college if they had it to do over again	Percent who would not
Ivy League 98%	2%
The Big Ten 84%	16%
17 Technical Schools 81%	19%
20 Famous Eastern Colleges 79%	21%
All Other Midwest Colleges 78%	22%
All Other Eastern Colleges 72%	28%

to little, to rich or to poor, the graduates by very substantial majorities have liked the experience and would gladly repeat it.

Perhaps the best advice the graduates offer to youngsters is this: Your choice of a college depends largely on your own likings and your own personalities. If you want a big puddle to swim in, during those important four years, and if you will not be appalled by the somewhat impersonal and assembly-line methods of the great university, you will probably enjoy the big campus. If you like small groups, informality, congeniality, and the virtue of knowing and being known by practically all the students and teachers who are sharing the same experience, you will probably enjoy the small campus.

If the college fits you, in other words, wear it. The whole business of this argument over big schools versus small may boil down, in the last analysis, to what type of experience you are ready for after leaving high school. How, for example, is your high school educational training? Are you in danger, because of your own personal background, of repeating the somewhat unfortunate experience of a big-school graduate who says:

I would not go to the University of Michigan directly from high school.

My high school, at the time, was not even on the accredited list; so my predicament was that I was faced with some 16 examinations before I could even be admitted as a student. Had I had a better background, I'm sure I could have made a better showing. As I look back, I realize that we were not even taught to think in my high school. The one who had a good memory could make quite a showing.

A large institution hasn't the facilities for personal contacts, and a youngster is lost and feels inferior with a group so superior mentally. It is a case of teaching algebra to one who hasn't had a grounding in arithmetic.

I was so impressed with my inadequacy that many times I felt that the Lord had forgotten to endow me with brains.

And what about the matter of social confidence? One of our women graduates who wishes she had gone to a smaller school is frank to admit that social and personality factors play a large part in her feelings:

My reasons for feeling that another college could have done more for me than my alma mater are that the school was too large and too impersonal to develop the personalities of its students as a smaller school might have done. I grew up as an only child with some of the timidity which often attends such individuals. I believe that a smaller college might have given me an opportunity to develop more along social lines than my school did.

A similar sort of motivation is cited by some of the graduates who are glad they went to smaller schools. A California librarian states:

I was very timid before I went to college, and I am glad that I went to a small school where it was easier for me to adjust.

Another woman who went to Western College in Ohio says much the same thing:

I had a taste of a larger school, Purdue, when I took graduate work. There is no comparison. At Western I got more of a chance to be a person instead of a mere cog in the wheels of education. Being shy and an average student, Western in its smallness gave me a chance for more personalized help and a chance to be drawn out of myself.

What the letter writers seem to be saying, when you get right down to it, is that it is a good idea to pick a campus that suits your family background, your ambitions, your high school training or lack of it, and your tendencies to be timid or self-assertive. But the nicest thing of all about the problem of choosing a college is this: no matter which type of school you select, the large or the small, the rich or the poor, the chances are at least three to one that you will find it satisfactory and will be glad you made the choice you did.

For the young woman, of course, there is an additional problem— namely, whether to go to a girls' school or a coeducational college. There are letters on both sides of this question, too. We can start right in with Vassar. On the pro-Vassar side we have first a young housewife who was graduated within the past decade:

I think more serious work can be and *is* done in a non-coed college. We concentrated on studying in large doses during the weeks and our social life was intensive on weekends. However I firmly believe that high school coeducation should precede such a college training, or the student seldom gains a *natural* attitude toward the other sex.

And second on this side we have a much older graduate, who has a daughter who in turn has also been graduated from Vassar:

Vassar is a college for women only—and for me, at least, that proved essential for my development. I do not know to what factor in my life to attribute my original distrust or disparagement of my sex. However, going to a college where, for companionship, it was essential to cultivate the friendship of other girls, gave me a fresh point of view—a new respect and healthy liking for women. It may be that coeducation is the prescription needed for some girls but in my case it would not have been the medicine needed. I was boy-crazy at that age and regarded all girls as natural competitors. To see them in any other light required the comparative absence of males.

For those who claim such segregation conducive to greater obsession with the subject of sex, I would assert that there was no visible dearth of young men around—the campus was flooded with them weekends, but during the week days there was that absence of girl-competition-for-boys which made for better attention in classes and for the cultivation of friendships that grow richer with every passing year.

But another housewife and mother who attended Vassar at about the same period has reached an antithetical conclusion:

No, I would not attend the same college because I feel that I would have been much happier in a coeducational setup. Men, at that time, were not very welcome by the faculty except on special occasions. We all felt the omission.

Another girls' school graduate, this time an unmarried teacher who went to Elmira College in New York, expresses the same general idea:

Although it was fun for girls to be "men" in dramatic presentations, it's a healthier situation when college girls have an opportunity to mix regularly with young men.

And another woman graduate, whose college shall be nameless, expresses some sharp criticisms of a certain type of girls' school:

The college was not geared so much to the pursuit of higher learning as to the correct social usages and "gracious living." The emphasis on these was a trifle juvenile, with such things as a demerit system with penalties for such trivia as not wearing a hat, carrying gloves, etc. Furthermore, since the enrollment was small, the administration relied, a trifle too evidently for the majority of students to digest, on a few who were the proverbial teacher's pets, apple-polishers, or whatever the word is today. The students in my time at the college complained about these matters at length, and I gather from conversations with present students that they are still continuing without change or abatement.

Strangely, although there are boys' schools as well as girls' schools, none of our men graduates seems to have been sufficiently exercised about this whole problem to have mentioned it in a letter. Or perhaps this is not so strange after all, since in statistical terms it seems to make very little difference among the graduates whether they went to a one-sex school or to a coeducational college. Of the graduates of men's and women's colleges, 82% state that they would choose their alma maters all over again. Among the graduates of coeducational schools, the vote is 78%.

The same statistical pattern holds for the graduates of denominational schools versus the graduates of colleges with no special religious affiliations. Those who went to denominational colleges vote 78% to return; those who went to secular colleges vote 80% to return. And the same sort of infinitesimal differences hold between the graduates of private schools, 79% of whom would return to their alma maters, and the graduates of state-supported schools, 80% of whom would return.

On all these matters of choosing a college, the ultimate message from our graduates seems to be just this: Don't worry too much. If you can't make up your mind any other way, flip a coin. Whether it comes up heads or tails makes very little difference. You will probably be glad either way.

19

To Study or To Play

To study hard (and perhaps run the risk of being known as a Greasy Grind)—or just to coast along (and perhaps run the risk of having a prospective employer decide that you are a little stupid)? To go or not to go out for the football team, debating team, mixed choral group, student council, school band, archery squad, rifle club, literary magazine, humor magazine, campus newspaper, square dancing club, intramural tennis, intramural field hockey, intramural soccer, and intramural quoits?

Next to choosing a college and a subject to study, these are the questions that most bother the beginning student—and are often a cause of joy, regret, or mixed emotions in later life. Many a graduate, finding now that it was possible to get barely passing grades without really learning very much, wishes in the retrospect of maturity that he had studied much harder. Many a graduate, finding that his Phi Beta Kappa key did not win him many friends, provide him much fun, or give him any social poise, wishes he had sacrificed at least one A to a little more extra-curricular life.

Four years are a long time. To the student himself, they may seem to be passing swiftly, to represent just a quick way station on the road to a career or to marriage. But in retrospect they often seem to our graduates like a long and golden period, a leisurely era of great opportunity before all the time-consuming responsibilities of adulthood descended. The business of being an adult is not nearly so thrilling to adults as it seems to youngsters; the college days often seem in later years like the last wonderful time of freedom before the world closes in.

The graduates who wish they had studied more seem to be the most articulate on this problem of wasted opportunities. This perhaps is only natural. After all, most extra-curricular activities on the campus are a mirroring of adult life, a kind of youthful imitation of the adult world's political organizations, journals, bowling clubs, bridge clubs, lodges, and Rotaries. The graduate who has become a successful journalist is not likely to regret that he never worked on the campus newspaper; the graduate who runs the local Junior League is not likely to be sorry she never served on the campus May Day Committee. But very few people ever again have the strictly educational opportunities that college affords. A Baltimore housewife who at the time of writing her letter was especially busy nursing three ill children says:

My strongest feeling is that I would devote much more time to real study, because those beautiful four years in college are the only adult leisure consistently open to follow all the intellectual leads that are so intriguing—and to gain a perspective that must last most of a lifetime. Extra-curricular activities are about on a par with ladies' sewing circles and can be indulged at any time.

A New Jersey minister's wife adds:

In four years one can never learn all one wishes he could—and never will he find such excellent conditions to store away knowledge in later years.

The men graduates feel just as strongly on the subject as the women. A Yale man living in California writes:

College is the last good chance one has to study. It becomes increasingly difficult while trying to raise a family and earn a living.

And an Arkansas minister, looking back at college 33 years later, comes to the same conclusion:

There is plenty of time for extra-curricular activity after we are beyond the curriculum. But once out in a busy life there isn't always time or inclination to grind on a college or university course.

Some of the graduates who wish they had studied more and engaged in fewer activities have come to the conclusion that there is really very little lasting pleasure or profit to be gained from extra-curricular matters. Witness this comment from a Pennsylvania woman who has had both a career (as a display artist) and then the experience of being a housewife and mother:

I consider extra-curricular activities, especially the social type, a waste of time and money.

And this one from a Virginia lawyer:

I would devote considerably more time to study and give a correspondingly smaller amount of my time to extra-curricular activities. The solid background of information that I would have derived from my studies, I think, would more than compensate for the, to me at least, overrated virtues of extra-curricular activities.

On the other hand many of the graduates believe that extra-curricular activities have a definite place on the campus and value in later life, but feel that the proportion of activities to studies has become distorted. Since the best advice is usually the most objective advice, and since these graduates have no particular complaint about extra-curricular activities except on the matter of over-emphasis, it may prove worthwhile to listen to a number of them. First, from a man in Oregon:

I believe college students generally do not devote enough time to study. Extra-curricular activities are useful, but they should not interfere with the real purpose of a college education.

From a Massachusetts man, a graduate of Holy Cross:

I would devote more time to study, because the ensuing years with their concurrent maturity have proven to me the value of the acquisition of as much knowledge as possible. By this I do not mean that social activities should be entirely neglected. But in my opinion entirely too much emphasis is placed on extra-curricular activities in the American college of today.

From a Midwestern banker who was graduated from the University of Iowa:

During my time at college I now think I directed entirely too much energy to extra-curricular activities. In retrospect I think it advisable to devote less time to the side show and more to the main tent.

From an Alabama man:

After all, study is the primary purpose of school. Occasionally extra-curricular activities equip one better than the education for a successful career— but more often, I believe, they only take him away from his school work.

And finally from a North Carolina banker:

At my age and experience, I certainly believe that I would devote more time to study rather than extra-curricular activities. As a seventeen- or eighteen-year-old boy I had more desire to take part in school activities and social life.

That was my greatest trouble, and I believe that most college boys I know today devote more time to activities than to study. I am not in any way opposed to the extra activities on the campus, but apparently they are very numerous and unregulated as to the amount of time consumed.

As for the practical economic advantages of more study or more extra-curricular participation, these have already been discussed in Chapter 13. But since we are now considering the opinions and advice of our graduates, as well as the statistical data, perhaps we had better conclude this brief survey of the graduates who favor more study with two letters written along highly pragmatic lines. The first is from a Milwaukee businessman:

Too much emphasis on outside activities sets a bad pattern for a person who must plan his own time in the business world.

The second is from an Ohio State graduate, now a successful business-man in New York, who believes in a little of each but feels that study is the *sine qua non*:

Extra-curricular activities are fine, if they do not detract from academic work. I have found that the men who made good marks in school, along with the achievement of popularity, are the men who are forging ahead in business today. In my opinion, they are forging ahead because they have a well-founded technical background to back up their personal leadership ability.

So much for the graduates who advocate more study. But there are just as many letters on the other side of the fence; this is another place where the graduates disagree among themselves and the prospective college student, after listening to all their arguments, will have to make up his own mind. We can begin the case for extra-curricular activities, indeed, at exactly the point where we left off the other side of the debate. Here is a businessman graduate who feels that any student will be seriously handicapped in the search for a job if he neglects the more social side of college:

The weight placed on activities and study by employers should be some indication of the emphasis to be placed by a student. Most companies determine whether the mental ability is there by examining grades—and then, for lack of any good guidepost to go by, judge the personality by the activities in which the prospective employee took part.

An architect who was graduated from the University of Minnesota thinks that extra-curricular activities help not only to obtain a job but also to succeed at one:

To go through school without taking a somewhat active part in the many varied non-scholastic activities is a terrible mistake.

Success in business of any type depends not only on the individual's technical skill, but on his ability to make himself acceptable, even sought-after in the business circle because he has that intangible asset of personality. This ability can be gained painlessly and pleasantly while at school, and it will serve as the key to the door to a fuller life in both the business and social world.

To which a Connecticut businessman adds:

My advice to any prospective college man would be to maintain average marks and get into every outside activity he possibly can. The teamwork, sense of responsibility, and friendships I acquired by engaging in outside activities have brought me a much fuller and more pleasant life both in business and in my private life.

Not only in business, but in the general matter of obtaining satisfactions from life after college, there are graduates who feel that extra-curricular activities provided the key. A male schoolteacher in St. Paul, who is naturally not particularly interested in the competitive commercial aspects of the college career, writes as follows:

I spent a good percentage of my time on extra-curricular activities and think that hour for hour I got more from them than from my studies.

And an Illinois schoolteacher, this time a woman, seconds the motion:

I find that I've gained more from extra-curriculars for the time spent than I did from many courses—in helping me adjust to situations and to work in social situations with pupils and with community.

Two housewives, completely removed from the business world, have similar opinions. The first is a Mount Holyoke graduate who was married after a short career as social worker:

I think the extra-curricular activities in college and the satisfaction I derived from them led me to get into community activities now that I'm a housewife— and I'm a lot less stodgy than I'd be otherwise.

The second is the graduate of a denominational school, now a housewife in Indiana:

I've observed that the best citizen and community-minded person is the one who can engage in various activities, not the studious type who is only mentally alert.

Some of the graduates feel that extra-curricular activities are worthwhile solely for the friendships gained, if for nothing else. Of the many letters mentioning this factor, this one from an engineering graduate of the University of Wisconsin is typical:

It was through the extra-curricular activities that I have made more friends who have stuck by me than through classroom activities, and these friendships surely have meant as much to me as the education I got.

Other graduates feel that the give-and-take of extra-curricular activities is somehow closer to life as actually lived than is the theoretical learning of the classroom. A man graduate who is a Y.M.C.A. executive in Pennsylvania expresses this feeling the most succinctly:

Extra-curricular activities have more potential growth possibilities than specific professional cultural subject material. I believe this for two reasons:
1. The classroom offers limited possibilities in human relationships. It is a pretty stilted experience compared to playing in a football game, leading a student forum, or developing some club project.
2. Where people gather together, work together, and an inter-play of human relations is involved, the art of getting along with people is developed. The classroom doesn't offer this sort of growth experience.

To round out the argument for extra-curricular activities, which has thus far been made by graduates who themselves participated in a great many such activities and are glad that they did, we need to hear from some graduates who neglected this side of campus life and are sorry. We have two which seem to summarize all the regrets of the graduates who never went out for a team, a club, or an organization; their what-might-have-beens are quite poignant. A retired army officer writes:

I'd decidedly devote more time to participation in extra-curricular activities. I needed to broaden, to meet people, know more about such things—for I was a very green country boy when I went to college.

And an Oklahoma tax accountant says:

In college I worked hard and graduated a wallflower. I was shy outside of everything but books and baseball. That has been overcome now, but now I see how much education I missed in association with and in dealings with other students.

There we have, in a condensed but fairly comprehensive selection of letters, the pro and con opinions of our graduates. The arguments on both sides sound pretty good; we seem to have a case of six on one side and a half dozen on the other. For a little more conclusive answer, we shall have to return to the statistics.

In the first place, our data seem to show that this whole problem will be more or less resolved for future students simply by the course of events. New social custom, or the new campus atmosphere, or fate, or whatever you want to call it, seems to insure that most of today's and tomorrow's students will be drawn into extra-curricular activities whether they plan it that way or not, or even whether they think about the problem at all. The whole trend on the campus is to involve more and more students in this type of activity, and to reduce the numbers of students who stay on the sidelines. Among the younger graduates, as can be seen in Chart 48, there are fewer and fewer "wallflowers." There is an extremely consistent decline, in each age bracket from oldest to youngest, in the number of graduates who took no part in extra-curricular activities, and also in the number who took part in only one. At the same time the number taking part in three or more activities has risen steadily and sharply.

The greatest increase—among women as well as men—has been in intramural athletics. Of the oldest graduates, only 33% of the men and 29% of the women took part in these non-varsity sports; of the youngest graduates, 64% of the men and 48% of the women did. Athletics, far from being confined to the football and basketball players, have in recent years become a general field of activity for nearly two-thirds of men students and nearly half the women. Campus politics have also been engaging the attention of more students of both sexes; of graduates over 50, only 21% of men and 13% of women took part, while among the youngest graduates the proportions have risen to 32% of men and 29% of women. Work on college publications has also increased: only from 23% to 28%, or negligibly, among men; but from 24% to 37% among women. Musical activities are about as popular among men (23% of the oldest and 20% of the youngest) but have noticeably increased among women (from 27% to 37%).

CHART 48

The new trend is toward a more active campus life

Percent of Graduates who participated in

| | NONE | ONE | TWO | THREE OR MORE |

extra-curricular activities

Graduates who are

	NONE	ONE	TWO	THREE OR MORE
50 AND OLDER	17%	33%	24%	26%
40 TO 49	14%	29%	27%	30%
30 TO 39	11%	27%	28%	34%
UNDER 30	7%	23%	28%	42%

The trend is steady and marked, and presumably it is still holding sway. Extra-curricular activities have become a standard feature of campus life. For better or worse, the youngster entering college this year or in coming years is almost certain to take part in at least one or two, and very likely in more.

Looking at our data from another direction, the strange thing is that on the average, considering the group as a whole, the amount of satisfaction our graduates obtained from college seems to depend very little on their extra-curricular roles. If we divide the graduates into separate categories, depending on whether they never took part in extra-curricular activities, took part in one, or in two, or in many, we find that this sort of separation has taught us nothing of how they feel about their college days. Each category votes about the same on whether to return to the same college.

To take an extreme case, let us consider just two groups—the graduates who had no extra-curricular activities at all, and the graduates who held offices (which would seem to represent the ultimate in active participation and personal satisfaction) in at least two extra-curricular groups. One might suppose that the "wallflowers" (again to use that term applied by the Oklahoma tax accountant) would be far less happy about their college careers. Yet 79% of them say they would return to the same campus if they had their lives to live over again. Among the graduates at the opposite pole, the leaders in extra-curricular groups, the proportion who would return is 78%.

The amount of study done, at least insofar as it is reflected in high grades versus low ones, is on the other hand very closely correlated with warm feelings about the college career. Let us go back to our old measure, used several times before, of the proportion of graduates who would repeat all three major decisions of their college careers—that is, would choose the same college, the same field of study, and the same degree of specialization or of generalized education. As a general index of satisfaction with the college experience, a yes vote on all three matters seems pretty significant. And on this index, the A students turn out to be much more content than poorer students.

Of the men graduates who made mostly A's, 40% would repeat all three decisions.

Of the men who made mostly B's, the yes-vote drops to 33%.

Among C and D men students, the yes-vote drops again to 25%.

It does not even matter what type of course they took, or whether their training was general or specialized. All the graduates, the humanities students, the social scientists, the physical scientists, and the engineers, rate on our satisfaction index in direct proportion to their grades. And among men students it does not matter whether they went into the professions, where we have seen that grades play a part in earnings, or into the business world where grades seem to have no relation to financial success. Wherever they went, whatever they studied, and whatever they are doing now, the graduates who made the best grades are more satisfied with college than those who made B grades, and the B students in turn are much more satisfied than the graduates who just got by. Whereas the number and intensity of extra-curricular activities have no effect whatever on our statistics, high grades and satisfied customers tend to go together.

Before we leave this field of advice to the youngsters, however, we have another type of letter which is worth serious attention. It is possible for any fairly bright young person, as all too many of them discover, to get through college without making any sort of outstanding effort of any kind along the lines of either study or activities. To the youngster with a quick ability to absorb enough facts from his lecture courses to make passing grades, college can be a period of pure vegetation, a snap, a breeze, an experience that makes very little dent of any kind. In our sample of U.S. graduates, there are undoubtedly many of these people, as the letters indeed prove. Unfortunately we cannot put them into any kind of statistical group and study their present feelings about college; while it is easy to subdivide the graduates by scholastic grades, or by the number of extra-curricular activities, it is impossible to separate out the graduates who just loafed along ticking on four or five of their eight cylinders.

But some of the graduates themselves, in their letters, have mentioned this problem—and always with intense regrets. What the letters say to today's and tomorrow's college students is something like this: Those four college years can never be repeated; they are your last days of freedom, before life becomes all too real and all too earnest; they are your last chance to experiment and test your wings, whether along scholastic or social lines; for heaven's sake do not waste them in idleness or indirection.

There is this from a Chicago businessman:

If I had it to do over again I would devote more time to both studies and extra-curricular activities and devote a little less time to general inactivity.

From a Wisconsin businessman:

I feel that I wasted considerable valuable time on unorganized recreation and "bull sessions."

From an Iowa housewife:

I now realize that I missed so much that was within my reach except for my own laziness and laxness.

From a Virginian:

In retrospect I would devote more time both to my studies and to extra-curricular activities and reduce the hours spent in idle and aimless "batting around."

And from a man in Des Moines who summarizes this whole matter in six simple but memorable words:

I wasted a lot of time.

CHAPTER **20**

Pulling Up Stakes

One good thing about college, according to many of the graduates, is that it takes you away from home and forces you to stand on your own two feet. Some of the graduates actually feel that this is one of the most important parts of a college education, and that any youngster who goes to a home town college, meanwhile living with his parents, is making a great mistake. A woman who went to Wheaton College writes:

The fact that Wheaton was approximately 2,000 miles away from my home counts in its favor, as I look back on my college experience. The jolt of suddenly being separated from my parents was good for me, although it seemed quite difficult at the time. I am convinced that it is good to have the experience of being completely separated from one's family.

A Vassar graduate concurs:

I think the experience of being away from home is invaluable. I learned to assume responsibilities and make decisions that I never would have had I lived at home and gone to college a few blocks away.

And a woman graduate of a state normal school adds:

I believe that learning and remembering the subject matter taught is of course important, but equally important is getting away from home influence and learning independence. This of course means that one must attend some school outside of the home town, otherwise a big share of one's educational experience is lost.

A schoolteacher, who incidentally has settled down in Chicago, writes of her experience at the University of Chicago:

Since my early life had been spent in the country and a small town, the life of the city of Chicago was a great feature of my college years. I shall always consider that becoming acquainted with this great city was a vital part of my advanced education.

And a graduate of Oklahoma A. & M. adds a slightly different angle to the same general idea:

Another thing that we gain from being in college, I think, is that we aren't around our parents or the old home town where our family had made our social place for us. We find out that the Joneses and the Browns are just as important, high-rating, and otherwise qualified to be accepted in the best circles as the Astors or Vanderbilts.

There are other graduates who take the opposite view; they went to their home town colleges, went on to live and work in the same city, and feel that the experience of getting their degrees right in their home territories was a big advantage. A schoolteacher who got her degree and still works in the same Ohio city writes:

I like my home town and have always wished to make and keep friends from my own town. Having attended my home town university, I know my city and its residents much better.

An engineer who took his degree at the University of Pennsylvania in Philadelphia says:

As I have lived most of my life in Philadelphia, I have been in constant contact with men with whom I went to college. They have been a great help to me.

But despite the pros and cons of going away to school or attending a home town school, the thing that the youngster about to enter college must really consider is this: when you leave home on registration day, whether to go to the campus around the corner or to one 3,000 miles away, you had better be prepared to say good-bye to your family and friends not only for the day, not only for the school term, but forever. Once you go to college, our statistics show, the chances are almost even that you will never settle down in your old neighborhood among your old friends—but that you will wind up living and working in quite different climes. Of the graduates in the survey, only 56% were even living in their home states. The other 44% had all found homes and jobs across the state line.

Many of them, in fact, had deserted their sections of the country as well as their own states, and were living in an entirely different part of the nation. Of the graduates from the West, 13% were no longer living there. Of the Southerners, 24% had left the South. Those who had left the Midwest numbered 26%, and those who had left the East, 30%. (There is nothing in the survey to explain this wide difference between the West and East. One guess might be that the West, which has been growing faster than any other part of the nation, has as much attraction for its own college people as for the "immigrants" who have been flocking there in such large numbers. It may also be that the East, which produces much more than its proportionate share of college graduates, cannot absorb them all.)

The men graduates are particularly prone to leave the home state. The mere percentages are not very striking: 46% of the men have moved away as opposed to 41% of the women. But a closer look at the figure for the women shows that this whole phenomenon is largely a masculine thing. The women who leave their own states are mostly women who have found husbands elsewhere, or have followed husbands who got the urge to travel. Of the unmarried career women only 33% have left their home states; for housewives the figure is 47%. The tendency for the career woman to stay close to home is especially pronounced among the younger ones; it appears that the women graduates, right after getting their diplomas, characteristically take jobs in their home towns. Then as the years pass more and more of those who have not married begin to follow job opportunities which take them away from home, probably with a growing realization that their status as single career women shows prospects of becoming permanent. More of the older men than the younger men have also moved; but the differences are not so pronounced.

While all graduates have a tendency to leave home—the men more than the women, the housewives more than the career women, the older career women more than the younger ones—their chances of leaving depend on a good many things. The first and most important is how far they have gone from home to get their educations. Of the graduates who went to college in their own states, as about two-thirds of all the graduates have done, only 35% had deserted the state at the time of the study. But among the graduates who went away to a school outside the state boundaries, the proportion of deserters was 62%. What this means in rough terms of mathematical chance is that while the odds are about even that any graduate will wind up living outside his home state, the odds are decreased to about one in three if he goes to school in his own state, and increased to about two out of three if he gets his diploma elsewhere.

Another important factor is the matter of family background—in other words, whether the graduate had to work his own way or had parents wealthy enough to send him. This matter of wealth or lack of it works in a rather devious way. First of all, the sons of richer families are more likely to go to a distant college than those whose parents are less well off. Our figures show that 47% of the men who were completely supported by their families left their home states to go to college, while only 34% of those who earned at least a part of their expenses went away, and only 30% of those who earned more than half their expenses. The figures for women follow a similar pattern.

Since students who leave home to go to college have the greatest tendency to stay away after they graduate, it would logically be expected from all this that the sons and daughters of richer families would be those most likely to settle down away from home. But it does not work out that way. Money in the family not only tends to send the sons and daughters away from home for a college education; it also tends to bring them right back home again. Of the men graduates in our study who left their home states to go to college, only 55% of the family-supported students stayed away, as opposed to 69% of the men who had to pay most of their own way. It is likely that men from wealthier families, by virtue of their connections, have better opportunities for careers near home. On the other hand men whose families cannot help them so much are more footloose; they must look for their job opportunities wherever the pastures are greenest. But whatever the reason, the figures show that while it is a better bet that the rich boy will go away to school than the poor boy, it is also a better bet that he will return home after he finishes. Conversely, although the poor boy is less likely to go away to school in the first place, when he does go away it is much more likely to be for keeps. The net result is that the home states actually lose somewhat more of the students who work their way through college than they do of the wealthier students. The over-all total works out to this: 48% of the men graduates who earned over half their expenses have settled outside their home states, while for the completely supported men the figure is 43%.

A lot depends also on the type of course that was studied in college. The real rolling stones are the graduates who majored in engineering,

59% of whom have left their home states. The physical science majors are well established in second place with 49%. Among those who majored in all other fields, the figure is only 38%. In fact enrolling for an engineering or physical science course is an even surer guarantee of leaving home than is going off to a distant college.

Looking at the present occupations of the graduates, it develops that there are more stay-at-homes among the doctors, lawyers, and dentists than in any other group; only 37% of them have left their original states. In contrast, the percentage among educators and clergymen is 43%; among businessmen 44%, and among government men—many of whom naturally gravitate toward Washington—52%. Probably the doctors, dentists, and lawyers find it easier to build up their practices at home, where they at least have their boyhood contacts to fall back upon, than anywhere else.

The good students leave home oftener than the poor students; among our graduates 49% of those with A grades were living outside their original home states at the time of the survey, as compared with 41% of the B students and 37% of the C or D students. And the chances of leaving increase with age; the proportion of those living in new states rises steadily from 40% in the under-30 group to 51% in the 50-and-over group. This seems only logical; the older men have had more opportunities to leave, and their pre-college home ties have probably weakened with the passage of years.

Besides the movement from state to state, there is also a great migratory wave of graduates from one type of town to another. The cities—and especially the big cities—have a pronounced attraction for college graduates. The small towns—and especially the farms—repel them. Chart 49 tells most of the story; 27 graduates out of 100 now work in the big cities of half a million or more, although only 17 out of 100 graduates were brought up in cities of this size. The medium-sized cities of 100,000 to 500,000 have also attracted more graduates than they sent to school, and the cities of 25,000 to 100,000 have held their own. All other communities, and especially the farm areas, have lost part of their graduates to the bigger cities. College is always the city's gain, and the rural area's loss.

There are other figures, on the home towns and present residences of the graduates, which indicate this: the chances that a graduate from a town of under 2,500 will decide to live in his own community or one of the same size are less than two out of five. Conversely, the chances

CHART 49

Getting a degree
means a move to the city

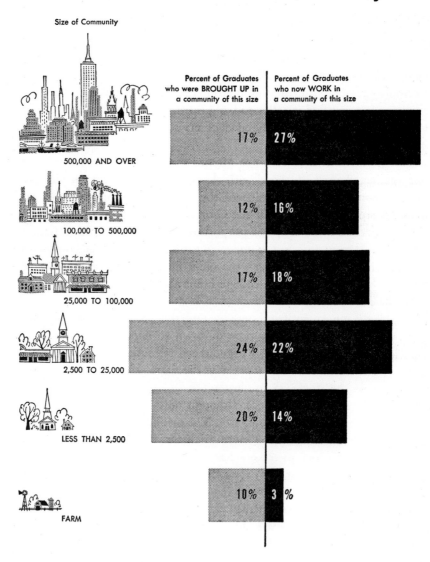

Size of Community

	Percent of Graduates who were BROUGHT UP in a community of this size	Percent of Graduates who now WORK in a community of this size
500,000 AND OVER	17%	27%
100,000 TO 500,000	12%	16%
25,000 TO 100,000	17%	18%
2,500 TO 25,000	24%	22%
LESS THAN 2,500	20%	14%
FARM	10%	3%

that young men and women from these communities will move to bigger cities after graduation are better than three out of five. But if a graduate is from a city of 100,000 or more, the chances are only three in ten that he will decide to settle down in a smaller community. It is definitely hard to keep the college man and woman down on the farm, or to attract them there.

Since so many graduates leave home, it is pertinent to inquire what becomes of the travelers. Obviously, they have a lot of adjustments to make. The small-town Southerner who goes to college and winds up working in Chicago has to get used to the fact that his neighbors do not automatically vote the Democratic ticket on election day and are not surprised if a Negro takes the next stool at a lunch counter. The girl from Pentwater, Michigan, who moves with her college-acquired husband into a gloomy remodeled brownstone in Brooklyn Heights finds the neighbors a good deal more aloof than she is used to. She may run into them now and then buying potato salad at the corner delicatessen, or snatching a copy of the morning tabloid from the newsstand in the St. George Hotel as they jostle their way toward the subway turnstiles, but in Brooklyn Heights neither she nor they seem to attend church socials or P.T.A. meetings. There do not appear to be so many children on the block, either.

As we have seen, nearly half the graduates in our sample had left their original home states. Did they take the home-state attitudes and behavior patterns along with them intact? Or do they resemble their new neighbors more than their old ones?

We can begin on a note which may be mildly encouraging or mildly discouraging, depending on point of view. Nothing in our figures indicates that leaving home, in itself, guarantees much greater earnings than staying put. Among the graduates, those who had crossed a state line did have an edge, but not a very big one, over the stay-at-homes; for example, 46% of them were earning $5,000 or better a year as opposed to 39% of the stay-at-homes. The very highest paid group among the graduates, the doctors, dentists, and lawyers, were all inclined to be stay-at-homes.

In the matter of politics, moving around seems to play a substantial role. It was noted in Chapter 10 that graduates from the Solid South who have moved North are less likely than their parents to be Democrats, while Northerners who have moved South are a little less likely to be Repub-

CHART 50

To leave the old home
is to leave the old party

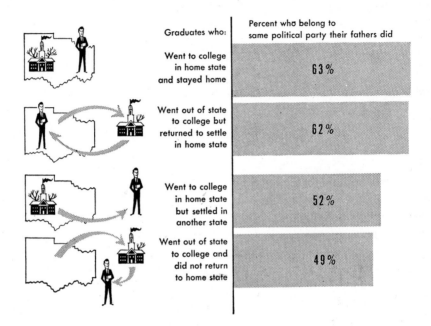

	Graduates who:	Percent who belong to same political party their fathers did
	Went to college in home state and stayed home	63%
	Went out of state to college but returned to settle in home state	62%
	Went to college in home state but settled in another state	52%
	Went out of state to college and did not return to home state	49%

licans. We can now add that any other kind of move from state to state after college is likely to involve changing political loyalties. All graduates tend to vote the same way their parents voted, but as Chart 50 shows, this tendency is greatest among the graduates who settle down close to home. Among those who leave their home states, there is a much stronger inclination to break away from the family pattern. Of those who go away to school and never return, indeed, less than half vote as their fathers did. But simply going away to college—provided the graduate returns home to settle down after getting his degree—does not involve this sort of insurgence.

The trek of graduates from small towns to cities, and the smaller counter-wave of migration from big city to smaller, involves another kind of adjustment. Two significant differences between big-city dwellers and small-town folk are the size of their families and their participation in community activities. In general, small-town residents have more children than big-city people. They also participate more actively in civic affairs—running church bazaars, joining Parent-Teachers Associations, and all the rest. Do our graduates who moved, after college, from small towns to big cities have the large families they became used to while they were growing up? Do they show the same interest in community affairs their parents did back home, or do they pattern their behavior on their new big-city neighbors? And how about the graduates who made the reverse move from the cities to the small towns?

Chart 51 gives the answer on the matter of family size. The similarity between the graduates who have lived in big cities all their lives, and those who moved there from a small town, are quite remarkable; the pattern of children for the two groups is almost identical. And among small-town dwellers, the graduates who had moved there from big cities actually had even more children than the graduates who had been reared in small towns in the first place. With respect to family size, our graduates had clearly conformed to their new environments. The patterns of the communities in which they were brought up were absolutely eradicated.

Chart 52 gives the story for civic activity. Just as in the matter of family size, the thing that seems to govern participation in civic affairs is not the size of the communities in which the graduates were originally brought up, but the size of the communities in which they settle down. The small-town backgrounds of the new urbanites did not prevent them from becoming virtually as apathetic in civic affairs as the veteran urbanites. And the veteran small-town dwellers were only slightly more active than their new neighbors who had been reared in the cities.

It turns out that college—and next year's freshmen may as well be prepared for it—is a pretty upsetting experience. It upsets geographical patterns and the urban-small town pattern; the college graduate tends to move around a great deal from town to town, state to state, and even section to section. Moreover the moving around implies a great many adjustments. The graduates who leave home physically often leave it in the political sense as well. The small-towners who move to the big city turn out to be citified, and the big-city graduates who move to a small town conform to the ways of the small-town society.

Whether the graduates actually change in accordance with their new environments—or simply were different to begin with from their old

CHART 51

Big towns, small towns and fertility

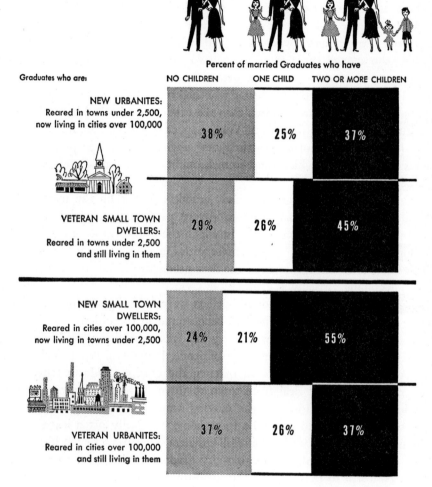

Percent of married Graduates who have

Graduates who are:

	NO CHILDREN	ONE CHILD	TWO OR MORE CHILDREN
NEW URBANITES: Reared in towns under 2,500, now living in cities over 100,000	38%	25%	37%
VETERAN SMALL TOWN DWELLERS: Reared in towns under 2,500 and still living in them	29%	26%	45%
NEW SMALL TOWN DWELLERS: Reared in cities over 100,000, now living in towns under 2,500	24%	21%	55%
VETERAN URBANITES: Reared in cities over 100,000 and still living in them	37%	26%	37%

CHART 52

Civic activity depends on where you live not where you came from

Percent who participate in

1 or 2	3 or 4	5 or more
	civic activities	

Graduates who are:

NEW URBANITES:
Reared in towns under 2,500,
now living in cities over 100,000

20%   36%   44%

VETERAN SMALL TOWN DWELLERS:
Reared in towns under 2,500
and still living in them

11%   25%   64%

NEW SMALL TOWN DWELLERS:
Reared in cities over 100,000,
now living in towns under 2,500

15%   27%   58%

VETERAN URBANITES:
Reared in cities over 100,000
and still living in them

20%   39%   41%

friends and neighbors—is something that the survey cannot answer. Probably both factors operate; we can assume that some graduates have a predisposition to leave their home neighborhoods for environments more congenial to their tastes, while on the other hand the new environment accentuates the differences or creates them where none existed. At any rate college does, for a great number of graduates, mean pulling up stakes. No one can foresee the end of the road that the student enters on registration day—but the chances are that it will be a strange one, and will take the graduates a long way from the paths that were familiar to their mothers and fathers.

PART SEVEN

Some Advice to the Colleges

CHAPTER **21**

The Dissatisfied Graduates Speak

Up to this point the colleges have come out pretty well in the survey. As we noted in Chapter 11, the great majority of all graduates are well satisfied with their training—and a good alert advertising man could run quite a nice little campaign on the basis of their testimonial letters. The only thing is that while the dissatisfied graduates are a minority, they are a very vocal, articulate, and hard-hitting group. They feel that college let them down, cheated them, failed to do the job it purported to do—and if a guarantee came with the entrance fee they would be asking for their money back. Their comments, while often angry, can hardly be dismissed. There are too many of them—and they make points that anyone who has ever seen a campus will concede to have merit.

We can begin with a woman graduate who majored in Spanish and music at a quite respectable and well-thought-of school in the Midwest. This is what she now thinks of the quality of training she got in her two chosen fields:

I could scarcely speak Spanish when I left school. Likewise in the fine arts school, I heard only enough good music to recognize a few of the simpler Beethoven sonatas, no concertos at all, most of Chopin, very little of any other composer's works—such a little that I did not even know their general style of writing. I learned almost nothing about chamber music nor symphonies. I learned almost nothing about stories of the operas nor did I hear enough of the arias to recognize them.

A lawyer defending the colleges could rise at this point to object that training in the languages and arts is a very difficult thing to judge. Perhaps this woman graduate, while not learning to speak Spanish very well—something that is very difficult to do anyway without living for a time among Spaniards—did learn a great deal about reading and writing

245

the language, which is even more important. As for music, how can the whole literature of an art be covered in a few college years?

Perhaps; certainly these are all factors that must be considered. But what would the lawyer say to this letter, from a distinguished physician, covering a much more technical and specific educational field:

> I have found a Navy corpsman who could assist me in a delicate operation almost as well as a man who had had four years of college, four years of medical school, three years of special training and resident work. Naturally I raised the question—"Is college required?", or is college necessary to become a surgeon, available to your community at the accepted level of good work?
>
> I am sure that the stratified educational planning of today is either intended to perpetuate the intellectual oligarchy that has already obtained good positions in the delightful old custom of educating our youth, or has failed to see that aptitude (meaning intelligence) is of far greater importance than intellectuality (meaning acquired knowledge) in the world of today and tomorrow. . . .
>
> So many years are wasted, devoted to worship at the shrine of stratified education, when there should be full consideration of the normal emotional adolescent problems of development, contact, and home construction, rather than courses and diplomas!

Can this physician, and the young college-trained doctors with whom he has come in contact, represent another special case—this time men whose education was necessarily so specific as to rule out anything but the hardest scientific facts? Perhaps—but a teachers' college graduate, a man exposed to a considerable amount of liberal arts training, and so interested in educating the young that he went on to take an M.A. at a big university to help prepare himself for the job, writes a quite similar letter from his own very different point of view:

> Like most college graduates with whom I talk, I regret most of all the prevailing emphasis on degrees, hours, and prescribed courses, rather than on the gaining of knowledge and training in the processes of reasoning. Vocationally, the colleges have done a good job. As promoters of general culture, they have failed.
>
> It seems to me that there is a desperate need for a re-evaluation of the aims and objectives of college faculties and officials to overthrow tradition and curricula wherever such action seems to be indicated.

The lawyer for the defense might here object that these are all letters from graduates who did not themselves make the most of college, and have subsequently been associated with other graduates who did not study hard enough either. We can only answer indirectly, with this comment by a graduate who is now an architect in Texas:

Our American college system leaves much to be desired. We think far too little and seem to cater to this state of childishness. Our college graduate does not know as much as a European high school graduate. I knew a Phi Beta Kappa in college who admitted he had never read a book in his life other than the prescribed work in his classes.

Or with this comment from a man in New York whose letter makes clear that he studied quite hard in his college days:

How could college have helped me more? By being even tougher academically!

The dissatisfied graduates seem to represent all types, and to criticize the colleges from many different points of view. There is a group of three letters, for example, that constitute a really striking study in contrasts. The first is from an engineering graduate of Ohio State:

I wish we would have had more knowledge of what industry expects of graduates instead of so much emphasis on theories, 80% of which I have never used. This is a pretty big order, however. If asked to set up such a curriculum I'm not sure I'd know where to begin.

The second is from a much less pragmatic Old Grad of the University of Pennsylvania:

The fine arts were, in my undergraduate days, shamefully neglected. No hint was ever given that Beethoven and Michelangelo were as important in the greatness of our heritage as were Plato and Galileo.

And the third is from a man who was graduated from the University of California:

Let speech classes, personality development courses, sociology courses train the modern mind to face modern situations—not the situations of Shakespeare's time. Seems to me that there's too much emphasis on the history of this, the philosophy of that, the theory of Aristotle on the other hand, etc., etc., ad nauseum. Sure, utilize the wisdom of the past, avoid the errors of yesteryear, but don't cram non-essentials down the throats of modern boys and girls with the idea in mind that the more you write on their mental slates the more educated they will be. Nonsense!

At this point, of course, the defense lawyer can smile broadly and interpose the very sensible argument that you can hardly please everyone. But it may be that the three graduates just quoted are not nearly so different by nature as their letters would indicate. Their complaints about college may merely be symptomatic of a more general and inclusive objection. Some of the most analytical letters from critical graduates reach the conclusion that the colleges are simply doing a bad job of presenting education as an integrated whole. Along these lines an engineer from Case states:

College (and all education) would gain considerably by a process of introducing disagreeable subjects in such a manner as to convince the student of their value. History stands out as a subject that is given too much value. I still am not convinced that the time I spent on it was well spent. The subject, teacher, student, could each or all be in the wrong, but I am so prejudiced as to blame the first two. Why ram a subject—Shakespeare for instance—down a student's throat if he naturally dislikes it and can see no reason for it? This procedure only makes the situation more difficult, less interesting, less helpful. I still do not like any part of Shakespeare and will probably never willingly read any part of it again, all because of its handling in the past.

And a man graduate with an M.S. from the University of Pennsylvania takes an even more philosophical view of the same problem:

College could have been more helpful to me had there been more effort made toward interpreting the subject matter with a broader perspective. There might have been more emphasis on the philosophy of life and importance of the various subjects that were being studied in relation to this philosophy. There seemed to be need for a bit more personal contact between professors and students—and the guidance aspects of education were well-nigh absent. It required a considerable amount of home training, church and community activity to give me a well-rounded perspective on life and to enable me to look at various subjects with a broader vision.

I cannot help but feel that for many men who went through school at the time that I did, and who did not have the advantages of the outside contacts that I have mentioned, that the college must have left them rather poorly prepared for a life of service and enjoyment. From discussions which I have had with other men I believe that the experience which I had at my school was somewhat typical.

All of which leads, by natural progression, into what is perhaps the most common complaint of all to be voiced by our graduates. It is on the matter of general preparation for life, for citizenship, for a mature adulthood—for all the many intangible things that make up a useful and happy existence in the post-graduate years—that our dissatisfied graduates feel the most disappointed. So many graduates of varying types express this thought, in so many different ways, that it is worthwhile to quote a good many letters here.

From an engineering graduate of Notre Dame, who at the time was in a Big Ten graduate school:

College training does not imply good citizenship. The main trouble with most colleges today is that they give the knowledge but do not teach for what end it should be used. The former without the latter is worse than not having just the former. A college which does not teach morality, ethics, business and professional ethics, religion, is a den, not a place of learning. College is teaching me a way to make a living; my religion taught me to be a good citizen.

From an engineering graduate of the University of California:

College training has been no help in furthering my enjoyment of life, very little in becoming a good citizen—and a "must" in furthering my career.

From a Chicago journalist:

As far as citizenship is concerned, I personally feel that college either added nothing or possibly detracted somewhat by inducing the usual juvenile cynicism which either makes for an indifferent citizen or leads one off the paths of rational political thinking.

From a man who was graduated from Arizona State College:

About citizenship, I believe that college doesn't do a damn thing along this line except to make one aware of the structure of government. Upon graduation one is usually broke, a trifle cynical, a little radical mayhap. However, as a few years pass, the graduate acquires a little property, a wife, a child or two, and he becomes aware of the fact that regularity, decency, etc., are necessary if he is to live a happy well-ordered life. Then he starts thinking about helping in his community—especially if he has a special sewer assessment or two to pay for.

From a Pittsburgh man:

Colleges should in my opinion attempt to teach students (1) to think and (2) social responsibility, rather than loading them with courses of facts and figures, and encouraging them to cut throats to make money above all things.

From a graduate in Virginia:

My college training has undoubtedly helped me to enjoy life more and has furthered my career. It is somewhat questionable whether as a citizen my usefulness has increased enough to repay society for the price which it paid for my education.

And finally from a New York chemist with long experience in graduate as well as undergraduate work:

College has helped me in my career and in my enjoyment of life mainly by enabling me to make several close friends, some of whom are now my dearest friends. As for making me a good citizen, I fear that college had little influence. A few facts from the history, economics, and other cultural and citizenship-type courses still float about in my mind, but I don't believe any fundamental impression was made.

In line with my last comment, I would like to say that the failure of college to make any impression on me with a view toward making me a better citizen is not atypical. This I believe is the major failure of our colleges and indeed our entire educational system from grade school up. Our schools and universities should, in addition to furnishing technical training for technicians, turn out citizens capable of independent and critical thinking, cognizant of their roles in a democracy, and desirous of improving it in every way. Instead of this, most of our teachers are spiritless and routine individuals, going through the motions of teaching history, economics, or elementary philosophy. They have no power to inspire their students with the spark of critical probing thinking, to make them realize that they are sovereign individuals in a great democracy and in a world of wonderful knowledge. This I say is not true of all teachers. A few possess this gift, and it is they who are remembered by their students. Their number is all too few.

All these letters, in varying language and by varying thought processes, make much the same point—a point which the lawyer for the defense would have a hard time answering. Indeed educators themselves have been worrying for years about the same thing—the whole question of what education is really for, how it can be integrated into the rest of modern life, the kind of living philosophy and character training that should go with the classroom facts. The colleges worry about the problem a lot and discuss it endlessly—but in the opinion of at least some of the graduates they have failed to provide the solution.

After these letters, it is not at all surprising to find that some graduates have actually come to the conclusion that the whole college experience is almost worthless. Even though they might return to college if living their lives over again, mostly for social or economic reasons, they would do so with tongue in cheek and very little hope of any real benefit. Two letters along this line serve to illustrate the most extreme critical position taken by the graduates, and also to wind up this chapter on the general comments of the dissatisfied college customers. A housewife graduate of Mary Washington College writes:

I sincerely think a college degree is grossly overrated by a great many potential employers. A lot of people have a degree and are uneducated; a great number have no degree and are very educated in every sense of the word.

And a career woman who attended both Smith and Columbia University adds:

I devoted as little time to study as possible and still managed to pass and I do not regret this, as I find I remember very little of what I learned. I think the fact that I have an A.B. is a practical help in getting a job—just as having a Ph.D. would impress some people—but I personally do not think one learns a great deal in college that one would not learn through experience.

22

The Sad Case of the Little Lost Sheep

In literature the college professor is a younger, more vigorous, but equally kindly Mr. Chips. He wears a brown tweed suit and smokes a pipe. He loves books, long walks, quiet conversations, flowers, birds, and students. He is absent-minded about such details as meals, appointments, combing his hair, and straightening his tie, but brilliant in discourse and gifted with a dry and penetrating sense of humor. A gentle and modest man, he is as friendly and reliable as a fine shaggy sheepdog. His students sometimes laugh at his unworldliness and take advantage of his good nature, but deep down they admire and adore him. In novels the college professor is often a sort of Scattergood Baines, straightening out the lives of his students without ever claiming credit or taking a bow; or he is valiantly fighting the cause of academic freedom against some villainous trustees; or he is stoically and heroically enduring a nagging and social-climbing wife. In detective stories it would be unthinkable to cast him as the murderer; indeed it is he, through casual but dazzling deduction, who traps the murderer at the end.

It is jarring, therefore, to discover what some of the dissatisfied graduates have to say about their professors. A young Pennsylvania housewife writes:

I had several instructors whom I respected very highly for their knowledge in their field, their contribution to it, and their sincere desire to help the students. But I also discovered that too many of the instructors were narrow-minded, prejudiced, selfish, and certainly disinterested in offering unbiased knowledge to the students.

A woman librarian says:

I think colleges would be wiser if they assigned superior teachers to teach their underclassmen. If one could get inspired or at least interesting instruction in the freshman and sophomore years, real study could be done in the last years. I have seen so many assigned to teach lower division courses. They are usually not too well prepared and often deadly bores. And not too adept in quashing the "brilliant" student (there is one in every class) who is all too eager to take over and air his pet theories and superior knowledge in long and rambling soliloquies while the rest of the class has to suffer.

In one instance I had the opportunity of studying under an intelligent and brilliant history teacher as a freshman and sophomore. His influence is still with me and the deadly bore who took his place is just an unhappy memory now.

A Pennsylvania businessman, who wishes now that he had taken more specific business training as an undergraduate, writes this bitter note:

Possibly I would have made that choice early in my college days if the dean of my alma mater had been more interested in why a student was getting bad grades rather than putting on an angered-father air and laying down the law. My grades in commercial subjects, which I took up as a post-grad course, will attest that there *is* some gray matter in the upper story.

A letter from a Harvard graduate, now a New England businessman, has echoes of both the last two. This man, although he feels very warm toward most of his teachers, also mentions dean trouble—and he also speaks particularly of the freshman and sophomore years. He writes:

There was no one to take me in hand during the first two years and help me organize my courses for the best over-all result. There was no person and no course to tie in the isolated courses. The one individual who had the most and worse influence on my college career was a shallow and vindictive dean, who had an obvious dislike for me; who went to great lengths to make certain formal requirements unnecessarily burdensome; and whose attitude went a long way toward negating the positive and optimistic and inspiring influence of most of the educational personnel.

The college professor, obviously, is not so universally loved as our literature would indicate. Perhaps this is only natural. Professors, after all, are human beings, subject to headaches, moodiness, hostilities, and billiousness. Being grossly underpaid, they are probably also subject to budget troubles which reduce their lovability around the first of the month. Moreover the professor has been so idealized in literature that any slight lapse from perfection is likely to be shocking to the onlooker. Students, as a matter of fact, tend to expect miracles from their teachers;

education is supposed to be both easy and thorough, entertaining and precise, as profound as the encyclopedia and as painless as a comic strip. If a professor seems too down-to-earth and pragmatic, many of his students will hardly think of him as a professor at all, but as a sort of football coach. On the other hand if he is bookish, some of his students will criticize him in terms like these from two of the graduates' letters:

I believe that college instructors need to get out into their respective fields and learn more about the practical uses of the things they teach.

I would have been helped more if the professors of business administration had been successful businessmen rather than theorists. . . . Colleges should attract as many practical businessmen to the teaching profession as they can—less theorists and government economists, etc.

It must also be considered that the relationship between young adults such as college students, and full-fledged adults like the professors, is always subject to a certain amount of strain. As every middle-aged parent knows, children around the age of 20 tend to regard adults with a certain patronizing curiosity, if not with outright contempt. And as every professor knows, growing older in the teaching profession involves a peculiar phenomenon in which freshmen seem to grow younger and more ignorant by the year. Viewing the whole situation in the most charitable terms, one might say that it is not easy to be a young student facing a professor or a dean—and it is not easy to be a professor or dean facing a class of young students. A certain amount of friction is almost bound to develop.

Yet the quality of college teaching is criticized so often in our graduates' letters that it would be foolish to write off the complaints as inevitable, or as exclusively the product of rebellious students who probably gave the teachers a much worse time than the teachers gave them. The colleges might well ponder their methods of selecting teachers, and their methods— or rather lack of methods—of determining whether a teacher is actually doing his job. It is more or less standard practice to select faculty members on a basis of their grades or research accomplishments, without inquiring into their actual ability to teach. And once a man has been appointed to a faculty, he has the closest thing to lifetime tenure that is known in this country. Very seldom does anyone bother to check up on whether he is offering his classes any real guidance and inspiration or just a sleepy rehash of his old lecture notes.

The colleges might also ask themselves, in view of some of the graduates' comments about the freshman and sophomore years, whether it is really such a good idea to let the faculty's scrub team handle the new-comers, meanwhile saving the first team for the junior and senior years and the graduate school. The theory, of course, is that it hardly pays to waste a brilliant authority on the beginning students, and that on the other hand the young and shaky teachers should get their practice on the be-ginners. This saves the tyro professors from being torn apart by more sophisticated students—and it also keeps the real faculty experts from hav-ing to look at the students until the youngsters have had a couple of years to accumulate some basic knowledge and a little more maturity. The arrangement is a happy one from the faculty point of view; it saves the young teachers from being thrown to the lions, and the old teachers from being bored by lambs. But it may not be such a fortunate scheme from the point of view of the students, or of the maximum effectiveness of the college.

There is another matter, already mentioned by the Harvard graduate in connection with his criticism of the dean, which turns out to be the most common complaint of all among our graduates—and something that should disturb every college president. This is the matter of how little guidance or advice of any kind the colleges have offered to their students. A great number of our graduates, from many varied viewpoints, cite this as an outstanding defect of the colleges. For example a businessman grad-uate of Susquehanna University feels that college graduated him without the faintest notion of what would happen to him:

A good sound program of aptitude testing followed by vocational counsel-ing would have been most helpful to me, since many years of my life were utilized in finding the field of endeavor for which I was best qualified.

An Ohio housewife, who had a taste of a career before her marriage, has a similar complaint:

The college should assist a student in finding his niche. I can see little value in a college education to a person who wanders aimlessly through the whole four years. They clutter up the college for those who are there with a pur-pose—and waste their own time when a little advice from experienced people could steer them into something which would suit them perfectly. I speak from experience in this.

After graduating from a university I drifted into library work, for which I had no training beyond a B.A. degree. I had never heard of library schools. This work was extremely fascinating to me yet my field was limited from lack of training. Vocational guidance would have steered me right.

A man who was graduated from Miami University feels much the same:

I feel that each college should have a highly developed vocational guidance department. For example, I should like most of all to be in museum work, diplomatic work, or teaching. Some college professor should have set me straight—I am an interior designer because during my teens an older person, whom I admired, suggested it.

And there is this letter from a graduate who took an engineering degree at Notre Dame, found he detested engineering, and was back in school at the time of the survey starting all over with a new major:

In my case college certainly missed the boat in not showing me my true talents. I had to find out the hard way.

A Holy Cross graduate, also having vocational trouble, makes the same point:

College could have helped me more by providing in some way a more definite guidance program whereby my natural inclinations and abilities could have been directed to a worthwhile career in the outside world.

It is not only the graduates thinking specifically in terms of careers, however, who make the point about lack of guidance. For example there are two letters from lawyers, presumably well satisfied with their own choice of career, who nevertheless feel that in a general way they did not get nearly so much out of college as they might have with a little more helpful advice. The first is from a man who took an A.B. at DePauw before becoming an attorney:

My college could have helped me more if it had directed me more. I think all colleges should maintain a faculty committee to offer and perhaps compel conferences with students on courses to be taken and objectives to be attained.

My experience was perhaps not so different from that of many other young men. I went to college just because I thought it was the thing to do, without purpose or plan. My real serious thinking and planning came after graduation.

The second lawyer, a Missourian, comments:

Looking back at my college career I think I was permitted too much election in my courses. Perhaps it is well to allow considerable election but I think I did not receive sufficient guidance. It seems to me that I picked a number of courses because I thought they were snaps, when I might have diversified a little more. Specifically, I might have taken a little more philosophy and less modern language. Perhaps a course or two in appreciation of music or art would have been helpful. I found history, economics, and languages relatively easy and neglected studies in other fields.

Other graduates make the point that the student just arriving at college faces a brand-new experience and needs help in adjusting to it; these graduates urge guidance not only during the college career but even before it. A Vassar graduate, now a housewife, writes:

More information and counseling should be made available to the girl about to enter college. The freshman-to-be needs much orientation and stimulation: the importance of friendships and the simple techniques of "how to win friends and influence people," a comprehensive presentation of the extra-curricular program and the advice to choose one or two specific groups, the suggestion that the summer preceding entrance may be an excellent time for typing instruction and gaining proficiency in this field. She should be encouraged to be friendly with the faculty, to seek their advice and friendship without fear and without "apple-polishing."

Study and research methods in colleges are very different from those in most high schools; lecture note-taking is a new tool for many. A brief, intensive course on study techniques would be very valuable: effective note-taking, best methods of reviewing, outlining, and executing term papers, testing of reading speed and comprehension and how to improve them, use of the library's varied materials, and the efficient use of time in studying and in taking exams.

A woman who has combined marriage with a career—part of which was spent observing a campus from the administrative point of view—adds this note:

I was only 17 years old when I first started college. If I had had tests to analyze my real interests, or if anyone capable of analyzing such things had talked with me, my courses would have been different. I was influenced to take secretarial work because I had done well in typing and shorthand in high school and felt that I needed to make a living and that seemed to be the popular thing to do. If I had been properly tested as to aptitudes and interests at that time and had realized that there was a future for house planners, I probably would have taken art and architecture. I have since wished many times that I could have done this.

I realize that colleges are now more and more giving aptitude tests, etc. I believe the University of Chicago gives these tests to children with fairly good results. I hope the time will come when all children, rich and poor, can have such tests early in life so that more time can be spent turning their talents to productive use. As a secretary in a college for seven years I had ample opportunity to see a great many youngsters come to our campus floundering around from one school to another trying to find out just what they really wanted. Then when they did find the thing they thought they wanted, they had lost quite a number of college hours which would have counted toward their degree. Not that the degree itself is so important—but most students (and their parents) cannot afford to spend the time and money to flounder around for a year or two.

A war veteran tells of his own experience, which seems to have been shared by many young men whose college days were interrupted by military service:

I entered college without advice of any kind; my questions were answered with, "Study what you want to," "Go there and find out." After three years of college I was leaving for active duty, and by then I had found out. Three years of indecision, jumping from course to course, left me at that time discontented. Navy, then the fourth year, were different. When at last I knew where I was going, I learned more in one year than in three previous years.

All in all it appears that the colleges, whether they know it or not, have a lot of little lost sheep on their campuses. To be sure, vocational and general guidance is much more common nowadays than a few decades ago; but the pattern of letters, coming from graduates of all ages, indicates that it is still too little, and not good enough. (A graduate who has had experience teaching says flatly: "A good counselor is a help but almost all that I have seen recently are a waste of the taxpayer's money.")

While this book was being written, the authors happened to discuss with a friend the remarkable number of letters that had turned up on the problem of guidance. This man was moved to write a little essay on the problem; and while he was not one of the subjects in the survey, his words seem to be such a good summation and commentary on the criticisms in this chapter that they are worth quoting at some length:

My first contact with the university was through a catalogue which the registrar sent to me in the summer before I enrolled. The catalogue described the physical plant of the university, told how many books were in the library, and informed me that I should take five subjects in addition to physical education. Two of these, it stated, must be English and mathematics. In addition, I would have to choose one of the physical sciences, a modern language, and either history or political science.

This catalogue was the first indication of what I was to find out later was the chief characteristic of the university's attitude toward me—its policy of laissez faire. There was nothing in the booklet to show why I was compelled to take English and mathematics. Nor was there anything to suggest which of the natural sciences I might find most profitable, or which modern language, or whether history or political science would be more desirable in my instance.

Left to my own guidance in this fashion, I chose my program on registration day in the way most students do. I was a little unsure of myself, a little worried that I might not make the grade; and so I chose the subjects that looked best suited to my background and tastes.

I had studied chemistry in high school; therefore I elected chemistry as my natural science. As my modern language I chose Spanish, which I also had studied in high school. I always had hated history—as a result of a whole succession of grade and high school teachers who thought that history was nothing more than the monotonous memorizing of dates—and so I chose political science.

Those first days at the university were puzzling ones. I went to my first mathematics class and the instructor began reviewing high school algebra. She didn't bother telling the class why she was doing this or what was to come, and certainly she made no attempt to tell us why we were studying mathematics in the first place. Perhaps she didn't know, either.

In the chemistry class, the professor started in to lecture on the elements, which I already knew about, and assigned us a chapter of our textbook to study. In English, the instructor asked us to write a review of some book we had read, so that she might get an idea what kind of students we were. The Spanish professor talked about the fact that Spanish verbs must be declined. The assistant professor of political science gave a lecture in which he said that the subject was the study of government and that he positively would not give a passing grade to any girl student who powdered her nose when he was lecturing.

This all seemed exactly like high school, and I was disappointed. I couldn't figure out just what I was doing, or why, or what was going to come of it; and nobody helped me find the answers. There were a few meetings of the entire beginning class in connection with something called freshman orientation, but these were of no aid. The university president and some deans delivered addresses in general terms about what a fine thing college education was, and how we should deem it a privilege to study hard and do all the assignments our instructors gave us; and that was all.

Youths and young women sixteen to nineteen years old are nothing if not realistic, and I can assure you that we did not take these talks very seriously. They sounded to our critical young ears like the same old stuff, and in point of fact they were the same old stuff. Study hard and the university will be proud of you. Remember that culture is more important than making money. Going to college carries a grave responsibility, for it is to you young men and young women that the leadership of the world will fall when the older generation dies.

We had heard all this before, and how it could have been expected to orient us I do not know.

In addition to these lectures by the president and the deans, the university provided me with a freshman adviser to whom I was to go when my first month's grades were turned in, and regularly thereafter once a month. My particular adviser was an ascetic-looking assistant professor in English, very scholarly and by no means interested in callow freshmen. He had a half-dozen other freshmen besides me to advise, and his technique was to get rid of us as quickly as possible.

Every month he gave me my grades and said, "That's fine; you're doing very well." I said, "Thank you," and walked out. In later years, when I became interested in the institution of freshman advisers, I questioned numerous students on the campus, and found not one who had received more advice from his than I had from mine.

These first days at the university set the tone for all that was to come. Each year, at registration time in September, I made out a program which included a few compulsory subjects—fewer each year—and was completed with whatever I felt at the moment like taking. Each course was more or less of a separate unit, and very little effort was made by the instructors to correlate their subject matter with anything else I might be learning.

After the university had "oriented" me by letting me listen to the president and the deans a few times, and had provided me with a freshman adviser to whom I talked for a total of about fifteen minutes, it apparently felt that it had fulfilled its responsibility. For the rest of the four years, it never once made an effort to show me why I was in college, what I could hope to gain from my presence there, or how I best might go about profiting from the experience. It provided no guidance whatever for my attempts to acquire an education, or for the personality I was developing.

It simply gave me a catalogue of courses and let me choose from them on a hit-or-miss basis, and like most students I made more misses than hits. I finished the four years without any knowledge of history because no one ever told me that history was an essential part of the well-educated man's equipment. I studied Spanish instead of French because no one ever suggested that French was culturally much more important. I didn't acquire any knowledge of physics because I had no way of discovering that physics was the most exciting field of natural science today.

Doubtless, among the many professors and instructors whose classes I attended in the four years, there were at least a few men of vast and detailed learning in their own fields coupled with a broad general knowledge of world affairs, literary trends, and social, economic, and political philosophy. An acquaintance with those men should have been a stimulating experience; their example should have guided me and shown me the way to culture.

But how was a student to become acquainted with these men, or with any other of his teachers? My contacts with the instructors were limited to the three hours a week in which they gave lectures on the subject matter of their courses, cut-and-dried lectures which they had been giving for years. If they had something more to offer, they didn't offer it. There was nothing in their contracts with the university to compel them to regard me and the other students in their classes as anything more than the occupants of chairs arranged in rows in front of them; and occupants of chairs we were. Their job was to teach us the subject matter of their courses, not to worry about how we were going to fit that subject matter into our lives.

It might be argued, in defense of the colleges against criticisms like these, that higher education is just what the phrase implies—something that cannot be spoon-fed, and is not really designed for the young person without sufficient background and maturity of intellect to make his own decisions and find his own way. But such an argument is perhaps rather snobbish. The young person from a highly cultured home, with college-trained parents whose education is reflected in every facet of their daily living, and from a first-rate prep or high school which has grounded him in all the techniques of study, may well find in the college all the educational tools he needs to round out his knowledge and pursue his own well-considered interests. But as we saw in Chapter 17, the expansion of the colleges has drawn an increasing number of students from less privileged homes; the tendency nowadays is for young people to be much better educated than their parents, and this is something that every democratic American must surely approve. What of the student to whom college is not just a routine extension of the education for life provided by his erudite and articulate parents and friends, but instead is the golden and only opportunity for acquaintance with better things?

The moral of all the comments we have been quoting here from graduates is perhaps this: by devoting insufficient thought to the quality and the inspiration of the teaching, and especially by failing to provide advice, guidance, and some rounded explanation of the curriculum, the colleges are succeeding the least with the type of students they could help the most. This is a serious criticism but it represents the feelings of far too many graduates to ignore.

CHAPTER **23**

But Maybe It's Not the College's Fault

One fine thing about a survey like this is that the facts it discloses—and even the opinions that it unearths—are so beautifully impartial. This is a great boon to the people who make surveys and the people who write about them, who ordinarily are not the type to be exactly spoiling for an argument. Among the graduates' letters, for every one praising the colleges there is another one condemning them, while for every point raised by the foes there is in turn a logical rebuttal by the friends. In the last two chapters our graduates have been trampling on the colleges; now they are about to let the colleges up, call bygones bygones, and shake hands.

In the last chapter, it will be recalled, one of the strongest cases for more guidance by the colleges was made by a Vassar graduate. Her letter was quite reasonable, objective, and convincing. In fact she is such a reasonable person that in another part of her letter she insists on taking some of the guilt off the college's shoulders and onto her own. She writes:

More maturity on my part—as well as more effective orientation on the college's part—would have made my college training more beneficial.

Maturity. This is a good word to ponder, for in the feelings of our graduates about their colleges it very often seems to play an overt or at least an implied role. When the word is just implied it often takes the form of criticism of the nation's high schools, as in this letter from a man in Texas:

High schools of today do not train students to study, and upon entering college they are lost.

Or this one from a businessman graduate in Ohio:

The time I spent studying would have been more efficient if my basic high school training had been better.

But most of the graduates, rather than blaming the secondary schools, come right out and admit that they wish they had been older and wiser when they went to college, as does this man from Missouri:

If I had been older with some experience, I believe my college work would have helped me more and I would have been able to study more intelligently.

And it is quite startling to note how many of the graduates actually use the word mature, or who look at the other side of the coin and use the word immature. A career woman office worker in Georgia writes:

Had I been more mature, I could have gotten a lot more out of college.

A Negro graduate who had taken his A.B. and was in law school at the time of the survey says:

I went to college at 18 but was still immature. Poor grades resulted. It was not in any way the fault of the college. I caught on in my third year and it was easy from there on in.

A man from Indiana, who wishes he could live his college days over again to more advantage, confesses:

My reading during my four years of college was far too skimpy and my interest in voluntary research non-existent. Probably I was too immature for it anyway.

There was also a very convincing letter in the last chapter from a man whose college career was interrupted by wartime service in the Navy. His complaint against his college was that nobody helped him to find himself during his early years on the campus, that he was just in the process of doing so by his own efforts when he had to go to war—and that then after his Navy experience he learned more in his last year of school than in all the previous years put together. Now we may logically inquire whether this war veteran was the victim in his early years of bad guidance—or simply the beneficiary in his final years of the greater maturity that comes with additional birthdays. For we have a letter from a young working wife whose education was also affected by the war. Her conclusions are quite different from the ex-sailor's:

I wish there were some way in which a college student could take part of his training, then leave and work for a year or two at his profession. After the actual experience he would go to school with a *reason* for learning. So many students try to "get by," simply because they do not see an actual need for the material they are studying.

During the war, while my husband was overseas, I went back to college for a year. That year, I feel, was more beneficial to me as a teacher and as an individual than any of the other years I spent at school.

The young woman who wrote this letter had an unusual experience, but the conclusion that she has reached is by no means unusual among our graduates. Many others have also decided that college would be more useful if it could be obtained a little later in life. A man graduate of Arizona State College writes:

I believe that unless a high school graduate drops out of school for a couple of years he doesn't have maturity enough to really knuckle down to specialized career study.

And an Ohio businessman says:

College could have helped me more if I had had two years in between high school and college. By that time I would have realized some of the things that were needed and would have had a more definite goal to attain.

Indeed it is quite amazing how many of the graduates of different schools and in different areas and occupations have arrived at the same thought, without any collusion, about an educational sabbatical between high school and college. An Illinois University engineer writes:

College is generally presented in too much of a "lump." The students are just a little too young. Their previous contact with business has been more or less confined to part-time jobs of an inferior nature. I offer no solution, but it would seem to me that if a two-year period just for growing older could be placed between high school and college, a majority of the students would benefit. The veterans have illustrated this more vividly than I can describe it.

And a liberal arts graduate in Chicago expounds the same theory from a somewhat different point of view:

I think that I, like many others, went to college totally unprepared, without sufficient maturity to apply intelligent self-direction or take advantage of whatever opportunities were presented. I feel that if I had deliberately allowed two to four years between high school and college to try my hand in a variety of occupations and to just plain grow up a little more, college might have proven a much more beneficial experience.

Like 95% of the other undergraduates whom I had the opportunity of observing, I went to school with no definite purpose, no concrete ambitions, and without the vaguest notion of what I was attempting to prepare myself for. I have always had an intense envy for those students who came to school with a specific ambition, who knew exactly what they wanted to do. As a result they selected their courses with a purpose and applied themselves more intensively. I think their chances of success were far greater than the great bulk of flounderers like myself—and even if they didn't become successful in their chosen careers, it is probably true that they could enjoy failure in an occupation which they had always desired far more than the rest of us can enjoy success in an occupation of no particular appeal but one into which we finally stumbled.

This last letter has a reminiscent quality. It recalls all the statistics in Chapter 12 on the number of humanities graduates who have wound up, to their vast or slight regret, in occupations which they never planned, never prepared for, and can never quite reconcile themselves to. But right here it has an even more important meaning. It adds another voice to the chorus of graduates who feel that college failed them—but that this was the result of their own immaturity and lack of planning, rather than any fault of the college.

There are also many other graduates who blame themselves for not taking full advantage of the campus, and their reasons range from the normal frivolity of youth to much more drastic self-criticisms. The following five letters are representative.

1. From a University of Michigan graduate:

Had I been able to decide earlier on a career, I should have profited. Guidance might have saved me something here. But I am not sure I would have harkened to it, for there are so many things that youth must learn for itself.

2. From a woman graduate of Simmons College:

I don't believe that college could have helped me more—but rather that I could have helped myself more by making better use of everything college has to offer.

3. From a man in New York City:

How could college have helped me more? If I had worked harder!

4. From another New Yorker, a graduate of Hobart College many years ago:

How could college have helped me more? By my paying more attention to the courses!

5. And finally from a man in the Midwest:

Without cynicism, and devoid of frustration or disappointment, I would, at my age of fifty years, state that education is the student's own personal task and never a compulsion of the institution. Knowledge is freely available for anyone seeking it seriously. . . .

And with that letter we come to the end of the facts, and of the opinions as well. As to how they add up, as to what they prove about the success or failure of the American college, we leave that to the reader. Some people may feel that the graduates as a group do not come off nearly so well in the figures as college graduates should; that the satisfied graduates have been willing to settle for too little, and that the dissatisfied graduates are justified in their complaints. Others, especially after reading the letters in this chapter, will probably feel that the picture is quite impressive—and that the only thing really wrong with college education today is that it, like youth, is wasted on the young.

Appendix

This book is based upon questionnaire replies from 9,064 graduates of U.S. colleges, universities, teachers' colleges, professional schools, and technical institutions. The 9,064 repliers are—with the partial exceptions which are noted later—believed to be generally representative of the living college graduate population of the United States.

These 9,064 graduates are the major part of a master sample of names which was compiled through the co-operation of over one thousand institutions of higher learning. The master sample was assembled from lists supplied by these colleges in response to *Time's* request made in the spring of 1947. The listing form sent to all degree-granting institutions (per the U.S. Office of Education's 1946-47 Educational Directory) specified as follows:

U. S. COLLEGE GRADUATE STUDY

INSTITUTION_____

CITY, STATE_____

In the space below kindly list and classify as indicated the full names of all living graduates of your institution whose last names begin with the letters "Fa", for example: Fairbanks, James Miller; Farley, Stephen Ashley, etc. So long as the information on each graduate is given in full (and we again beg your earnest cooperation in giving complete data in order to attain our goal of 100% accuracy), the graduates may be listed in any order most convenient to you. In the case of women graduates whose names began with the letters "Fa" at the time of graduation and who subsequently married, please also list their married names. Use this sheet and as many of the "continued" sheets as may be required to list your "Fa" graduates. Should you need more room, continue your listing on plain paper similarly arranged.

Full Name	Class	Latest Known Address	Degrees Earned	Major Subject	Sex (M or F)	Color (W or N)

Return to: Director of Special Research, TIME, Inc., 9 Rockefeller Plaza, New York 20, N. Y.

The names resulting from this alphabetical selection ranged from Faarborg to Fazzone. The same alphabetical cross section was employed in *Time's* 1940 study—see F. Lawrence Babcock, *The U.S. College Graduate*, The Macmillan Co., New York, 1941.

The 1946-47 Educational Directory lists 1,244 institutions of higher learning, of which—according to *Time's* correspondence with them—1,229 are degree-granting. Of these, 1,037 (84.4%) co-operated in assembling the sample. This 1,037 includes 850 colleges, universities, and teachers' colleges which accounted for 95.2% of the 1947 enrollment in institutions of this type. (Enrollment data for professional and technical schools are generally not available in reference form.) The geographic location of the co-operating institutions is as follows:

	Co-operating Institutions (Number, and % of total)		
Geographic Area	Colleges, Universities	Teachers' Colleges	Professional, Technical
New England	53 (95%)	18 (67%)	15 (71%)
Middle Atlantic	108 (94%)	33 (89%)	49 (75%)
East North Central	135 (94%)	27 (87%)	49 (71%)
West North Central	85 (86%)	25 (93%)	15 (68%)
South Atlantic	116 (81%)	20 (83%)	25 (83%)
East South Central	54 (86%)	12 (71%)	10 (63%)
West South Central	58 (77%)	14 (88%)	7 (88%)
Mountain	22 (92%)	8 (67%)	4 (67%)
Pacific	54 (93%)	8 (100%)	13 (81%)
Total *	685 88.2%	165 82.9%	187 73.9%

The names received from these institutions totaled 17,053—after elimination of duplications and of names of persons who were found through correspondence to be deceased or not to be graduates.

A 13-page questionnaire was mailed to this list in October, 1947. The questionnaires were keyed by serial number, and a follow-up mailing was made to the non-respondents in November, 1947. The two mailings produced a

* Includes Negro institutions.

total of 9,064 replies—53.1% of the total sample or 59.1% of the net sample exclusive of bad addresses.

In addition, a sample of the remaining non-respondents was interviewed in January, 1948, with 419 interviews being taken.

The total sample, then, breaks down as follows:

Replied to first mailing	6,180	36.2%
Replied to second mailing	2,884	16.9
Were interviewed	419	2.5
Total—with full data	9,483	55.6
Bad addresses	1,726	10.1
Wrote, refusing to answer questionnaire	234	1.4
Refused to be interviewed	188	1.1
Non-repliers (all other)	5,422	31.8
Total—with college listing data	7,570	44.4
Total sample	17,053	100.0

Results from each of the two mailings and from the interviews were tested statistically. In all, 173 characteristics or question responses were tested by Chi Square or other appropriate method. In 89 cases there were indeed real differences between one or the other of the three sets of data. However, the magnitudes of the differences were so small in most instances as to have little practical meaning. There were no differences in the 84 remaining cases.

The sample of 17,053 "Fa" names is somewhat smaller than might be expected from other national distributions. A sample of telephone directory listings, for example, indicates that "Fa's" account for about 0.57 per cent of total name listings,* whereas this sample's 17,053 names account for 0.36 per cent of the 4,717,000 persons who had completed four years of college.† One reason may be that 15.6% of the colleges are not included. Another and more important reason is that probably few college rolls are complete. The sample is a little younger than the national estimate—repliers' median age, 36.9 years; nationwide graduate median age, 39.9 years †—perhaps because recency of graduation makes for better alumni address records. And the repliers include only 1% of non-whites where the national figure is about 4%.†

* This sample consisted of 189 places, stratified by city size; it included 100% of the cities over 500,000 and a randomly selected approximate 20% of 100,000-499,999 cities, 10% of 25,000-99,999 cities, 2% of 2,500-24,999 cities, and ½ of 1% of places under 2,500.

† U.S. Bureau of the Census, April, 1947 sample census.

The question as to whether a sample based on an alphabetical selection is representative of the whole requires a qualified answer. Sampling theory argues for a randomized selection of names, of course. But in the present instance practical problems of control of listings (among over a thousand suppliers of lists) argue for a specific alphabetical selection. It would seem that the only point at which such a question might arise is in consideration of possible biases with respect to ethnic, racial, or national origins; and it must be said that the "Fa's" were selected as a sampling base with no such biases known or intended.

In sum, this study has aimed at the objective of creating a large body of knowledge about the more interesting characteristics, both past and present, of U.S. college graduates. The sample on which the study is based is a workable representation of the total graduate population—and is considered to be sufficient to support broad conclusions.

Index

A.B.'s. *See* Education, general

Accountants, incomes of, 35

Activities. *See* Community; Extra-curricular; Politics

Advisers. *See* Freshman advisers

Age, and children, number of, 46-48; and divorce, 71; and earning power, 28-30, 35-37, 76, 170, 174; median, in survey, 12-13; and migration, 233-35; and opinions, 98-100, 104, 115, 122; of women, and marriage, 61-63, 70. *See also* Longevity

All-Around Girls, and marriage, 59-60

All-Around Students, 10-11; incomes of, 163-65

Amherst College, 179

Aptitude testing, need for, 255-61

Arizona State College, 249, 264

Arts, incomes in, 150-51, 153; proportion of graduates in, 32

Atheism, 104-7

Babcock, F. Lawrence, *The U.S. College Graduate,* 268

Bachelors, proportion of graduates, 39-40, 43, 50; and size of city, 43-45

Bankers, incomes of, 32-35

Baruch, Bernard M., 97

Bates College, 179

Ben Greet Open Air Players, 135

Big Men on Campus, 5, 10-11, 18; grades of, 157; incomes of, 163-65

Big Ten universities, graduates of, earning power of, 179-85; increase in proportion of, 208; loyalty to school of, 214

Big Women on Campus, 10-11; and marriage, 59-60

Birth control, 46, 50, 55

Birthplace, as factor in whether one goes to college, 14

Birthrate, national, 38

Bowdoin College, 179

Brooklyn, Polytechnic Institute of, 179

Brown University, 179

Business administration, 9

Business, age and earning power in, 174-75; extra-curricular activities and success in, 163; grades and success in, 157-63; incomes in, 32-35, 157-63; increase in career choice of, 22, 206-7; leadership on campus and success in, 163; and migration, 235; occupational types in, 35-37; proportion of graduates in, 32; specialized education and success in, 150-51, 153; women in, 74; working one's way through college and success in, 172-77

Business executives, earning power of, 26, 32-37; political opinions of, 113; and religion, 187

California Institute of Technology, 178

California, University of, 210, 247, 249

Career women, unmarried, 70-77, 80-81, 85; age and earning power of, 76; and choice of curriculum, 77; and community activities, 81-82; on education, value of, 133-36; incomes of, 74, 85; leisure time of, 80-81; and migration, 233; proportion of graduates, 70-72; reading habits of, 81; specialization and earning power of, 148-49; types of jobs of, 72-74, 76-77, 85; as voters, 82

Carnegie Institute of Technology, 178

Case Institute of Technology, 178, 248

Catholics, 11; and community activities, 191; earning power of, 186-91; increased enrollment of, 207-9; political opinions of, 191-95; and religion, 105-7; women, and marriage, 55-56

Census Bureau, 25, 46, 270

Chicago, University of, 7, 179, 231, 257

Child care, need for training in, 65-66

Children, number of, of all graduates, 46-50, 53-54, 60; of housewives, 78-80; and income, 46-48; and migration, 238-39; and size of city, 48, 238-39; of women graduates, 53-54, 78-80, 85-88, 90; of working wives, 85-88, 90

271